Gendertrolling

Gendertrolling

How Misogyny Went Viral

Karla Mantilla

PRAEGER™

An Imprint of ABC-CLIO, LLC
Santa Barbara, California • Denver, Colorado

Copyright © 2015 by Karla Mantilla

All rights reserved. No part of this publication may be reproduced, stored in a retrieval system, or transmitted, in any form or by any means, electronic, mechanical, photocopying, recording, or otherwise, except for the inclusion of brief quotations in a review, without prior permission in writing from the publisher.

Library of Congress Cataloging-in-Publication Data

Mantilla, Karla.
  Gendertrolling : how misogyny went viral / Karla Mantilla.
    pages cm
   ISBN 978-1-4408-3317-5 (hardback) — ISBN 978-1-4408-3318-2 (ebk)   1. Internet and women.   2. Misogyny.   3. Sexual harassment.   4. Internet users—Attitudes.   5. Computer crimes.   I. Title.
   HQ1178.M36 2015
   004.67'8082—dc23   2015019524

ISBN: 978-1-4408-3317-5
EISBN: 978-1-4408-3318-2

19 18 17 16 15   1 2 3 4 5

This book is also available on the World Wide Web as an eBook.
Visit www.abc-clio.com for details.

Praeger
An Imprint of ABC-CLIO, LLC

ABC-CLIO, LLC
130 Cremona Drive, P.O. Box 1911
Santa Barbara, California 93116–1911

This book is printed on acid-free paper ∞

Manufactured in the United States of America

Contents

Acknowledgments	vii
PART I: GENDERTROLLING AND ITS EFFECTS	
Chapter 1: Introduction	3
Chapter 2: Characteristics of Gendertrolling	21
Chapter 3: Responses to Gendertrolling Campaigns	99
Chapter 4: Fighting Back	117
PART II: GENDERTROLLING IN HISTORICAL AND SOCIAL CONTEXT	
Chapter 5: Gendertrolling: It's Not about the Internet	131
Chapter 6: The Power of Naming	149
Chapter 7: Cultural Defense Mechanisms as Backlash	159
Chapter 8: Gendertrolling: Cultural Defense Mechanisms at Work	175
Chapter 9: Recommendations for Change	195
Epilogue	219
Notes	221
Index	263

Acknowledgments

The gifts I have been given by the following people have been life-altering and have literally (not figuratively) saved me at times that I desperately needed saving. That this book was ever begun, much less completed, is due entirely to them.

Ashwini Tambe, who believed in me, both professionally and personally, at a time when I was so far from believing in myself.

Brittany Fremaux, without whose sage advice and understanding I surely would not be here, and who promised/warned me that my initial article on this topic was important in ways I couldn't see.

Amy Hummel Corbin, who continually sent me updates and needed information, helped with proofreading, and has been a steadfast friend and advisor.

Kate Davison, whose neighborly pep talks were as insightful as they were wise, and who provided much support, both material and emotional.

Charlotte McNaughton, who kept me from abandoning the project just in time and thereafter was a steady supporter and cheerleader.

Julie Harris, faithful and true friend and demon-chaser extraordinaire, who understands the power of the demons and gave me untold ways of combating them.

Laurel Long, ever-loyal friend and persevering research assistant, who did much work on the manuscript when it needed it the most and diligently proofread every chapter in their rough forms.

Nina Mantilla, my beloved daughter, for endless (and more) hours of support, tangible and otherwise, and for dragging my "dead horse over the finish line," notwithstanding my dogged insistence on giving up on myself. And for rendering indispensably incisive, perceptive, and well-deserved critiques on every chapter.

This book is dedicated to my adored children, Marcel and Nina Mantilla, whose wisdom, maturity, support, integrity, and kindness have been the biggest light in my life. In my wildest dreams, I would never have dared hope to have children as wonderful and talented as they have turned out to be.

Part I

Gendertrolling and Its Effects

Chapter 1

Introduction

You may be surfing the Internet and come across a topic being discussed in the comments of an article that you care deeply about, say, perhaps, recycling. You read comments debating whether it really makes a difference to recycle, given the scope of environmental problems on the planet. Fair enough. But then someone starts contributing what seems to you a slew of inane or irrational posts. This person writes that he (you won't know the gender, but trolls are most often male[1]) never recycles and encourages his friends not to recycle, even going so far as to throw unrecyclable materials in recycling containers he sees so as to destroy others' attempts at recycling. He expresses scorn for people who care about the planet and swears that he leaves his car running "just to piss off those dirty eco-hippies." You become incensed and start explaining to him that environmental concerns are real and provide data and links to sites with solid and well-researched information about environmental issues. But it seems that the more information you provide, the more outrageous his claims are and the more insulting he becomes. You become angry and insult him back, telling him he is illogical, stupid, and obtuse, and asking him to educate himself on these topics. But he continues to spout his insulting and infuriating nonsense. In response, you become increasingly frustrated, but nothing you say seems to have any effect on his stance.

In all probability, you've been trolled.

This means the person you have encountered who has been expressing the anti-environmental sentiments may not actually believe anything he writes; he may even be an avid recycler IRL ("in real life"; IRL is an

Internet term for distinguishing between online activity and real-life activity). His intention was only to get a rise out of you—and he did. You've been trolled.

It is unclear whether the etymology of the name "troll" derives from the word's use in fishing, so that online trolling is seen as analogous to the fishing technique in which a baited line is dragged in water in the hopes of catching fish; or from the mythological creature who waits under a bridge to surprise unsuspecting people. However, the first known use of the word "troll" as an Internet phenomenon dates back to the early 1990s, when a user who called himself "Troll" posted on July 8, 1992.[2] In his post titled "Hi boyz and girlz," he (again, he is presumably male) writes,

> Just some credentials. I am called Troll. I didn't get the name because I'm a fun guy. I am the the [sic] champion of channel +insult on irc and I have thrice defended the title before the channel went down, so I can flame with the best. Flame away if you like, but "I'm gonna deal it back to you in spades. 'Cause when I'm havin' fun ya know I can't conceal it. Because I know you'd never cut it in my game."—Guns N' Roses Troll[3]

Trolling on the Internet consists of making online comments or engaging in behaviors that are purposely meant to be annoying or disruptive. People who engage in trolling activities use a variety of strategies to disrupt online discussions such as being obnoxiously illogical, feigning ignorance, bringing up extraneous or irrelevant topics, or otherwise derailing conversations. The behavior is committed with the express purpose of tweaking, upsetting, or enraging others. Online trolls relish the resulting fallout of their strategies, which includes the target becoming angry, perplexed, insulted, or frustrated.

There are online forums where trolls brainstorm strategies and brag about their exploits to their fellow trolls. In the early 2000s, trolls began to congregate in various Internet sectors, most notably on a subsection of the website 4chan called the /b/ board. 4chan currently has over 20 million visitors each month,[4] with a rank of 275th most frequently visited website in the United States according to Alexa.com, a provider of Internet metrics that rate website popularity.[5] Although that means 4chan is among the top 500 most frequented websites, the /b/ boards are only a subset of the website, and so 4chan's high ranking does not mean that Internet trolls are comprised of huge numbers of people. Trolls often boast about their exploits on sites such as 4chan and Reddit where they develop and refine their strategies and techniques. Out of such forums, trolls have developed a variety of recognizable strategies that they use to provoke their targets.

TROLLING STRATEGIES

Many trolling tactics, although they can certainly be upsetting and disruptive, fall under the category of annoying or sometimes even humorous, albeit a rather twisted or even acerbic kind of humor, regardless of whether the person they target shares in thinking the tactic was funny.

Bait and Switch

One such tactic is "bait and switch." A fairly common one is "rickrolling," in which a troll provides a link, ostensibly related to the topic of an online discussion, that is actually a link to a 1987 music video of the Rick Astley song "Never Gonna Give You Up." People who click on the link have been "rickrolled" in trolls' lexicon. Rickrolling emerged out of the website 4chan as an iteration of an earlier practice called "duckrolling," in which the troll provides a link purportedly to a dramatic or sensational news item or image, but which actually leads to an image of a duck on wheels.

Rickrolling has spread to become the theme of several pranks. On April 1, 2008, every featured video on YouTube's front page redirected the user to the Rick Astley music video. The song was also played, performed, and sung at many of February 2008 protests against the Church of Scientology, which were organized by Anonymous through its Project Chanology, a protest movement against the Church of Scientology in response to its attempts to remove material from an interview with Tom Cruise from the Internet. In addition, in April 2008, there was an online poll to determine a song for a sing-along during the eighth inning of a New York Mets game. Users of the website Fark.com, a news aggregator and social networking site that mocks current news and events, voted overwhelmingly to select the song "Never Gonna Give You Up," which garnered over 5 million votes and so won the poll.[6]

Concern Trolling

Trolls also employ tactics such as "concern trolling," when a troll pretends to share the opinions or ideas of the people he is conversing with, but expresses trumped-up but seemingly earnest "concerns" in order to foment doubts, dissent, or disagreement about the opinion that the troll ostensibly agrees with. An example of this might be someone who pretends to support reducing the use of disposable plastic bags, but then evinces numerous "concerns" about, say, people's "rights" to prefer disposable over reusable bags or about the manufacturing process of disposable bags. Concern trolls also use "sock puppets," a fake account in which the troll pretends to be someone else, sometimes engaging his own sock puppet in heated and vitriolic disagreement. This tactic tends to induce others engaged in the discussion to make numerous attempts to resolve the resulting confusion, to attempt to intercede in the inevitable arguments that arise, or to end up taking a more polarized stance as a result of the inflammatory statements by the troll.

Advice Trolling

Advice trolling occurs when trolls offer misleading, erroneous, or malicious advice to others who are less savvy about computers or the Internet. One such scheme involves instructing a user to "download more RAM." Since random access memory (RAM) is hardware, it cannot be downloaded. Trolls have created fake webpages where a user could select the amount of RAM to download.[7] Trolls have even gone so far as to create YouTube videos to instruct users on how to download more RAM, which cannot be in fact done.

Another, potentially more destructive instance of advice trolling is known as "delete System 32."[8] Trolls instruct users that System 32 is a virus that should be deleted and that doing so will speed up the user's computer. In reality it is a file that is essential to running the Windows operating system and deleting it will cause the computer to no longer be operational. This hoax peaked in 2006–2007, although Google Trend data indicate that searches for "delete System 32" are still common.

Practical Jokes

Trolls sometimes coordinate efforts to sow mischief or to make a point. For example, a large number of trolls coordinated together to weigh in on a website that asked readers to vote on which country Justin Bieber should perform in next. They all voted that he should go to North Korea.[9] In another similar effort, trolls got together to disrupt a corporate media campaign conducted by Walmart and Sheets Energy Strips in which they announced that Miami rap star Pitbull would visit whichever Walmart store received the most "likes." The trolls organized to get people to "like" the Kodiak, Alaska, Walmart store so that Pitbull would have to go to that very remote and, in their view, less desirable location. In the end, the Kodiak store received 70,000 "likes," despite the fact that the town has only 6,100 inhabitants. Pitbull visited Kodiak in July 2012, as a result of the trolls' campaign. Finally, in a more politically motivated effort, when it was revealed in 2013 that the National Security Agency (NSA) was monitoring people's telephone calls and web activity, a website, trollthensa.com, was created. The website coordinated a campaign for large numbers of people to call or email a specific script to a friend on the same day that contained many of the keywords that NSA had flagged for monitoring. The following are excerpts of that script (with the NSA-flagged keywords in bold):

> My job is so shitty I wish I could **overthrow** my boss. It's like this **oppressive regime** where only **true believers** in his management techniques will stay around. . . . I just read this article about how these free **radical** particles can cause the **downfall** of good health and accelerate aging. They could actually cause **death to millions of Americans**. . . . Okay, I gotta run! I'm late for **flight school. I missed the last class where we learn how to land**, so I really can't miss another one. Talk to you later![10]

Flaming

Flaming is a somewhat more hostile form of trolling where a person attacks someone else verbally through insults, name-calling, or other forms of antagonism, often over hot-button topics such as religion, politics, or sexism. There have been many "flame wars"[11] over such topics as which computer operating systems are preferable (Windows, Mac OS, or Linux) or whether Mac versus PC computers are better. Flame wars occur in public settings such as on blogs, in the comments section of articles, or on online discussion boards. Flaming is often not a one-sided attack by trolls as much as a disagreement that devolves into insults and name-calling on all sides. Flame wars, rather than being attacks by one or more trolls on unsuspecting targets, tend to be engaged in by multiple parties, many of whom become increasingly hostile and insulting to people who express opposing opinions as the conflict progresses. Flaming and flame wars can be thought of as analogous to fights that people might engage in offline where the participants, rather than attempting to fight fairly, use as many hurtful and insulting words as they can in order to provoke the people with whom they are having a disagreement.

While some trolling tactics can be considered annoying, even highly annoying, they nevertheless have more in common with pranks or other mischievous behavior. However, other trolling tactics consist of meaner, more vicious activities.

Griefing

Video game players are targeted in "griefing," which occurs when players in massively multiplayer online role-playing games (MMORPGs) deliberately harass or bully the other players in the game. Griefers are more concerned with deliberately ruining others' experiences of the game rather than with playing the game or winning.[12]

Raiding, Shock, and RIP Trolling

Although many of the previously mentioned tactics of trolls can be fairly easily dismissed as an aggravation, trolls have also developed strategies that are less easily ignored, for example, "raiding," which is an attack on a target by a coordinated group of trolls who, by virtue of their numbers, can dramatically increase the scale and intensity of the attack. Another less amusing and more offensive tactic is "shock trolling," where trolls post a link that purports to be something innocuous but instead links to shock sites, websites that contain content or images that are shocking and offensive, such as graphic pornography, extremely violent images, or profane or scatological content.[13]

Trolling becomes even more of a malicious and unconscionable attack when trolls go out of their way to target vulnerable people, as in the case of RIP trolling. RIP trolls search for social media or web pages that are put up in tribute to someone who has died, and they post nasty, critical, and insulting comments about the deceased person. Trolls have gone so far as to flood Facebook pages that were put up by parents to commemorate their dead child with gruesome photos of dead children. RIP trolls also make fun of or mock the way people have died, as in the case of a woman who was hit by a passenger train or a Sea World trainer who was killed by a whale during a performance in front of an audience.[14]

Impersonation/Sock Puppets

Trolls use "sock puppets," which is when a person takes on a fake identity, often in order to sow mischief or confusion. A troll might use a sock puppet to argue viciously with himself in the comments section of a blog in order to rile others up; or he might use a sock puppet to voice exaggerated, bigoted, or foolish opinions in order to undermine those who hold similar, but more reasoned opinions. Trolls also use sock puppets to impersonate someone whose reputation the troll is trying to damage by making others think that person would say the terrible things the troll espouses using the sock puppet identity.

IRL (IN REAL LIFE) TROLLING

Other forms of trolling extend into offline life, often to instill a sense of threat by letting the targeted person know they know where she lives. One way this is done is by sending food orders, such as pizza, from restaurants that deliver. Often the orders are especially unappealing, such as sending pizzas with anchovies, double sausage, double meat, and pineapple as toppings. The orders are not paid for, causing confusion and sometimes pressure by the delivery person to pay for the order. In one ominous case, trolls sent a pizza to the address of their victim, but the order was in the name of an accused murderer who the trolls knew the victim knew.[15]

Swatting

Another offline trolling behavior that is even more harassing and potentially dangerous is "swatting." Swatting occurs when trolls call an emergency service such as the police or fire department and report a serious threat such as a bomb, a shooting, a fire, a kidnapping, or other emergency at the home of a person they are targeting. Such incidents have resulted in the deployment of bomb squads, SWAT units, or numbers of police or other emergency personnel. Rapper Lil Wayne was swatted in March 2015 when someone called the police and reported that four people had been shot at his Miami Beach mansion.[16] Swatting is a trolling activity that crosses a line into real-life danger because of the possibility that law enforcement might kill or injure someone due to having received false information about an emergency. FBI agent Kevin Kolbye explained that "it's only a matter of time before somebody gets seriously injured as a result of one of these incidents."[17]

A commonality of these trolling tactics, even the most destructive or reprehensible, is that the goal is the enjoyment and amusement that the trolls derive out of having annoyed, upset, angered, or hurt others. Whitney Phillips, a scholar who studies online trolls, explains that "trolls are motivated by what they call lulz, a particular kind of unsympathetic, ambiguous laughter. Lulz is similar to Schadenfreude—loosely translated from German as reveling in the misfortune of someone you dislike—but has much sharper teeth."[18] Claire Hardaker, a linguist and scholar who researches online aggression, deception, and manipulation, says that "behaviors that fail to generate and/or celebrate lulz do not qualify as trolling."[19] Danielle Keats Citron, a law professor and author of *Hate Crimes in Cyberspace*, cites an ex-troll who describes what "lulz" means to him: "Lulz is watching someone lose their mind at their computer 2,000 miles away while you chat with friends and laugh."[20] A hallmark of generic trolling, then, is the troll's intention of annoying or upsetting others for the "lulz." Trolling for the sake of enjoying upsetting and disturbing others is a defining feature of what I call generic trolling.

Because their primary motive is lulz, despite any appearances to the contrary, generic trolls generally are not trying to make a sincere point or seriously engage on a topic. Phillips explains that "as a general rule, trolls don't take principled stands, they provoke."[21] Hardaker elaborates: "Trolls believe that nothing should be taken seriously, and therefore regard public displays of sentimentality, political conviction, and/or ideological rigidity as a call to trolling arms."[22] Laura Miller, staff writer and cofounder of Salon.com, says that trolls' "objective is not even to win the argument, but to delight in making his target ever more incensed and distressed, and then to crow over the resulting spectacle with his troll pals."[23]

While types of generic trolling range from annoying to upsetting to maliciously destructive, there is a very different pattern of harassing, abusive, and threatening behaviors that is specifically targeted to women, which has been increasingly occurring on the Internet. I am making the case in this book that these particular forms of harassment, abuse, and threats of which women have been the targets are a separate and distinct category from generic trolling, which I am calling "gendertrolling."

Gendertrolling arises out of different motivations than generic trolling. Blogger and 11-time *Jeopardy!* champion Arthur Chu explains that the kinds of trolls who target women are engaged in a very different project than generic trolls. In contrast with generic trolls, Chu says that "the emotions [of the people who attack women online] are entirely sincere and the people are entirely earnest."[24] Gendertrolls, more often than not, believe ardently, even obsessively, in the stances they take and act against their targets out of their sincerely held convictions. While, like generic trolls, they often try to provoke their targets, they are not doing it for the lulz. Gendertrolls more often hope to inspire abject fear in their targets and to win the battle they believe they are waging, which is to drive the target, along with her objectionable opinions (usually that women deserve social, political, and economic equality with men), out of public discourse online. One troll succinctly points out that he considers that behaviors typical of gendertrolling are not trolling: "Threatening to rape someone on Twitter isn't trolling.... That's just threatening to rape someone. On Twitter."[25]

Gendertrolling is often mistakenly conflated with the name-calling and general unpleasantness that is characteristic of generic trolling and is more likely to be men's experience of online harassment. A recent study on online harassment conducted by the Pew Research Center confirmed a difference in men's and women's experiences of online trolling. In a report on the study's findings, Maeve Duggan, a research assistant at Pew Research Center's Internet Project, says: "In broad trends, the data show that men are more likely to experience name-calling and embarrassment, while young women are particularly vulnerable to sexual harassment and stalking."[26] In addition, there are some data that show that women are disproportionately targeted for online harassment. An organization that tracks online harassment, Working to Halt Online Abuse, reports that, of those who have filed online harassment cases with them from 2000 to 2013, fully 70 percent are women.[27] While many people think gendertrolling is best handled by ignoring it or laughing it off, as may be the case for generic trolling, because gendertrolling arises from entirely different motivations and manifests in very different ways, this strategy is for the most part ineffective.

CHARACTERISTICS OF GENDERTROLLING

There are many ways that gendertrolling is distinct from generic trolling, among which is the different motivation on the part of the perpetrators. More significant, however, are the ways that gendertrolling is exponentially more vicious, virulent, aggressive, threatening, pervasive, and enduring than generic trolling. As discussed earlier, gendertrolls, as opposed to generic trolls, take their cause seriously, so they are therefore able to rally others who share in their convictions to take up the effort alongside them, resulting in a mob, or swarm, of gendertrolls who are devoted to targeting the designated person. Because of the numbers of people involved in the attacks, gendertrolls are able to sustain their attacks for an extended period of time—for months and, not atypically, even for years. Another distinctive feature of gendertrolling is that gendertrolls use graphic sexualized and gender-based insults to demean women as sexual objects and to insult them for being women. In gendertrolling attacks, women are typically called "cunts," "sluts," "whores," and the like; their appearance is insulted by calling them "ugly," "fat," and much worse; and graphic pornographic depictions are frequently made of images of the targeted women. An additional feature that distinguishes gendertrolling from generic trolling is that, while generic trolling tends to remain on the online forum, discussion board, comments section, or blog post on which it originated, gendertrolls launch a more aggressive and proactive campaign that branches out to and involves multiple online sites, social media, and forums. Although the initial remark or opinion that gendertrolls object to may appear, for example, on a particular blog, gendertrolls then use

Twitter, Facebook, Tumblr, YouTube, Storify, email, and discussion boards simultaneously to carry out their multifaceted attacks. Gendertrolls also employ a variety of tactics concurrently such as hacking a *Wikipedia* page about the target or creating a blog as if in the target's name where they espouse horrendous views that are then attributed to the targeted woman. They may also post and repost graphic Photoshopped pornographic images involving the target or seek out the target's family members, friends, and supporters to harass them as well. Gendertrolls are so committed to their campaigns that they become quite creative and inventive in using a wide variety of means to achieve their ends. Finally, the feature that is possibly the most common in all gendertrolling attacks is that they inundate their target with explicit rape and death threats, many of which are credible. They also commonly induce fear in the target by posting her home address, telephone number, or other real-life data about her, while egging others on to use that information, thus increasing the possibility of a real-life, physical attack.

These features are common to online campaigns against women, and they characterize a unique and unprecedented form of online abuse, which is clearly distinct from other kinds of generic trolling. After reviewing the experiences of large numbers of women and the attacks waged against them, as well as conducting in-depth interviews with many other women who have been subject to these vicious online campaigns, the following seven characteristics emerged as common features of these online attack campaigns against women:

1. Gendertrolling attacks are precipitated by women asserting their opinions online.
2. They feature graphic sexualized and gender-based insults.
3. They include rape and death threats—often credible ones—and frequently involve IRL targeting, which adds to the credibility of the threats.
4. They cross multiple social media or online platforms.
5. They occur at unusually high levels of intensity and frequency (numerous threats or messages per day or even per hour).
6. They are perpetuated for an unusual duration (months or even years).
7. They involve many attackers in a concerted and often coordinated campaign.

Certainly not all cases of gendertrolling evince every one of these seven characteristics; nevertheless, this general pattern of characteristics describes a unique constellation of tactics that recurs in a significant number of online attacks on women.

OTHER KINDS OF ONLINE HARASSMENT

The Internet is certainly rich territory for spawning any number of pernicious and innovative forms of harassment and abuse. Other abusive and harassing behaviors that have also arisen from the Internet include cyberharassment, cyberbullying, cyberstalking, posting of upskirting photos, revenge pornography, rape blackmail videos, and bullying campaigns that result in Internet-induced suicides. Although these are all also damaging and destructive forms of harassment and abuse, they are distinct phenomena from gendertrolling. Cyberharassment is the use of the Internet to bully or harass an individual or group and involves the intentional infliction of emotional distress on the target. (Gendertrolling is a discrete subcategory of cyberharassment.) Cyberbullying, another subcategory of cyberharassment, is generally seen as online harassment directed at children or underage teens. Cyberstalking is characterized by the relentless pursuit of a targeted person online, and often occurs in conjunction with offline stalking. The motivation for cyberstalkers often involves revenge against, anger at, or obsession with the target, and the stalker and the target have typically had some kind of personal relationship, whether off- or online.

Posting upskirting photos, revenge pornography, rape blackmail videos, and often cyberbullying that results in suicides are forms of online harassment that, like gendertrolling, often have a gender component to them. "Upskirting" is when someone, usually a male, surreptitiously photographs up an unsuspecting woman's skirt in a public place and subsequently posts the photograph online. Revenge pornography occurs when someone obtains a nude image of the target, nearly always a woman, either voluntarily, such as in the case of a woman sending a nude photo of herself to her partner, or without the woman's permission, in the case where the photo is obtained through hacking or other illicit means. The photo is then posted to a website devoted to posting revenge pornography with identifying information about the woman pictured in order to embarrass and humiliate her by the exposure.

Rape blackmail videos are a somewhat newer phenomenon, although it is becoming more common, especially in India. Rape blackmail videos occur when a woman is raped or gang raped, and the rape is videoed. Thereafter, she is threatened that if she reports the rape, the assailants will post the video online, where she will be shamed.[28] Shamina Shafiq, a member of the National Commission for Women in India, reports that "more and more women are reporting that men are recording the act of rape with their smartphones, and they are using these recordings to threaten women into silence."[29] In Canada, the suicide of Rehtaeh Parsons was motivated by a similar dynamic: the 17-year-old killed herself after she was gang-raped at a party and a photo of the rape was posted online, which resulted in a long campaign of bullying, shaming, and intimidating her for having been raped.

Other Internet-induced suicides include 14-year-old Jill Naber, who hanged herself after a photo of her topless went viral,[30] and Amanda Todd, a 14-year-old girl who committed suicide after she was persistently bullied and blackmailed because of a photo of her topless, which she had sent to a stranger when she was in the seventh grade. Both of these girls were relentlessly bullied by countless others because of their photos. Some Internet-related suicides of young men are also gender related in that they were bullied and tormented for being gay or for being perceived to be gay, effeminate, or insufficiently masculine. (Because of strict gender norms that define heterosexual masculine behavior, men who deviate from those norms by presenting as effeminate or by being gay often become the target of extreme forms of abuse and derision. In this manner, harassment of gay men can be considered gender related.) Two examples of this are Tyler Clementi, an 18-year-old college student who committed suicide after his roommate made a video of him, without his knowledge, kissing another man, which the roommate then showed to other people who participated in ridiculing him; and Ryan Halligan, a 13-year-old who was bullied and cyberbullied for nearly three years by schoolmates and others online who taunted him about being gay (although he apparently was not), inducing him to kill himself.

While cyberbullying, cyberstalking, posting of upskirting photos, revenge pornography, rape blackmail videos, and Internet-induced suicides are all gravely serious problems that have been made possible or intensified by the Internet, they are distinct from gendertrolling and are therefore beyond the scope of this book. Instead, this book is devoted to laying out and detailing the phenomenon of gendertrolling, in the hopes that doing so will result in greater awareness that will lead to the changes—legal, policy, cultural, and social—and that will lessen and hopefully bring an end this new threat to women's freedom and agency online.

In Part I of the book, I lay out the experiences of women who have been gendertrolled, giving examples and detailing how gendertrolling has played out in their lives. Chapter 2 consists of seven sections, one for each of the seven characteristics of gendertrolling described earlier. Each section features the story of a particular gendertrolling campaign that illustrates the wrenching experiences of women who are gendertrolled. Each section then gives examples of the respective gendertrolling characteristic, with anecdotes to illustrate how that particular feature of gendertrolling plays out. At the start of each section of Chapter 2, I include a few statements that are typical of the kinds of messages that are sent to targeted women during gendertrolling campaigns. As horrific as they are to read, I include them because it can sometimes be too easy to dismiss the harassment that women receive as merely negative comments, insults, or name-calling. Although I am loathe to repeat them, I believe that by including examples of these offensively graphic and upsetting statements, it will allow the reader to gain a better understanding of the horrific content to which gendertrolled women are exposed, often on a daily basis.

Chapter 3 provides examples of the range of reactions that women have had in response to being targets of gendertrolling attacks. Many women experience the attacks as quite, to extremely, upsetting, with a full range of attendant emotional reactions including frequent crying, anxiety, shock, and, not uncommonly, especially after prolonged exposure to the graphic and horrific content and threats, the onset of post-traumatic stress disorder (PTSD) symptoms. Women respond to the attacks in a variety of ways, such as by limiting what they write about online or withdrawing partially or completely from online activity. Some women manage to become inured to the abuse, although they point out that hardening oneself to such vicious attacks can also have drawbacks. Finally, many women find that, for their safety and that of their family, they must make significant adjustments to their offline activities and circumstances. Some women have had to leave their homes temporarily; while others have been forced to move to another home in order to protect themselves in the face of the ongoing specific and credible threats that involve posting their home address.

Chapter 4 illustrates the multitude of ways that women have attempted to fight back or take control in the face of the onslaught of gendertrolling attacks. Some women have attempted to fight back by reaching out to law enforcement, although that tactic is generally met with limited success. Other women have shown considerable fortitude in resolving to stand strong and resolute in the face of the attacks, remaining determined not to be silenced regardless of the threats they receive. Finally, some women have found ways, through humor and creativity, to use the horrific attacks against them to raise public awareness about online harassment against women.

Part II of the book is an analytical overview of gendertrolling that situates it within other English-speaking, European and American historical and contemporary patterns of misogyny. I also lay out what I call "cultural defense mechanisms," a patterned form of backlash that has emerged with other forms of misogyny, which also comes into play when women attempt to describe their experiences with gendertrolling. I argue that clearly recognizing and naming harassment and abuse of women, in this case gendertrolling, is an indispensable step toward enacting laws and policies that will protect women online as well as making the legal, cultural, and social changes to ensure women's full equality and participation.

Chapter 5 explores how gendertrolling is situated in a long-standing historical tradition of harassment and abuse of women, in which women have been barred from full participation in cultural, social, and political discourse and have been thereby shut out of professional opportunities. I make the case that gendertrolling is not a unique phenomenon that has emerged out of the particular qualities of the Internet, as many people have suggested, but that it is instead an adaptation of offline misogyny to the specific features of the Internet. I also make the case that, in general, women are treated differently online from men and that the constellation of characteristics that define gendertrolling happen for the most part to women, or, when they do happen to men, it is most often when men show public support for women who are being gendertrolled. Finally, I assert that, despite any number of reasons given as to why gendertrolling happens, such as that the women provoked it in some manner, it happens to women *because they are women*—and for no other reason.

In Chapter 6, I examine gendertrolling in the context of contemporary misogynistic behaviors: domestic violence, rape and date rape, stalking, street harassment, and sexual harassment in the workplace. Gendertrolling has much in common with these forms of harassment, abuse, and violence against women, which are varied expressions of misogyny. They are primarily aimed at and harm women, are pervasive rather than idiosyncratic or rare, and have a major impact and effect on women's lives. While these forms of misogyny have been widespread, they have been paradoxically unacknowledged and unseen until feminists campaigned to raise awareness about them. Before feminist activism brought them into public consciousness, these forms of misogyny were unacknowledged, and they therefore had no recognizable social existence. When they did occur, they were often construed as matters of private and individual shame by the women who experienced them. Gendertrolling, much like these other behaviors, is also widespread, but is largely unseen and unrecognized. I maintain that there is great power in bringing these widespread and destructive patterns into social awareness—and in naming them. I argue that naming is a powerful and indispensable step toward implementing the changes to policies, laws, and social and cultural values that are needed in order to counter these behaviors. Like the other named misogynistic behaviors, gendertrolling is a form of misogyny that needs to be clearly named and defined so that changes can be implemented to address its harms.

Chapter 7 explores the multipronged backlash that arises in response to recognizing, naming, and defining a pattern of social behavior, especially those patterns of behavior that uphold and preserve power and privilege for certain groups. As feminists mobilized to bring attention to other forms of misogynistic harassment, abuse, and attacks on women—domestic violence, rape and date rape, stalking, street harassment, and sexual harassment in the workplace—they faced a sizeable cultural pushback against that mobilization. This pushback can be likened to a massive cultural defense mechanism, which tends to consist of common forms: "shooting the messenger," denial, shifting culpability, and assertions of inevitability. "Shooting the messenger" occurs when accusations are made against the integrity or trustworthiness of the people describing what happened to them, or, particularly in the case of women, when they are shamed sexually as a way of creating a barrier to speaking out. Denial takes the form of discounting the seriousness of the phenomena, making accusations that women are exaggerating or lying, or claiming oversensitivity on the part of the targets. Shifting culpability occurs when culpability of those doing abusive or harassing behavior is blurred or even reversed through blaming the victim, asserting that the behavior of both parties is at fault, switching the focus to the perpetrator's intentions rather than actions, or seeing the perpetrator as the real victim. Finally, the offending behaviors are seen as unchangeable when they are made out to be natural and therefore inevitable. These multipronged defense mechanisms help ensure that even when women begin to develop a social awareness of a patterned behavior that is targeting them, they will face significant counter attacks.

In Chapter 8, I discuss how the same cultural defense mechanisms that have been employed in the past to stave off full recognition of myriad abuses against women are also used to stymie women's attempts to name and explore remedies for their unique experiences of harassment, abuse, and threats online. The same pattern of defenses—"shooting the messenger," denial, shifting culpability, and assertions of inevitability—comes into play when women bring public attention to gendertrolling. In this chapter, I also detail the ways that segments of online denizens have created an ideology where abuse against women has been construed as an unavoidable feature of the Internet. Some of the tenets of these beliefs are that online interactions are an expression of "natural" human behavior patterns; that the Internet is a separate world, special, distinct, and apart from offline life; that anonymity is essential to maintain the Internet as a uniquely free place where there are no consequences for antisocial behavior; that whatever ideas or memes proliferate are "naturally" meritorious due to the mere fact that they are popular; and that free speech should be absolute, without even the exceptions to free speech in offline life, such as for credible threats. In the end, the pushback effect of this pattern of cultural defense mechanisms thwarts naming and defining gendertrolling as well as coming up with solutions that might address or ameliorate it. In order to have an effect on diminishing gendertrolling attacks on women, feminists must therefore do the double work of clearly describing and naming the rampant harassment and abuse of women online, while also effectively countering the array of defenses brought to bear against their efforts.

Finally, in Chapter 9, I lay out a variety of recommendations for change, from legal remedies to changes in policies of online content providers, to suggestions for coping with gendertrolling attacks, to proposals for ways to institute cultural changes that would reshape values and ideas so that gendertrolling attacks on women would no longer be acceptable or tolerated. Legal scholars advocate increasing the enforcement of existing laws, especially laws against true threats, and training law enforcement to become more familiar with patterns of stalking and threats that take place online. Other legal scholars advocate amending or implementing new laws that specifically address the unique kinds of abuse and harassment that occur online. Many commentators recommend making changes to Internet policies and protocols, for example, eliminating or discouraging anonymity online or increasing comment moderation. Most of those who attempt to bring attention to this topic recommend that online content providers, especially social media, implement policy changes that might alleviate the problem. Finally, because online life is a reflection of offline life, a preponderance of activists have come to the conclusion that widespread cultural change regarding attitudes toward women must take place before gendertrolling attacks will diminish.

I have purposely included a plethora of quotes in this book so that my analysis would not drown out or override the experiences of the multitudes of women who have experienced the online campaigns of harassment, abuse, and threats that I am calling gendertrolling. It is my hope that this book will serve as a way to gain a wider audience for their voices, especially in view of the fact that gendertrolling campaigns have often resulted in silencing them.

I also hope that by bringing this phenomenon into social consciousness, women who grapple with gendertrolling campaigns in the future will be less devastated by them. Seeing gendertrolling as a pattern that has happened to many other women can help remove the sense that the insults, abuse, and harassment occurred as a result of some personal failing, characteristic, or flaw on the part of the woman being attacked, which is what gendertrolls assert. The tendency to self-blame when gendertrolling attacks happen is lessened when women become aware that so many other women have been similarly attacked and that they are being targeted, not for something they did or said individually, but for being a woman.

Finally, I wish to raise public awareness about gendertrolling in the hopes of galvanizing support for finding some creative and effective solutions to this problem. It is my sincere hope that conveying the experiences of the many courageous and outspoken women who have withstood the horrific onslaught of gendertrolling campaigns will result in changes in laws, online policies, and cultural attitudes that will reduce gendertrolling attacks. Coming up with solutions to reduce these attacks will ensure that the remarkable and impressive level of courage and strength shown by the women profiled in this book in the face of horrific attacks will not have been in vain.

Chapter 2

Characteristics of Gendertrolling

There are seven sections in this chapter, one for each of the seven characteristics of gendertrolling.

1. Gendertrolling attacks are precipitated by women asserting their opinions online.
2. They feature graphic sexualized and gender-based insults.
3. They include rape and death threats—often credible ones—and frequently involve "in-real-life" (IRL) targeting, which adds to the credibility of the threats.
4. They cross multiple social media or online platforms.
5. They occur at unusually high levels of intensity and frequency (numerous threats or messages per day or even per hour).
6. They are perpetuated for an unusual duration (months or even years).
7. They involve many attackers in a concerted and often coordinated campaign.

Each section features a brief story that details a particular gendertrolling campaign, as well as quotes and examples that illustrate the characteristic discussed in that section.

SECTION 1: WOMAN HAS AN OPINION ON THE INTERNET

What a long winded bitch. You certainly do need to be gagged.[1]

Shut your whore mouth now, or I'll shut it for you, and choke you with my dick.[2]

the only time your mouth should be open is when I'm putting my d-k in it.[3]

Women that talk too much need to get raped.[4]

FEMINISTA JONES

"Feminista Jones," an online pseudonym, is an activist who works on issues of street harassment, domestic violence, and sexual assault, particularly as they relate to black women and other women of color. In July 2014, Jones started her #YouOkSis Twitter campaign to provide support and solidarity to women of color who are harassed on the street. The campaign emphasizes that bystander intervention can be an important form of support to women who are harassed. She explains that "the whole reason why YouOkSis exists is because I feel like the stories of black women and women of color have been erased from a lot of the street harassment stuff." But since she started her campaign, she reports that "I don't think there's a day that goes by where there is not somebody attacking me because of #YouOkSis."[5]

Because Jones is open online about being both black and a woman—and she frequently writes about issues of concern to black women—she receives harassment that is both sexualized and racialized. Jones finds that some issues she writes about elicit harassment from both black and white men: "When I'm talking about issues related to women and women's rights and things like that, then it's both. It's both black men and white men."[6] She reports, however, that it is mostly black men who harass her when she speaks about feminist issues that relate specifically to black women:

> Every time I write something new, I can expect that there is going to be some level of trolling and harassment from this particular group of black men who feel that I am exposing them or making them look bad in front of white people. . . . There are a lot of men who are responding to [#YouOkSis] with "you're trying to put us in jail. You're trying to create something that's going to criminalize black men." . . .

They're saying I'm a . . . pawn for white feminism to help put more black men in prison by putting up this mantle against street harassment. . . . I had people saying that they don't condone violence against women while telling me I deserved to be raped and killed and lynched . . . and that I'm a traitor, and they hope somebody kills me. . . . When I'm talking about black women, then it's black men [who harass me]. It's almost 100 percent black men whenever I'm speaking specifically about black women.[7]

Jones finds it particularly dismaying that her black male harassers imitate "the kind of trolling and threats that I see white men do, talking about how I need to be raped and lynched and calling me a savage and all these kind of things. And I think [they] don't sound any different from the white men who are doing this."[8]

On the other hand, when she speaks out online about topics related to racism, such as police brutality, she finds that it is mostly white men who do the harassing: "So, if I'm talking about something like police brutality, or . . . the Trayvon situation, or Michael Brown, then I would get a lot of white male trolls. But a lot of their comments were gendered. So there's the gendered racial commentary. And it would be harsher."[9]

Jones finds it particularly dismaying that the tactics of her black male harassers are so similar to the kind of insults and threats that she receives from white men, that they both send her graphic threats about how she should be raped and lynched and call her a "savage" and the like. She marvels at how similar their tactics are and even jokes that they must have all gotten the same script.

Like most women who have been harassed online, Jones takes pains to distinguish between generic trolling, or as she calls it, "heckling," and the kind of sustained and relentless harassment that she has received:

You expect a certain amount of heckling or things like that when you say things that people don't agree with, right? I mean everyone kind of engages in that . . . I think we all do that. . . . But that's a lot different than what seemed to be almost constructed efforts, like somebody went somewhere [online] and said, "We're going to do this to this person.". . . And when you look at the 4chan boards or you look at these other message boards where they congregate, you see them planning this stuff. You see them giving them the words to say and giving them the tools: "This is what we need to say to this person. This is the person we need to attack today. This is what we need to go after." And it's really kind of sad, because it is primarily men.[10]

As is characteristic of most gendertrolling cases, Jones was harassed across a wide variety of online platforms and social media including on her Twitter and Facebook accounts, in the comments to her blog, in emails sent to her, and in the comments sections of online articles she authored that appeared in *Ebony*, *Time*, and *Salon*. She believes the perpetrators are often the same people writing in different media.

Jones has also been harassed over an extended period of time. When I spoke with her, she estimated that she had been experiencing these types of attacks for at least 18 months, although the intensity and viciousness of the trolling had picked up following the start of the #YouOkSis anti-harassment campaign. As is typical in gendertrolling cases, she has also been harassed not just by one or two people, but, in her estimates, by between 100 and 150 different accounts. She thinks that some of these may be the same people who use several accounts in order to multiply the effects of the harassment on her. One of her harassers, who goes by the name Johnny, has at least four or five different accounts that he has used to target her. As Jones blocked him on one account, he would create other ones to continue to harass her.

Like so many other women who are gendertrolled, Jones was also "doxxed," which is when personal information such as a person's real name, home address, telephone number, social security number, or other personally identifying information is posted online for others to see. Although Jones has tried to keep her online presence anonymous by using a pseudonym, gendertrolls spent the considerable time and effort required to dig around on the Internet until they found her real name, address, and telephone number. They posted this information in a Pastebin, a web application where people can post in plain text, which makes it much harder to trace who posted the information. Although the postings are anonymous, Pastebin can be viewed by anyone so Jones's personal information was available to anyone who wished to access it. Her personal information was then sent out on Twitter and tagged with her anti-street-harassment hashtag #YouOkSis, which meant it would be called to the attention of the people who were already bent on attacking her.

Shortly after being doxxed, she began to receive phone calls from telephone numbers that she didn't recognize. She found that many of them were using Google voice numbers, which indicated they were probably temporary telephone numbers and are not easily traceable. When she decided to answer one of the calls, the person who picked up tried to convince her he was her neighbor, and in the conversation, he revealed that he knew her real name and address.

The harassment campaign against her, like many other gendertrolling campaigns, had effects that extended beyond the Internet. Jones explained that one of her harassers, identified as "Lord Jamar," took her image from her avatar, along with other images of her, and tweeted them so people could identify her in person. Along with the pictures he tweeted, "Hey fellas. If you see Feminista Jones on the street, go up to her and tell her I said, 'Have a blessed day.'" She reports that the next day she was out having lunch with her son when a man who looked to be in his 40s approached her. Because his age was the general age of people who she knew followed Lord Jamar, she felt it not unlikely that he could have been among his followers. The man told her that she looked familiar and asked her where she worked. She replied that she would not tell him where she worked, but he reiterated that she looked "really familiar" to him and asked if he could talk to her. Another woman at the restaurant defended her, saying "Yo, she obviously don't want to talk to you! Why are you bugging her?" He replied that he was not trying to cause any trouble, said "Have a blessed day," and walked away.

Jones says she felt panicked at the thought that this could have been a result of her online harasser's request. She reported thinking "Oh my god. Please don't let this be reality right now. Please don't let this be somebody who was following what this guy said."[11]

Jones points out that the statement "Have a blessed day" is so frequently said that it serves to keep her off balance, because she can never know for sure whether someone saying it to her is doing so at the behest of her harasser. About this particular incident, she was uncertain whether it was the man's usual approach or whether he follows Lord Jamar on Twitter and was responding to his request. In any case, the event was extraordinarily unnerving to her.

The online campaign against Jones bled over into her real life in other ways as well. One man posted a photo on Twitter that he had taken of himself as he was standing behind Jones and her son at an event. He tweeted the photograph with the message, "I see Feminista Jones is at this event, too."[12]

Jones describes a kind of doubling down on the part of her harassers when she asks them to back off:

I can say, "please don't tweet me," and they will tweet me 10 more times, just because I said please don't tweet me. It's their way of asserting that kind of dominance. And it's their way of [expressing that] "No woman is going to tell me what to do. If I want to talk to women, I'm going to talk to women, and I don't care what you think."[13]

Like many other women, Jones has found that men experience a different reception online, both in response to their own comments and for trying to defend women against harassment:

If it's a man who steps in, the trolls tend to back down. If it's another woman, they kind of go at them as well. The tone absolutely changes when a guy speaks up. I have a group of guys who regularly step up for me. They jump in, and they try to bring the attention to [the trolls], because the trolls won't say anything after that. My boyfriend has even replied to certain people. There was this one white guy who was coming at me really hard. My boyfriend responded—[the guy] didn't know it was my boyfriend—but his whole tone changed! He was like, "Come on man, she was just saying blah, blah, blah," and my boyfriend just said, "No she wasn't. Why are you attacking her?" And the guy said, "I'm sorry. I shouldn't have done that." [My boyfriend said], "You could apologize to her!" But the guy never apologized to me—he apologized to this man he did not know was my boyfriend. For all he knew, this was a perfect stranger to me. But he was okay apologizing to him and not to me, and his whole tone changed. And that happens a lot. My male friends who are [online], they'll tweet the same exact things that we [women] do, and they say, "Nobody comes after us like us. I wish they would come for me like this!" And they just don't, you know. They just don't.[14]

Jones sees a connection between street harassment and online harassment: "Masculinity is being able to dominate and control women. And it's being able to have access to women at any chance. So, [the gendertrolls are] taking it from the streets to online."[15] She also sees the connection between online harassment and political harassment in real life, drawing a comparison with the kinds of harassment that civil rights activists have experienced: "It's kind of like back in the day when they would send bricks through people's houses or they would call their phones and threaten them. It's the same thing."[16]

Jones makes the important point that, although women of color have been harassed online as much as white women, "women of color don't get the same kind of media attention and support when they go through these kinds of cyber harassments. If you look at something like Gamergate [a campaign of harassment against women in the video game industry that received widespread media attention in August 2014], it's all white women. It's important to include the discrepancy in the ways in which people pay attention to how black women are treated and women of color are treated versus white women."[17]

She expressed frustration "to the point where I don't even want to go online sometimes," but she says that that is what the trolls want:

> They want us to stop tweeting. They want us to stop writing. They want us to go away. They want us to be silent. And that's what they do with this trolling and these insults, and the harassment. It's really terrorism! It's really trying to keep us from doing things. And I've spoken to other women who are going through similar things. I mean, children being threatened. . . . And people say, just ignore the trolls. And I'm like, you're telling me to ignore a troll who is putting my personal information or who is threatening harm to my son. What would you do if it were you?[18]

Like so many of the women who have been the targets of prolonged extensive harassment campaigns, however, Jones remains defiant:

> And [their attempts to silence Jones are] not working because I'm just going to be me, and I'm committed to this. But it's tiresome when I wake up in the morning and I log on to Twitter, and the first thing I see is somebody talking about how I'm a hateful bitch who needs to die. It gets annoying sometimes.[19]

In spite of her determination, like so many women who have been gendertrolled, Jones reports very significant adverse mental health and other real-life effects:

> I started thinking about [the online harassment] and processing it and realizing that it was triggering anxiety in me. I started seeing a therapist. I saw a psychiatrist. And they were saying, "we think you have PTSD from a number of things, but also from this level of harassment." . . . But as I'm talking about [the effects of the online abuse], I have more people coming at me in ways that are making me even more anxious. I've had some days, like this particular summer, where I don't want to go outside. I just didn't want to be in the street. And I would log on and there would be so many people

attacking me and the anxiety would just be through the roof, and I would just have to sign off. I was just feeling like I can't deal with this. I *cannot* deal with this. I'm not going to survive this. And I've had to kind of pull back. I've become a bit of a recluse. . . . I was declining social invitations. My friends are doing really amazing things, and I was just saying, "I can't make it," because of not wanting to be in public spaces. I went to a book signing the other day, and there were a lot of people who were recognizing me, and I just kind of put on my hood and thought, "I have to get out of here." I was just starting to feel the anxiety, like, what if one of these people is someone who trolls me online?[20]

In the end, Jones makes a plea for more empathy:

But it's just the fact that people don't have the same empathy. . . . A lot of people forget that there are human beings behind these accounts. And we go through these things, and we deal with these things, and we have emotions. As a black woman, I think people look at me with such a racist and sexist lens that they don't even realize they're looking at me. . . . They're seeing me as somebody who can handle anything and deal with anything, because I'm supposed to be the strong black woman. And I have people saying to me . . . "I just kind of see you as this superwoman. You're so used to it, that I just figure that you're okay." [But] that's a really fucked-up assumption to make. I'm a human being. I'm a mother. I go to work every day. I'm just like you.[21]

The events that have precipitated online harassment campaigns against women are extraordinarily varied. Whether speaking out or writing about controversial feminist or political topics, or expressing opinions on topics that are decidedly mundane, when women assert their right to voice their opinions in the new public sphere that is the Internet, that act alone can precipitate gendertrolling campaigns.

Many women have been subjected to online harassment campaigns when they were speaking out about topics entirely unrelated to women's rights or women's equality. For example, Laurie Penny, a British journalist, author, and a contributing editor at the *New Statesman*, was the target of vicious attacks toward her and members of her family for her opinions on economics:

Like many others, I have also received more direct threats, like the men who hunted down and threatened to publish old photographs of me which are relevant to my work only if one believes that any budding feminist journalist should remain entirely sober, fully clothed and completely vertical for the entirety of her first year of university. Efforts, too, were made to track down and harass my family, including my two school-age sisters. After one particular round of rape threats, including the suggestion that, for criticising neoliberal economic policymaking, I should be made to fellate a row of bankers at knifepoint, I was informed that people were searching for my home address.[22]

Secular humanist/atheist blogger Rebecca Watson began to receive what is, as of this writing, more than three years of intense harassment after she posted a video reporting on an atheist conference where she (very politely) objected to a male conference attendee asking her to "coffee" in a hotel elevator at 4:00 A.M.

Dawn Foster, a British writer and editor whose work focuses on sustainable housing, remarked that even a topic as seemingly innocuous as cycling could elicit abusive responses: "Even posts about cycling drew vitriolic emails or requests for dates and sex. Being a woman on the Internet seemed to be enough to anger people, regardless of what you were writing."[23]

Mary Beard, a professor of classics at the University of Cambridge in England, got harassed starting the day following her appearance on the BBC television program *Question Time* to discuss immigration. In the ensuing months, she experienced an onslaught of online abuse. Beard commented on the "gobsmacking" misogyny, adding,

> The whole "cunt" talk and the kind of stuff represented by the photo [someone created an image of her face superimposed onto a photo of female genitalia] ... is more than a few steps into sadism. It would be quite enough to put many women off appearing in public, contributing to political debate, especially as all of this comes up on Google.[24]

Janelle Asselin, an editor of various DC Comics titles, a frequent contributor to several online comic magazines, and an academic researcher on comics, was targeted for a harassment campaign after she criticized the cover of a comic book.

> Last weekend I called [my father] and explained that I had finally hit that magical level and had received my first rape threats. What had I done to garner this level of ire from Internet trolls, you ask?
> I'd written a review of a comic book cover and its company's marketing strategy.[25]

Ashley Judd, actor and women's rights advocate, was targeted for tweeting about a play in a championship basketball game. She concludes that there are "dangers that invariably accompany being a woman and having an opinion about sports or, frankly, anything else."[26]

Courtney Caldwell, a Texas-based activist and blogger at Skepchick, incurred a harassment campaign against her after she criticized on Twitter some Open Carry proponents whom she saw in her neighborhood.

> I was leaving a restaurant one evening. I was with a friend and we looked out the window, and we saw a bunch of people walking down the street. . . . we saw that they all had guns. . . . These were large guns, rifles, semi-automatics, and they were loaded. You could tell that a lot of them had scopes. . . . So I tweeted about it and I tagged the group that organized the protest, Open Carry Texas, in one of the tweets. . . . What happened next was that they started sending all of these tweets at me . . . so that all of their followers would see them too. . . . It was very obvious that they wanted to send people my way, and they did.[27]

Shauna James Ahern was shocked to be the recipient of gendertrolling attacks as a result of writing a blog on food:

> It's more than offhand comments on Twitter or raging emails. It's the systematic way that cruel comments come into my website inbox with every single post. When I posted the recipe for soft pretzels, within moments I received the comment: "I hope you choke on your own pretzels and die, you bitch." Every day, there is some nasty, vituperative comment on a post, something I skim quickly then delete. It could be comments about my husband ("He's obviously retarded. Look in his eyes. There's something wrong.") about our life on Vashon ("Oh that's right, everything is perfect on your fucking IS-LAND."), about our food ("That looks like dog vomit. Why does anyone pay you to do this?"), and mostly about me (my weight? my writing? my hair? my mere presence in the world? take your pick). New posts and posts from five years ago—it doesn't seem to matter.
>
> This happens nearly every day. Just from tonight: "i thought your kid cried all night and thats why you ate so much god damn pie. liar."[28]

An anonymous commenter was threatened and harassed for advocating breastfeeding online; she had verbal abuse sent to her along with threats of violence, including threats of death against her and her family and her young children. She remarks, "It's almost unimaginable that because I support women who want to breastfeed I am subjected to sexual harassment, verbal abuse, and threats of physical violence and death."[29]

Caroline Farrow, who blogs on Catholicism from a right-wing and religious perspective, was targeted for sexualized abuse and threats:

I am often told how my mouth would be put to better use giving fellatio or that I am uptight and sexually repressed, someone who could clearly benefit from a "regular seeing-to" and how my defence of conservative values stems from a deep-seated need to be anally penetrated. I am crying out for anal rape to be put in my place, preferably by an HIV-positive male who is not wearing a condom.[30]

Targeted for Achieving Prominence

Some women were apparently targeted because they had achieved prominence of some sort. For Kathy Sierra, a programming instructor and video game developer, the onslaught of harassment and explicit rape and death threats against her began when her blog about sexism in technology, called "Creating Passionate Users," became extremely popular, even making the Technorati Top 100 blog list. (Technorati was a search engine that was the gold standard for rating blogs in terms of their popularity and links; its blog index function has since been discontinued.) In 2014, she described the beginning of the years-long harassment campaign against her:

> Later I learned that the first threat had nothing to do with what I actually made or said in my books, blog posts, articles, and conference presentations. The real problem—as my first harasser described—was that others were beginning to pay attention to me. He wrote as if mere exposure to my work was harming his world.
>
> But here's the key: it turned out he wasn't outraged about my work. His rage was because, in his mind, my work didn't deserve the attention....
>
> I now believe the most dangerous time for a woman with online visibility is the point at which others are seen to be listening, "following", "liking", "favoriting", retweeting....
>
> From the hater's POV [point of view], you ... are "stealing" an audience....
>
> You must be stopped. And if they cannot stop you, they can at least ruin your quality of life.[31]

Feminista Jones, whose story is discussed earlier, also found that her online harassment increased dramatically when she achieved more prominence:

> I wrote an article about the Ray Rice situation [Rice's videotaped assault of his then-girlfriend Janay Palmer in an elevator in 2014] for *Time* magazine, and the trolling and harassment from that was just out of this world.... My profile has been growing for the last two years, but in 2014, I really started doing more public speaking, which was a goal of mine. So, now I'm doing a lot of public speaking and traveling around the country and around the world giving talks and lectures at colleges and universities and panels and

things like that. As I've become more visible in that way, there are people who see my visibility as a threat. And so they're doing whatever they can to try to intimidate me out of it.[32]

Targeted for Talking about Women's Rights

It also appears that women who speak out about women's rights or advocate feminism are particularly subject to threats and harassment. Cheryl Lindsey Seelhoff, whose story is detailed in Section 4 of this chapter, was one of the early recipients of a virulent online harassment campaign, in 2007, for writing a blog in which she discussed feminist issues.

Anita Sarkeesian (whose story is recounted in Section 5 of this chapter) is a media critic and blogger whose harassment began when she launched a Kickstarter page to fund a series of videos to expose gender stereotypes in video games. Lindy West, writer on the feminist blog Jezebel and commentator about comedy (her experiences are detailed in Section 2 of this chapter), was inundated with harassment along with rape and death threats after she went on television to debate a male comedian about whether rape jokes are appropriate in comedy routines. Jenny Haniver, a blogger and online videogamer, was harassed after she objected to the sexist and degrading insults she received from men while playing online video games. Caroline Criado-Perez, whose story is featured in Section 3 of this chapter, was shocked and surprised that something as inoffensive and innocuous as petitioning for a woman's face on just one British banknote provoked such an unheralded onslaught of harassment, abuse, and threats.

Amanda Hess, *Slate* contributor and freelance writer, speaking on the National Public Radio talk show *Tell Me More*, points out that women who either object to sexism or discuss sexuality openly are particularly vulnerable:

> When I speak with other women who talk about women's issues, whether it's, you know, from abortion to dating—by the way, I don't find dating to be a particularly racy topic—there will . . . be people who sort of use gendered harassment to lash out against people who are specifically taking on misogyny or discussing sexuality, frankly.[33]

Eleanor O'Hagan, a freelance writer who contributes to the *Guardian*, observed that certain kinds of speech seemed to elicit more attention and therefore harassment:

I became conscious of how my opinions would be received and began watering them down, or not expressing them at all. I noticed that making feminist arguments led to more abuse and, as a result, I rarely wrote about feminism at all.[34]

O'Hagan noted that advocating for women's rights or equality seemed to ramp up the harassment:

I noticed that making feminist arguments led to more abuse and, as a result, I rarely wrote about feminism at all. I was so nervous about the abuse I would receive when I wrote an article about cultural misogyny. . . . To me, misogynistic abuse is an attempt to silence women. Traditionally, men have been the ones who influence the direction of society: I think there is still a sense that it's not women's place to be involved in politics.[35]

Targeted for Supporting Other Women

For other women, the coordinated harassment campaigns targeting them occurred when they stepped up to defend other women who were being harassed. British Member of Parliament Stella Creasy, English journalist and broadcaster Grace Dent, and journalist Hadley Freeman publicly supported Caroline Criado-Perez (whose story is recounted in Section 3 of this chapter) when she was being harassed and were targeted with bomb threats as a result.

Melody Hensley, executive director of the Washington, DC, branch of the secular advocacy organization Center for Inquiry, began to receive widespread harassment and rape and death threats against her after she spoke out on behalf of Rebecca Watson, who was the target of a harassment campaign (see her story in Section 6). Hensley explains how her harassment began:

At first I was watching other women getting attacked, and I couldn't stand by because I am not the sort of person who stands by and watches that sort of thing. So I started speaking up in defense of women who were getting attacked, and that made me a target instantly. I started getting targeted by hundreds of people overnight, literally. That involved people attacking me on Twitter—constant—all day on Twitter. There were dozens of tweets a day at the beginning. And I was being monitored constantly.[36]

Amy Davis Roth, multimedia artist and blogger on atheist and secular humanist issues, also became the target of a campaign of harassment when she publicly allied herself with Rebecca Watson's concerns about the treatment of women at national atheist conferences and was therefore apparently seen as a stand-in for Watson:

> When I [wrote about problems with sexism at an atheist conference], suddenly the focus got put on me, because I had dared to speak up. Then after that time I started getting death threats, rape threats, I had my address posted, I was written about on MRA [men's rights activists] sites. From the point when I dared to speak up and I was no longer supporting what was considered to be the status quo is when the focus got directed on me. I became Rebecca [Watson] when I chose to go to the event that she was supposed to speak at. So people were mad at me because she wasn't there.[37]

Women Targeted for Their Race and Ethnicity

Many women are also targeted for being both women and of color. Danielle Keats Citron, a law professor whose work focuses on cyber law and author of *Hate Crimes in Cyberspace*, writes about harassment and abuse at the intersection of gender and race:

> Online mobs target African American and Hispanic women as well. As blogger "La Chola" explains, women-of-color bloggers consistently receive horrific emails and comments threatening violent sexual assault, death, and attacks against family members.... After the author of "Ask This Black Woman" posted commentary about a video game... [s]he received death threats. Posters told her to "[g]et back into the cotton fields, you filthy [n***r]."[38]

Malorie Blackman, a British writer designated Children's Laureate for 2013–2015, writes about harassment against her after voicing her opinion in a series of interviews that children's literature should be more inclusive of different kinds of people. When one of the interviews with Blackman was posted online, with the unfortunate headline "Children's Books 'Have Too Many White Faces,'"—a phrase Blackman had never used—the onslaught of harassment began. At her request, the news outlet changed the headline, but, as she reported,

> By then the damage had been done, with a number of publications publishing the ... article with its original inflammatory headline. A deluge of racist abuse then descended upon my head. My Twitter feed was inundated with racist comments thinly disguised as indignation.[39]

Zerlina Maxwell, political analyst and contributing writer for the *New York Daily News*, Feministing.com, theGrio.com, BET.com, and EBONY.

com, was harassed after she spoke out on the television show *Hannity* on Fox News about rape. As an example, she received a tweet that said, "Nigger! I hope you get raped and your throat slit! May be then you understand why white women have to be armed. DIE BITCH?" Although she had appeared on Fox News before without incurring rape and death threats, after she "talked about her experience being raped by someone she knew, disagreed that arming women with guns would be an effective way to reduce rape, and suggested that men should take some responsibility for ending [rape]," she began to be inundated with rape and death threats on Facebook, Twitter, and by email.[40] Maxwell explained,

> Clearly this is gendered and it has to do with the fact that I'm black. . . . Because the rape threats I received are not the same as the rape threats and death threats Lindy West got. Mine had the N-word all over them."[41]

Imani Gandy, attorney, political blogger, journalist, and women's rights activist, recounts the racialized and sexualized harassment she receives: "In my five years on Twitter, I've been called 'nigger' so many times that it barely registers as an insult anymore. . . . Let's just say that my 'nigger cunt' cup runneth over."[42]

In addition to racist, anti-African American abuse and harassment, gendertrolls have engaged in anti-Semitic harassment. The following message, among hundreds and hundreds of other harassing comments, was posted in response to a YouTube video that Anita Sarkeesian posted: "So you're a Bolshevik feminist jewess that hates White people . . . fucking ovendodger."[43]

Mikki Kendall, writer and contributor to *XO Jane*, *Salon*, and the *Guardian*, explained that, although her harassment was the result of being both black and a women, she believes that the topic women are writing on is irrelevant to whether they get harassed:

> So my experience has been both gendered and racial. I'm going to get called the B-word. I'm going to get called the N-word. I'm often going to be called them together. You get a lot of this—I think we all can all agree that it comes almost regardless of your topic.[44]

Kendall adds, "There is a tendency . . . to assume that these threats only happen to well known light/white women because that's who gets the most media attention. But [as far as I know,] they can happen to any woman who is online."[45]

Biological anthropologist Robin Nelson talks about the dangers of speaking or writing about black women's health and safety, policing practices in back communities, or sexual harassment and assault: "While I am finding myself speaking out more about these issues—I know I do so with considerable risk to my career and perhaps my physical safety. I have been trolled on Twitter following tweets about sexism and sexual harassment in academe, and racist policing in black communities. I have genuine concerns about being doxxed."[46]

Native American women have also experienced online harassment that is racialized. Erica Lee, a Canadian aboriginal woman, was targeted for online harassment after she participated in a campaign to get a Saskatoon high school to change its team name from "Redmen" and in the Idle No More movement, which was formed to protest legislative abuses of Indigenous treaty rights by the Canadian government. She received rape and death threats and reported that the harassers called her a "savage" and a "drunk."[47]

What Precipitates Gendertrolling Is Women Speaking Out

Women have been targeted online because they confronted sexism, or because they have gained notoriety, or because they supported other women who are being harassed. Many women have come to the conclusion that opining on pretty much any topic online can render a woman vulnerable for being targeted with rape and death threats, which can go on for months or even years. As Laurie Penny wrote in an article provocatively titled "A Woman's Opinion Is the Mini-Skirt of the Internet,"

> You come to expect it, as a woman writer, particularly if you're political. You come to expect the vitriol, the insults, the death threats. After a while, the emails and tweets and comments containing graphic fantasies of how and where and with what kitchen implements certain pseudonymous people would like to rape you cease to be shocking.[48]

Beard believes that online harassment and abuse happens regardless of the subject that a woman writes about:

> For a start it doesn't much matter what line you take as a woman, if you venture into traditional male territory, the abuse comes anyway. It's not what you say that prompts it, it's the fact you're saying it. And that matches the detail of the threats themselves. They include a fairly predictable menu of rape, bombing, murder and so forth (I may sound very relaxed about it now; that doesn't mean it's not scary when it comes late at night).[49]

Chris Kover, a contributor to *Vice News*, an online international news organization, sums up:

In most of these cases, if you look at it closely, what the woman being targeted has done turns out to be either nothing or something that has been exaggerated in all sorts of bizarre ways. Something that normal people wouldn't see as provocation.[50]

Dr. Nerdlove, online pseudonym for Harris O'Malley, who writes an advice column on love and relationships for "nerds and geeks," describes what he sees as a troubling phenomenon in geek culture:

> And yet [for] so many of my friends—just about every single woman I know who's active in geek culture, in fact—this isn't an abstract thought exercise. This is their daily lives. They are deluged with anonymous threats promising rape and worse . . . because some rando has decided that they must suffer for the crime of being a woman with an opinion online . . . and they know what you look like and where you live. . . . And nobody seems to care. Because this is the new normal. This is what, apparently, is accepted in geek culture now.[51]

The bottom line is that women who have opinions online are at risk of incurring a harassment campaign against them. It appears that it hardly matters what the opinion is, although having opinions affirmatively in favor of any aspect of women's rights seems to incur the most attention of the harassers. While women have been targeted for speaking or writing about an incredibly wide range of topics—from videogaming to women in technology, from comedy to comics, from atheism to gun control, even to cycling, sports, cooking, or breastfeeding—the commonality is that some woman somewhere on the Internet takes it upon herself to speak out publicly on a topic. And it is often worse if she advocates for women's self-respect, equal representation, or self-determination, however mildly and to however limited an audience. In response, groups of men from various sites on the Internet find out that a woman has taken such a stand, often going out of their way to search out such assertiveness on the part of women, and then rally their too-numerous troops to wage an all-out campaign to seek retribution on the targeted women in whatever ways they can. The unifying factor in common with all of these topics that women have talked about on the Internet is not the topic itself; it is that it is a woman who is doing the talking.

SECTION 2: SEXUALIZED AND GENDER-BASED INSULTS

> *You stupid ugly fucking slut I'll go to your flat and cut your fucking head off you inbred whore.*[52]

> *No one would fuck you, you're so ugly you look like you have downs syndrome, you'd be thankful to be raped.*[53]

> *You don't have to worry about being sexually harassed because you are hideous.*[54]

> *Good game, Jenny from the block. . . . But you'd be a lot cooler if you sucked on Fast Eddie's COCK!*[55]

LINDY WEST

On July 6, 2012, comedian Daniel Tosh appeared at the Laugh Factory, a comedy club in Los Angeles. A woman who attended the performance reported that Tosh started "making some very generalizing, declarative statements about rape jokes always being funny, how can a rape joke not be funny, rape is hilarious, etc." In response, the woman "yelled out, 'Actually, rape jokes are never funny!'"[56] According to the woman, Tosh handled the situation by taunting, "Wouldn't it be funny if that girl got raped by, like, five guys right now? Like right now?" as she and her friend exited the theater.[57]

In response to the controversy surrounding the Daniel Tosh rape jokes, Lindy West, a performer, editor, and writer, gained notoriety through some blog posts she wrote titled "How to Make a Rape Joke" and "An Open Letter to White Male Comedians" on the popular feminist blog Jezebel. In an interview, West explained about how she sees rape jokes being used in comedy:

> So what I saw happening was a lot of—especially white male comedians—using rape as a punchy buzzword to get a reaction. It was really cheap, it was really cruel and inconsiderate, and it really made no statement whatsoever. It accomplished nothing, and it was self-serving, and it traumatized victims and made women feel even more unwelcome in that space than they already were.[58]

West was subsequently invited to go on the FX television show *Totally Biased* to debate comedian Jim Norton about whether rape jokes were ever appropriate in comedy, which brought additional attention to the rape joke incident involving Tosh. Only six minutes of the debate between West and Norton ended up being aired on *Totally Biased*. The ensuing online response to West's appearance on the show was what she called "a suffocating deluge of violent misogyny" in the form of rape and death threats and other sexualized insults.[59] West described her harassment, which in her case also emphasized her appearance along with rape and death threats:

> It started immediately after the show aired, and for at least a week, it was constant. I didn't look at all of it. Every time I opened Twitter I had a hundred new mentions. I don't know how many posts the Jezebel post got. I get trolled on YouTube every day. But hundreds a day, for sure, for at least a week. And I still get trolling comments every once in a while because of that debate. As a fat woman, I get a lot of "Don't worry, you won't get raped," "You'd be grateful to be raped," "You're just jealous because no one wants to rape you," "Don't worry, no one would ever rape that fat bitch"—just a lot of that. There were some straight-ahead threats, like "Someone should rape some sense into you." Someone said they wanted to impale me and roast me on a spit. You know, all the classics. So a lot of graphic sexualized comments.[60]

West points out the irony of the response she received:

> How did [the people who attacked her] try to demonstrate that comedy, in general, doesn't have issues with women? By threatening to rape and kill me, telling me I'm just bitter because I'm too fat to get raped, and suggesting that the debate would have been better if it had just been Jim raping me.[61]

Many of the threats she received were such that she "considered getting a dog and a security system for my house."[62] Harassers warned her, "don't go walking alone, honey." Although West downplays the level of threat in the harassment she received in comparison with threats other women have received, she reports that, "They do talk about the city where I live. People definitely make it clear that they are looking into my personal life." She also found that there were whole threads on one particular forum commenting about her personal life as well as that of her fiancé. She reports that "they dug up pictures of his ex-wife to say, like, why would he go from this to that? It's really intrusive and alarming."[63]

West described feeling afraid and speaking about it to Jessica Valenti, feminist, author, and founder of the blog *Feministing*, who has also been gendertrolled. Valenti told West that she had spoken with someone from the FBI who had assured her that "it's not the loud ones you have to worry about," a thought that West did not find comforting.[64]

In a particularly disturbing incident, one of West's harassers spent enough time researching her life to discover that her father had died 18 months earlier. Because that troll managed to find out what her father had died from, where he was treated, and that West had siblings, West concluded that he must have found her father's obituary (something that would be rather difficult since her father's name is fairly generic, which means the troll would have had to spend considerable time and effort sifting through many similarly named people online to find him).[65] The harasser then went to the trouble of making a parody account on Twitter in her father's name, the bio of which said "embarrassed father of an idiot, other 2 kids are fine though."[66]

When Norton became aware of the level of vitriol and harassment that was being directed at West, although he did not know West before he debated her on *Totally Biased* and he holds a different opinion from her on the topic of rape jokes in comedy, he wrote a blog post in support of her:

> The reason I'm writing this is . . . to say how disgusted I am by the way many people have chosen to respond [to the debate]. I am very careful about telling people what they should write or how they should express themselves, but I truly hate a lot of the things that have been directed at Lindy. The anger she's facing is wrong and misguided. If you have [a] problem with her opinion, that's one thing, but to tweet that you hope she get's [sic] raped, or that you'd want her to be raped is fucking ignorant. She did nothing to deserve the vitriolic response she's gotten. She simply gave a well thought out opinion.[67]

West describes her feelings at the time of what she has humorously dubbed "Rape Joke Apocalypse 2013":

> It was very, very intense. It was very frightening. . . . It just makes you sick. . . . It's very jarring because you feel like, suddenly, civilization has fallen away, civilization has abandoned you, because this is not the way people talk to each other. . . . I live a very pleasant life. I am nice to people and people are nice to me. And it's so jarring to be just

ripped out of that and to have everyone's poison just coming at you from all sides. . . . Even people just saying the mean stuff to you, even people saying the meanest thing they can think of—when you multiply that by hundreds of people all day, every day, it's just exhausting, and it's this reminder that you're not a person. . . . I used to be more trusting and outgoing. And I wanted to go places and I wanted to talk to people and to meet people and I don't want to anymore. I'm tired. I feel like it's made my life smaller. . . . Because the amount of emotional energy it takes to feel okay when a bunch of strangers are trying to make you feel like shit all the time. . . . It's debilitating.[68]

Even though West says she has not received any specific or concrete threats, she says she still experiences "this sort of blanket hate, just all the time," which makes her uncertain about the level of danger she actually faces:

If I'm out and there's a man staring at me, honestly, I always think, is that a troll, is that one of the people who harasses me online? Is he going to take my picture and post it on some forum? It feels totally irrational, but these people are real and they live in my community, I'm sure, at least some of them do.[69]

West says the worst of her trolling occurred over the span of about a month following her appearance on the television show. In spite of the fact that she blocks known trolls continually, she says she "still get[s] comments about it. Just two days ago, I got a 'you're too fat to get raped.'"[70]

An overwhelming proportion of the harassing and abusing comments toward women on the Internet relate to women's physical appearance and sexuality. Women are especially attacked for being not sexually attractive enough to men, usually based on mainstream, conventional standards of attractiveness. Women are typically insulted for being, in the eye of the gendertroll, fat, "ugly," old, or a "dyke." Women are criticized for being too sexual (they are whores or sluts), or they are disparaged for having female body parts, which are used as insults (they are "cunts" or their genitalia are especially disparaged). Often these comments devolve into the gendertroll's determination as to a woman's rape-ability or the degree to which she deserves to be raped: for example, she is deemed too fat or ugly to be raped and/or she ought to be raped. These contradictory assessments are frequently made simultaneously.

Women Criticized for Being Fat or Ugly

One of the predominant ways that women are criticized is by judging their physical attractiveness as being deficient; that is, they are called "ugly" or "fat" most commonly. In this manner, their sexual attractiveness—or what is deemed a lack thereof—is at the forefront of the commentary about the targeted woman. Lindy West, for example, has been extensively targeted because of her weight as well as for being an outspoken woman on the Internet. "Georgia," an anonymous online gamer, wrote about receiving abusive comments about being unattractive and overweight, being called a slut, and receiving rape threats. She explained that she had enjoyed playing video games since she was young, but that when she was 15 years old, she started receiving rape threats along with comments about her weight and accusations about her "sluttiness." She says that she continued receiving these kinds of comments for years, concluding that "It's a sad world we live in where a 15-year-old girl must learn how to manage the onslaught of rape threats just to be able to play online games."[71] "Georgia" received these comments about her appearance even though she interacted with the harassers only through online video games, where they were unable to see what she actually looked like and had no way of knowing her actual weight.

Another woman video game player who blogs about her experiences wrote a post about being constantly harassed, abused, and stalked by male gamers. On the post, she reported receiving a comment "basically telling me I'm a joke for playing male-dominated video games, that I must be a hideous fat girl that has no life, and that I am an overall a pathetic person."[72] She explains that, "Between getting asked for my phone number, nudes, and my bra size, I'm being told how I'm obviously 300 pounds or butt ugly or worse when I refuse to respond or kindly ask to be left alone."[73]

Jennifer Pozner, journalist, media critic, and founder and executive director of Women in Media and News, an organization dedicated to increasing women's presence in the media, describes the gendered insults sent to her: "Very rarely have I gotten negative feedback that doesn't include either a rape threat or calling me ugly and fat. Or sometimes they tell me I'm hot, but they hate what I'm saying—they'd rather watch me on TV with the mute on."[74]

Kate Smurthwaite, feminist activist, comedian, and author of Cruellablog, gives examples of how the insults leveled at her are nearly always gender related:

> I get abusive comments on my blog or under my videos. Some is straight up hate-speech: fat, ugly, desperate or a bitch who deserves to be slapped, hit or gang-raped....

> The vast majority of the abuse is gender-related. There is a clear link to Internet pornography. Much of the language used could have come straight from pornographic sites. For example, from this week: "IF THIS TRASH TALKING K*NT HAD HER F*CKNG, TONGUE RIPPED OUT OF HER SUCK-HOLE...."[75]

Natalie Dzerins, a British law school graduate and social justice activist, laughed off being targeted for being, in a gendertroll's opinion, too unattractive to rape:

> Last night, I was informed that if all women looked like me, there would be no more rape in the world. I have to admit that I laughed when I read it, as it was exactly the level of response I was expecting. If there is one thing I have learned about being a woman with vocal opinions, it is that everything I ever do or say is wrong because of my physical appearance.[76]

Dawn Foster, a British writer and editor, commented about how the topics she discusses online get sidelined in the comments section by insults directed at her for being a woman: "The emails rarely mentioned the topic at hand: instead they focussed on my age, used phrases like 'little girl', described rape fantasies involving me and called me 'ugly' and 'disgusting.'"[77]

Melody Hensley, executive director of the Washington, DC, branch of the atheist/secular humanist organization Center for Inquiry, typically receives graphic images and other insults about her appearance:

> People would make these horrible videos about me calling me a "cunt" and a "feminazi" and stupid. And they would body shame me and say I am a professional victim. They would create these videos, taking the worst photos of me and making fun of me. And I would watch those videos and something in my head just snapped. The videos started replaying in my head. I cried for 6 months. That's when the PTSD started....
>
> [The insults] usually involve some type of insult to either my appearance or some sort of sexual epithet.... There's always some sexist element.[78]

Gendertrolls don't seem to be deterred by the contradiction of insulting a woman's lack of sexual attractiveness and his simultaneous—apparently notwithstanding—desire to engage in sex with the targeted woman. Caroline Farrow, a right-wing Catholic blogger, observes,

> The comments about my appearance tend to focus upon the fact that I am unattractive but yet paradoxically inviting sexual advances. People would deign to have sex with me either out of pity or to teach me a lesson.[79]

Genital-Related Insults

In addition to being told they are fat or ugly, women are frequently insulted in ways specifically related to female genitalia. Laurie Penny, an English journalist and contributor at the *New Statesman* and the *Guardian*, writes about typically receiving genital-related insults, among other gender-related insults:

> Most mornings, when I go to check my email, Twitter and Facebook accounts, I have to sift through threats of violence, public speculations about my sexual preference and the odour and capacity of my genitals, and attempts to write off challenging ideas with the declaration that, since I and my friends are so very unattractive, anything we have to say must be irrelevant.[80]

Actor and women's rights activist Ashley Judd writes about the flood of tweets that she received after criticizing a play in a basketball game: "I read in vivid language the various ways, humiliating and violent, in which my genitals, vaginal and anal, should be violated, shamed, exploited and dominated."[81]

Courtney Caldwell, who was targeted after she was publicly critical of some Open Carry gun owners, also reports attempts to shame her by insulting her genitalia:

> I got pornographic pictures sent my way. People took my profile picture and photoshopped words onto it. I don't use the c-word, but they used the c word. My Twitter handle is "Cult of Courtney." They changed it to "c-u-n-t of Courtney." [There were] a lot of very gendered threats and general harassment. They were talking about wetting my panties, really, really grotesque things that shouldn't be sent to women.[82]

Women Criticized for Being Old

Women are also targeted for being old. Mary Beard, a professor of classics at the University of Cambridge who is in her 50s, became the target of a slew of harassment after her appearance on the British television program *Question Time*. Much of the harassment involved gendertrolls declaring her unattractive, especially because of her age and her gray hair. A 20-year-old university student tweeted at Beard, "You filthy old slut. I bet your vagina is disgusting."[83] Gendertrolls also superimposed her face onto an image of female genitalia, and she was called "a vile, spiteful excuse for a woman, who eats too much cabbage and has cheese straws for teeth."[84] There was also, according to Beard, a "web post that has . . . discussed my pubic hair (do I brush the floor with it), whether I need rogering (that comment was taken down, as was the speculation about the capaciousness of my vagina, and the plan to plant a d*** in my mouth).[85]

Ophelia Benson, an atheist blogger who is also in her 50s and who writes for a popular atheist multiauthor blog titled Free Thought Blogs, reported that most of the abuse and harassment directed toward her was "about how ugly, old, and sexually repulsive I am."[86]

Other Gender-Specific Insults

Women receive a slew of typically sexualized forms of harassment, such as being called "whore," "slut," "cunt," or "bitch," and other derogatory sex-specific insults. An anonymous commenter identified as "Indiana" related her experience in an explicitly nonsexual chat room on the Internet where two men targeted her, calling her "'whore,' 'slut,' 'cunt,' 'fuckhole,' 'bitch.'"[87] Another commenter identified as "New York" cites some of the sex-specific harassment she has received:

> "Fuck you, E-skank! C*nt! You're a fat whore!" (never mind that they've never laid eyes on me.), "Shut up or I'll rape your ass! Cancel your account, slut!" It goes on and on. There are days I've been called every name in the book, simply because I've made my gender known.[88]

Miri Mogilevsky, blogger at Free Thought Blogs, stresses that the insults and harassment she gets are sexualized and specific to being a woman, rather than generic insults:

> The threats are almost always sexualized threats. I get very few nonsexualized threats. It's usually graphic: [they are] slurs, but they are gendered slurs like "bitch," "cunt," "whore," "slut." Or it will be graphic descriptions of rape. It's almost never the typical "LOL, you suck, go die."[89]

A defining characteristic of gendertrolling is that women are insulted in ways that are specific to their gender: belittling them for being ugly or fat; evaluating them as not being sexually attractive, or for being overly sexual ("whore," "slut"); attempting to shame and insult their genitalia; disparaging them for being old and thus no longer sexually attractive; and using gender-specific insults such as "whore," "bitch," or "cunt." These kinds of attacks are attempts to make women feel unworthy and to instill sexual shame. Being insulted by being called fat, ugly, or old is a way to make a woman feel that she is unworthy of respect or attention. Calling women "whores" or "sluts" and insulting and disparaging their genitalia are intended as ways of shaming women about their sexuality.

Rather than engage women on the merits (or demerits) of their arguments, activities, or writing, gendertrolls zero in on insulting the women's sexuality or sexual attributes. These gender-based and sexualized insults serve to distract and derail attention from the content of what women are writing and to cause online discussions and forums authored by women to devolve into personal insults.

SECTION 3: CREDIBLE RAPE AND DEATH THREATS

I will fuck your ass to death you filthy fucking whore. Your only worth on this planet is as a warm hole to stick my cock in.[90]

I daily receive headaches from selfrighteous rejects like yourself. I've had enough. . . now I seek you out. I rape you through the eye socket.[91]

You better watch your back . . . Im gonna rape your ass at 8pm and put the video all over the Internet.[92]

CAROLINE CRIADO-PEREZ

In April 2013, the Bank of England announced its decision to replace the image of Elizabeth Fry, a 19th-century English social reformer, with the image of Winston Churchill on the British 5-pound note. Fry was the only woman, other than Queen Elizabeth II, featured on any British banknote. In response to the announcement, Caroline Criado-Perez, a British journalist and cofounder of the feminist blog the Women's Room, began a campaign to try to get the Bank of England to feature another woman on a British banknote when it retired Fry. She launched a petition on change.org called "Bank of England: Keep a Woman on English Banknotes," which got more than 35,000 signatures.[93]

After an initial resistance to Criado-Perez's campaign, in the end, the Bank of England announced on July 24, 2013, that it would feature Jane Austen on the 10-pound note. The day after the bank's announcement, Criado-Perez began to receive a surge of threatening, abusive, and misogynistic messages, including rape and death threats—up to 50 threats and abusive tweets an hour at their peak.[94]

One person, who identified himself as Johnny@beware0088, targeted Criado-Perez with threats and insults all day and late into the night. He sent her messages in which he fantasized about raping her, and at one point, he threatened, "I will find you." He also tweeted "Could I help you with that" when another man tweeted, "you need to get f***** until you die."

Criado-Perez was shocked that such an innocuous campaign could have resulted in such an overwhelmingly vicious and negative response. She described being unable to eat or sleep, losing weight, and even having a "kind of breakdown," in which she cried continuously, was unable to function, and felt on "an emotional edge all the time."[95] In an online interview with the BBC, Criado-Perez elaborated on the effects of the torrent of online abuse aimed at her:

> It's . . . consumed my life both physically and emotionally. I've not really had much sleep. The threats have been so explicit and so graphic . . . they have sort of stuck with me in my head and have really put me in fear . . . when a journalist came to my house last night at 10:15 and I just had this huge reaction of total and utter terror . . . I feel under siege . . . because the threats have been so graphic and people specifically saying they are going to come find me, and people have posted what they thought was my address online. Luckily it wasn't my address, but the fact that they have actually tried to do that is really disturbing.[96]

Criado-Perez described the kinds of graphic abuse and threats that she found so horrifying:

> I remember the man who told me I'd never track him down, only feel his cock while he was raping me; the man who told me he would pistol-whip me over and over until I lost consciousness, while my children watched, and then burn my flesh; the man who told me he had a sniper rifle aimed directly at my head and did I have any last words, fugly piece of shit? I remember the man who told me to put both hands on his cock and stroke it till he came on my eyeballs or he would slit my throat; the man who told me I would be dead and gone that night, and that I should kiss my pussy goodbye, as a group of them would "break it irreparably"; the man who told me a group of them would mutilate my genitals with scissors and set my house on fire while I begged to die. I can see their words on the screen. I remember where I was when I got them. I remember the fear, the horror, the despair. I remember feeling sick. I remember not being able to sleep. I remember thinking it would never end.[97]

Criado-Perez felt that she had "stumbled into a nest of men who co-ordinate attacks on women."[98] She later commented,

> The head of WHO [World Health Organization] called violence against women a "global health problem of epidemic proportions"; she should take a look at twitter, where we have our own nasty little epidemic: an epidemic of misogynistic men who feel so threatened

by any woman speaking up, that they feel they must immediately silence her with a threat of sexual violence.[99]

Other women who were vocal in defending Criado-Perez online were similarly besieged with rape and death threats. Journalists Caitlin Moran and Suzanne Moore and Member of Parliament Stella Creasy showed public support for Criado-Perez and were subsequently targeted by many of the same harassers.[100] Creasy published a supportive opinion column in the *Guardian* in which she defended Criado-Perez and criticized the virulent nature of the attacks. Shortly thereafter she was sent threatening messages herself, including one that read, "YOU BETTER WATCH YOUR BACK. . . .IM GONNA RAPE YOUR ASS AT 8PM AND PUT THE VIDEO ALL OVER THE INTERNET."[101] Creasy was also targeted by Twitter user Johnny@beware0088, who called her a "dumb, blonde bitch" and menacingly suggested to her, "The things I could do to you."[102] Creasy defiantly tweeted back in response, "You send me a rape threat you morons I will report you to the police & ensure action taken."[103]

By early August 2013, however, the online campaign against women protesting online abuse turned even more alarming: a series of bomb threats were sent on August 2 via Twitter to numerous women journalists, including Hadley Freeman, a columnist with the *Guardian* newspaper; Mary Beard, professor of classics at the University of Cambridge; Grace Dent, a journalist who writes for the *Independent*; Catherine Mayer, *Time* magazine's Europe editor; and Emma Barnett, women's editor at the *Telegraph* newspaper. They had all been calling publicly for actions to prevent abuse against women on social media, including Twitter.[104] Freeman received a message saying, "A BOMB HAS BEEN PLACED OUTSIDE YOUR HOME. IT WILL GO OFF AT 10:47 ON A TIMER AND TRIGGER DESTROYING EVERYTHING," ostensibly in response to her writing a July 30 column in the *Guardian* that was critical of online misogyny and abuse. Other women targeted with similar bomb threats included Sara Lang, a social media manager at the American Association of Retired Persons; Katie Hartwill, assistant to a member of parliament; Laurie Penny, journalist and contributor to the *New Statesman*; and Anna Leskiewicz, editor of Oxford University's student newspaper.[105]

The police and Scotland Yard were alerted and investigated the threats. Although no bombs were found at the women's homes, the concrete details of the threat invoked an understandable level of fear in the recipients.

Criado-Perez said that when she contacted the police regarding the threats, they appeared "a bit flummoxed," but that they did eventually investigate the threats made against her. She still felt "frustrated" that the police didn't seem to be taking threats received by women other than herself as seriously.[106]

Since most of the rape, death, and bomb threats Criado-Perez and her supporters received occurred via Twitter, Criado-Perez tried appealing to Twitter for help. However, the only avenue available at that time on Twitter in England was to fill out a report form and wait for a response. As Criado-Perez explained, "If you're someone who's receiving . . . about 50 rape threats an hour, it's just not practical to expect you to go and fill in this form every single tweet. They're [Twitter] on the side of the abusers, not the victims, and they really, really need to get on the side of the victims."[107] A petition began circulating to make it easier to report abuse on Twitter, demanding a "zero tolerance policy on abuse"; as of August 2013, over a hundred thousand people had signed it.[108] On August 3, 2013, Tony Wang, Twitter's general manager in Britain, apologized to the women who had received abuse via Twitter and announced that Twitter had instituted a one-click option on all tweets, which would enable abusive postings to be more easily reported.

Because England has stricter laws than the United States about sending electronic messages that are "grossly offensive or of indecent, obscene, or menacing character," as set forth in Section 127 of the British Communications Act of 2003, several arrests have been made in connection with the rape, death, and bomb threats.[109] One of those arrested on suspicion of harassing both Criado-Perez and Creasy was John Nimmo, who was established to be Twitter-user Johnny@beware0088.[110] English law sets forth punishment for these crimes as up to six months in prison, and in January 2014, Nimmo was sentenced to eight weeks in prison for his threats on Twitter.[111]

Rather than withdrawing from public and online activities, as many women might understandably do under similar circumstances, Criado-Perez was determined to not let the online abusers silence or intimidate her. She felt strongly that if the harassers are out to silence women, then the last thing she would do is silence herself. She articulated the power she sees in standing strong:

> The don't feed the trolls adage is one that suggests they have the power. But if my experience from the last 48 hours does anything, it

is to give the lie to this impression. Troll accounts have been going private left right and centre. My twitter mentions are now overflowing with messages of support, messages from people saying that they want to shout back too. Messages from people realising that if we use our voice in unison, we are legion. . . . Over the past few days I have been overwhelmed by abuse, and I have been overwhelmed by support. I have felt elated—and I have felt close to defeat. But as I watch my timeline, it is clear which group is bigger. It is clear which group is louder. It is clear which group is stronger.[112]

Women who have been harassed online report that rape and death threats are by far the most common type of threats or abuse that they receive. Indeed, they are so common that Laurie Penny, the British journalist who wrote the widely read article about online abuse titled "A Woman's Opinion Is the Mini-Skirt of the Internet," makes the case that, much like the idea that miniskirts provoke rape, the mere fact of a woman having an opinion on the Internet is all it can take to for some men to feel justified in issuing rape and death threats.[113]

Rape and death threats are so common that they are almost the rule rather than the exception when women are trolled or harassed online. Soraya Chemaly, feminist writer, media critic, and activist, writes about her realization that rape and death threats are common experiences for women online:

The first time I received an online threat it was in response to an article in which I suggested the benefits of allowing boys to cross-gender empathize the way girls do. A man suggested that I should and would hang high. Since then I, like millions of other women, regularly am called any number of gender-based, usually sexually inflected insults, for expressing my opinions. And, like others, I get threats that include being stalked and raped. Most recently, one man explained—with this actual photography and name in Facebook, "if you guys ever gain ground, we will take that ground back with guns. I will make sure there are roving squads in every community going from house to house looking for feminists to kill."[114]

An anonymous woman identified as "New Jersey" described receiving rape threats along with other kinds of harassment:

I was threatened with rape. I had my father's death made fun of. My name and address were posted along with "gives good head." My phone number was posted in a fake online ad for casual encounters. All this online harassment was in conjunction with cell phone harassment and actual physical stalking for three years. The police did nothing.[115]

An online gamer identified as "Michigan" told her story of experiencing a virtual or simulated rape at the hands of other online gamers when she was just 11 years old:

> I know no one can do anything about this since it was indirect but they basically raped me in Minecraft and said that they were livestreaming it on Twitch.tv. If I tried to log off, they would threaten me. . . . In the Skype call, the last thing they wanted me to do before I had my parents shut off the Internet was that they wanted me to moan for them. Of course, I was only 11. I didn't know what rape was. I didn't exactly know what sex was.[116]

Actor and women's rights advocate Ashley Judd reported on receiving a deluge of vitriol and rape threats after tweeting a remark about a championship basketball game:

> Tweets rolled in, calling me a cunt, a whore or a bitch, or telling me to suck a two-inch dick. Some even threatened rape, or "anal anal anal."[117]

Rebecca Watson, an atheist/skeptic blogger whose gendertrolling experience is detailed in Section 6 of this chapter, describes the threats made against her: "The vast majority of threats are rape threats. The vast majority say I hope you get raped, you deserve to be raped."[118]

Miri Mogilevsky was targeted after she started writing at the atheist multiauthor blog Free Thought Blogs. She keeps a record of the rape and death threats she received (e.g., "I am going to rape you with my huge 5-inch cock").[119] In addition to the rape threats, someone created a Facebook page titled "Should Miri Mogilevsky Be Murdered?" On the page, it was posted,

> We should not ever break the law. Rather, we should advocate, through lawful and constitutional processes, to have the law changed so that it is legal to kill Miri Mogilevsy [sic]. Alternatively, we should, where legal, request that Miria [sic] Mogilevsky kill herself. Relevant laws should be changed so that suicide, and advocating suicide, is legal."[120]

Facebook was asked to remove the page. Mike Shaver, director of engineering at Facebook, tweeted the company's initial response to the request, declaring that the page did not violate Facebook's Terms and Conditions. After considerable protest and widespread reporting on the issue, Facebook did remove the page. However, even after the page was removed from Facebook, Shaver tweeted, "The title [of the Facebook page about murdering Mogilevsky] isn't a threat, though it might violate other of our terms."[121]

In another instance of a woman receiving rape and death threats, an actor, posting anonymously, who works in commercials and television in Los Angeles explained that when the commercials she works in are posted on YouTube, as is the custom by advertising agencies, the comments about her on the videos are often threatening and graphically violent. She said that videos and images of her were edited into violent depictions of women being brutalized, with people commenting below saying they wished to see her murdered and raped.[122]

Chris Kover, a journalist who writes for *Vice News*, an international news organization, talks about the harm that receiving rape and death threats causes, regardless of whether they are credible:

> But regardless of actual physical violence, just the threats in themselves already do an incredible amount of damage....
>
> Many of these men are trying to manipulate the Google results. Antifeminist activists very clearly try to harass women by making sure that all sorts of nasty things show up in their Google results. They say: We try to fuck things up for them and make sure they don't get hired in the future.[123]

Stella Creasy explained the effects of rape threats on Twitter: "It's not about sexual attraction, it's about power. It is somebody trying to make you frightened. It is about sex as a weapon."[124]

Graphic Threats

In addition to rape and death threats, many of the threats received by women are extremely graphic and evoke an extraordinary level of horror and revulsion. An anonymous commenter identified as "Virginia" recounted that when she gave her opinion in a discussion about the 2012 presidential election, a man threatened to rape her, saying he would "tear my ass up." She described herself as "shaking as she re-read the threats" in order to send screenshots of the threats to the website host.[125]

Another anonymous commenter, who is the executive director of a gun violence prevention organization, tells of graphic messages and images that she was sent, including voicemail messages telling her that she doesn't deserve to live because of her views on gun violence. She also describes being mailed a photograph of a "victim of the Mexican drug cartel with nearly 50 knives stuck in their body that said I should be concerned about 'kitchen knife violence.'"[126]

"Texas" reported that, although her blog is fairly unknown and is read by very few people, when she blogged about how her toddler daughter had affected her views on feminism, a commenter "appeared out of the blue and said that he would like to rape us both to death."[127]

Amanda Hess, *Slate* contributor and freelance writer, details a small part of her experience of online harassment:

> HeadlessFemalePig set up a Twitter account this summer expressly for the purpose of threatening to rape me and cut off my head. He's just sort of the latest abuser in a long line of mostly anonymous people who have taken to the Internet to make sexual comments against me and threaten my life.[128]

Anita Sarkeesian, media critic and author of the blog Feminist Frequency whose story is recounted in Section 5, experienced an ongoing and widespread campaign of harassment for speaking up about objectification in depictions of women in video games. In response, she received especially graphic comments, such as this one from her YouTube channel: "And bitches like to bake cake, lick da dick, suck anus, and deepthroat ballz."[129]

A troll who was later identified to be Frank Zimmerman sent Louise Mensch, a conservative member of the British Parliament from 2010 to 2012, an email that contained a horrific threat against her children. The email read, in part:

> We are Anonymous and we do not like rude cunts like you and your nouveau rich husband Peter Mensch. . . . So get off Twitter, cuntface. We see you are still on Twitter. We have sent a camera crew to photograph you and your kids and we will post it over the net including Twitter, cuntface. You now have Sophie's Choice: which kid is to go. One will. Count on it cunt. Have a nice day.[130]

As a result of the stricter laws about what is permitted speech in England, Zimmerman was convicted and given a suspended 26-week prison sentence for sending an "offensive, indecent, menacing message," and he was banned from contacting a list of celebrities.[131]

In illustration of an extremely graphic threat, Cheryl Lindsey Seelhoff, feminist blogger (whose story is detailed in Section 4), was sent the following message: "I'd like to tie you down, take a knife, and slit your throat. I'd penetrate you over and over in all orifices, and crate [*sic*] some of my own to stick myself in."[132]

Another woman, "Kim B.," who was a victim of the same early instance of gendertrolling as Seelhoff, was sent an image that she described as follows: "My image . . . was photoshopped to depict a hand-drawn male dog standing over me ejaculating on my face."[133] She was also sent a message in which "a man explained how he would rape me until I bled to death before burning my body and 'skull fucking your eye sockets.'"[134]

In a more recent attack, this time on the feminist website Jezebel, anonymous commenters repeatedly posted violent pornographic images in the discussion section of the website for a period of months. In an article written by Jezebel staff, they reported that men were "bragging about it on 4chan in conversations staffers [at Jezebel] have followed."[135] Because Jezebel is run by Gawker, which does not allow editors to ban users by IP address (an Internet Protocol address is a unique number assigned to each computer or device accessing the Internet that can be used to determine the identity and location of the user), and because most of the posters used "burner accounts," which are untraceable anonymous accounts allowed by Gawker, Jezebel staff were forced to view each image and delete them one by one, an experience they likened to "playing whack-a-mole with a sociopathic Hydra."[136]

It is clear that this aspect of gendertrolling, that of posting extremely horrifying and graphically violent content, is geared toward being as shocking and intimidating as possible to the targeted woman, in the hopes she will withdraw either from voicing her opinion or from the Internet entirely. The shock value and graphic nature of these kinds of messages and images, whether or not they were perceived by the recipients as credible threats, have an overwhelmingly upsetting effect. Receiving an unrelentingly sustained level of unthinkable viciousness, vile expressions of hate, and graphic and horrifying descriptions of sexual violence is not something that can be easily sloughed off, which is indeed the effect that women who have been the targets of these kinds of messages report.

Credible Threats

While the rape and death threats as well as the extremely graphic content of online harassment are especially disturbing, another characteristic aspect of gendertrolling is that many of the threats are perceived by the targeted women as particularly credible; that is, the threats are made in such a way that the recipients cannot feel certain that the threats are simply idle talk that won't result in their actually being physically harmed.

Although it may seem easy—from a remote location and when personally removed from the situation—to think that one could determine whether a particular threat might be carried out, there is no reliable way of ascertaining whether a particular harasser is likely to back up his threats with action. Posting a targeted woman's address, phone number, and often even information about her family can seem especially menacing. Harassers create the impression that they are able—and perhaps even intend—to carry out their threats. Indeed, the threats are often worded in such a way as most effectively to scare, intimidate, upset, or worry the targeted woman so that she will be induced to cease doing whatever the behavior is that the gendertrolls are upset about in order to safeguard her health and safety, which most often means silencing her opinions.

British feminist and trade union activist Cath Elliot speaks of just such an uncertainty as to whether to take the threats she has received seriously:

> There have been a couple of times recently when I've thought about going to the police. How am I supposed to know for instance whether "Let's hope she doesn't end up getting stabbed in the head or something" is a throwaway comment by a sad little man [sitting] in his bedsit in his underpants, or whether it's something slightly more sinister that means I need to keep looking over my shoulder whenever I leave the house? At what point does "a bit of online abuse" cross over into sexual harassment or hate speech? And how do you determine when a "nasty comment" has crossed a line and become a genuine threat to kill?[137]

In a particularly menacing move, harassers sometimes post information online that reveals that they have seen the targeted woman in real life. In a case in which gendertrolls targeted female law students through the online discussion board AutoAdmit, "discussion threads suggested that the posters had physical access to the women. A poster described a woman's attire at the school gym."[138] That one of the harassers had seen the woman in person and could describe what she was wearing lent an added credibility to the threats made against her.

Kover emphasizes that because rape is such a common occurrence in women's lives, rape threats can seem particularly credible:

> When a guy is threatened with rape, he doesn't actually say, "Oh, that has me worried." At least outside of prison men don't spend any amount of their time worrying about rape. But rape is something that women worry about. And some of these guys have the mentality of stalkers. When you look at men who stalk romantic partners, a lot of times it ends in violence. So there is a very real threat.[139]

Caitlin Dewey, a writer who covers social media and Internet culture for the *Washington Post*, writes about receiving what she considers credible threats:

> Like virtually every woman with any kind of public Internet profile, I regularly receive threats, slurs and other [types of] invective in the course of doing my job. Sometimes they're fairly benign: "get raped," while definitely not the first thing you want to see on a Friday morning, doesn't prompt a serious chat between me, my editor and building security.

But there have been other messages, too, messages that had me leaving work early, or consulting with The Post's lawyers, or calling my dad out of a business meeting in New York to explain what he and my mom should do if someone calls a bomb squad on them, as someone on Twitter promised.[140]

It's important to see the deluge of rape and death threats as occurring in a culture where nearly one in five women is raped during her lifetime.[141] Given the statistics on rape, even women who don't receive explicit rape threats fear rape and alter their behavior by avoiding going out alone after dark, carrying car keys in their hands when approaching their cars, or showing extra care about locking their doors at night. Bearing in mind that most women already live with a keen awareness that they could be raped at any time, the sense of fear and danger of women who also receive constant, express, and specific threats of rape (and physical violence and death) is understandably compounded.

Doxxing

Doxxing, in combination with rape and death threats, is also fairly common among women who are harassed by gendertrolls. Rape and death threats seem particularly alarming when the gendertroll demonstrates that he knows where the woman lives by doxxing her, that is, conducting extensive online searches until he finds her address and then posting it online for others to see. Targeted women have expressed feeling especially afraid when their real names, addresses, and other identifying information are posted on forums where targeting them is the topic of discussion.

In 2007, Kathy Sierra, a programming instructor and game developer, was the target of a campaign against her in which her social security number and former home address were posted, along with a fictionalized account of her past, her career, and her family, and a call was made for others to step up the harassment and threats against her. Her experience with being threatened and doxxed led to her shutting down her popular blog and retiring from her career-related Internet presence.[142]

Marcela Kunova, a London-based freelance journalist and photographer, writes about the effect of doxxing in combination with threats of violence:

> It now seems to be an established fact: women who speak publicly get threatened with rape, physical violence, harming their relatives and murder. It is not just a bit of fun. Many are stalked and get their home addresses published. And it doesn't really matter whether those threats will subsequently come true—they are already an act of violence.[143]

Amy Davis Roth, an atheist blogger, recounted how upsetting the experience of being doxxed was for her and how it added to her level of fear that the threats made against her might be realized:

> When it first happened to me, I was absolutely thrown back.... I had no idea that I was going to get start getting death threats and rape threats, and that my home address was going to be posted.... It was absolutely jaw droppingly terrifying to me at the time.[144]

Kate Smurthwaite, a British comedian and political activist, describes an increased sense of fear after being doxxed:

> What frightens me the most is when an abusive message includes my personal details. I've had my own address quoted at me with a rape threat and—yes—that is terrifying. That's when I call the police; they're not much help.[145]

Dawn Foster, a blogger, recounts how being doxxed, along with threats about her specific real-world activities, shook her sense of safety:

> The worst instance of online abuse I've encountered happened when I blogged about the Julian Assange extradition case.... Initially it was shocking: in the space of a week, I received a rabid email that included my home address, phone number and workplace address, included as a kind of threat. Then, after tweeting that I'd been waiting for a night bus for ages, someone replied that they hoped I'd get raped at the bus stop.[146]

Melissa McEwan, writer and founder of the feminist blog Shakesville, not only had her address and telephone number published along with statements encouraging online participants to harass her, but one site, *Encyclopedia Dramatica*, a haven for online trolls, offered a reward to anyone who could prove they had raped or killed her.[147] In addition, McEwan's website was targeted for a "DDoS-ing," a distributed denial of service attack. DDoS and DoS (denial of service) attacks occur when one user (in the case of DoS attacks) or multiple users (in the case of DDoS attacks) flood the bandwidth of a system such as a web server in an attempt to interrupt or suspend the service, rendering the server unavailable to users. Kelly Diels, contributor to *Salon* and Jezebel, writes about the online forum that fomented the gendertrolling campaign against McEwan:

> [McEwan's] address and phone number are published and so are suggestions about how to troll her, ranging from emailing her penis pictures, to "revenge-raping her," to targeting a Shakesville audience member who also owns a blog by extracting "their info from whois database, Facebook, or a phone book then proceed to raep." (Rape, deliberately misspelled as "raep,"

can mean a dos or Ddos attack.) In 2007, the Shakesville website, along with several other feminist blogs, was the subject of Ddos attacks—but the primary tool used to harass McEwan, year after year, is threats of sexual violence and death.[148]

A woman identified as "Ohio" recounted not only being doxxed, in spite of having been extremely careful to try to maintain an anonymous online identity, but that people online were being encouraged to physically assault or shoot her, her family, or her pets. Her harassment began in 2010 when, using an anonymous user name, she debated political issues in an online magazine. She later found in the forums where she had posted that people had created

> dozens of posts listing my real name, real address, email, phone number, and, worst of all, links to GoogleEarth photos of my home, along with detailed instructions on how to get there. Some were solicitations to beat me up or shoot me. One suggested killing my pets; another said "and if anyone in her family gets shot by accident—too bad!"[149]

The harassers managed to find out her husband's name, even though it was different than her name, and then harassed him by requesting to be added to his LinkedIn account, trying to set up fake interviews with him, and attempting to slander him professionally online. Several of those harassing her followed her to other sites where she posted. She said that it took about a year after deleting her accounts, including changing her email and her service provider and closing her Twitter account, for the harassment to abate. She describes how terrifying the experience was: "I won't easily forget how awful it was, and the cold chill that goes up your spine when someone who knows who you are and where you live threatens to murder you or your family. And yes, my attackers were all men."[150]

The combined effects of rape and death threats and graphic violent and sexualized content and images, along with finding out and posting online the women's physical whereabouts, are sufficient to instill fear and even terror in the women who are targeted in this manner. Regardless of whether these behaviors remain online, the constantly implied threats that they might not is sufficient to create high anxiety among the recipients of the harassment. However, not all of the harassment remains only virtual.

"IRL" Encounters

In addition to credible and graphic rape and death threats as well as posting women's real-life contact information online, some women have had IRL encounters with trolls. Jill Filipovic, a law school student at the time her online harassment began, saw the harassment cross over into her real life when she became aware that people who had interactions with her in her daily life were being encouraged to take photographs of her and to rape her.

> I've received more rape threats than I can count. . . . I've had stalkers and creeps show up at my school, email my coworkers, post my personal information online, call my cell phone, describe everything I was wearing on a particular day, and encourage my classmates to take surreptitious photos of me or rape me.[151]

Ultimately, one of the people who had been posting online on the forum where Filipovic was being targeted, AutoAdmit, showed up at the office where she was studying for the bar exam, which was on a nearly empty floor of her law school. She recounts that "he was having a psychological breakdown for which he was later hospitalized, but of course I didn't know that at the time. He was ranting about AutoAdmit, how I misunderstood him, how I was sending him coded messages and how he knew that I had told the whole Internet he was a bad person." She did not recognize him, but he had an imposing presence and was blocking the exit door. She reported that he was "towering over me, his pupils dilated and his fists clenched and his face bright red and sweaty. . . ." Filipovic recalls, "I was doing the calculations in my head: No one will hear me if I scream, so how fast can I get to the phone before he grabs me? What number do I even call? It's an NYU phone—what's NYU security's number? Do I have to dial 9 before I call 911?" Luckily, she had the wits about her to interrupt him, telling him that "I didn't think we had actually met, and that my name was Jill, and what was his?" He reacted by becoming confused and eventually left.[152] Filipovic said that thereafter she became much more careful about locking the door where she was whenever possible.

In another case, an online harasser was found to have visited his target's home. Jennifer Pozner, journalist, media critic, and founder of Women in Media and News, found a letter at her door saying that the man who had been harassing her online was going to "find you and your mom and rape you both."[153]

Real-Life Misogynistic Violence

Although many people dismiss online threats as "virtual" and not likely to actually be carried out, several real-life massacres by men have been preceded by misogynistic rhetoric that is similar to the online rhetoric of many gendertrolls who conduct harassment campaigns against women.

For example, the misogynistic writings of Elliot Rodger, the May 23, 2014, Isla Vista, California, shooter, were eerily similar to that of many online harassers, a point that was not lost on the women who have been harassed by men who frequent the same online sites as Rodger. Lindy West, whose story was detailed in the previous section, talked about her reaction to the Isla Vista shootings:

> This weekend [of the mass shooting by Elliot Rodger] has actually been really emotionally traumatizing. . . . I don't mean to make any of that about myself, but there is something so, so frightening about the exact same rhetoric that people throw at me turning up in a mass murderer's manifesto. I mean he sounds exactly like the people who harass me. It's such a concrete example of that kind of hatred of women turning into a real life danger.[154]

Rodger even frequented some of the same online forums where gendertrolls have tended to congregate, for example, BodyBuilding.com and PUAHate.com, the latter of which was shut down shortly after the shooting.[155] PUAHate.com was a forum that arose in opposition to "Pick-Up Artists" (PUAs), who offer lessons and even workshops for heterosexual men on how to pick up women. These programs tend to be highly misogynistic and view women as objects of contempt; accordingly they teach men techniques to deceive and "game" women in order to convince them to have sex. The men who visit PUA hate sites are frustrated with the idea of learning techniques to pick up women, although not out of an idea that people ought to be honest and not try to deceive each other, but more out of a frustration that the techniques taught either don't work or that women are not worth putting forth the effort involved. The PUA hate sites tend to coalesce around a deep-seated resentment toward women for not allowing the men who visit the sites access to sex with them (as if women owed the men sex). On these sites, women are frequently blamed for many if not all of the men's problems. Kat Stoeffel, contributor to *New York Magazine*, explains some of the terminology and misogynistic themes of PUAs as well as PUA haters:

> In headlines Isla Vista shooter Elliot Rodgers is the Virgin Killer, but online he was an "incel." Short for "involuntary celibates," incels are part of a subgroup of the many sexually frustrated men, would-be pickup artists, and Men's Rights activists who share sleazy seduction tips and air grievances about women in the forums orbiting Reddit's Seduction subreddit. The most extreme of them was a forum called PUAHate (since shuttered, read about its refugees at Jezebel), which Rodger claimed to have discovered about a year ago. "It is a forum full of men who are starved of sex, just like me," he

wrote in his manifesto. "Reading the posts on that site only confirmed many of the theories I had about how wicked and degenerate women really are."[156]

Rodger's manifesto, which he posted online, reflects many of the ideas espoused on the PUA hate discussion boards and revealed his animosity toward women in general. Katie J. M. Baker, national reporter for *BuzzFeed* and contributor to the *New York Times* and the *San Francisco Chronicle*, visited the PUAHate.com boards in 2012, prior to the Isla Vista shooting, and summarized the general misogynistic atmosphere she observed there:

> We browsed the forums for a few hours and failed to find one user who wondered whether women are unfairly targeted (as well as stereotyped, pigeonholed, and marketed) by the seduction community. . . . On their predominately male, heterosexual planet it's the poor, gullible men who are the true victims. . . . And it's the partners—and women in general—who are the villains to these outcasts.[157]

Significantly, other men, in addition to Rodger, have murdered women after expressing misogyny and, especially, bitterness and blame toward women for not wanting to be their sexual or romantic partners. In 2009, George Sodini killed three women and injured nine in an attack on an aerobics class at a fitness center near Pittsburgh. His online writings reflect frustration and bitter resentment at not being able to find women who were willing to date or become involved with him. The police officer investigating the massacre reported that, in the note found at the scene, Sodini "complains he had never spent a weekend with a woman, never vacationed with a woman and never lived with a woman, and that he had had limited sexual experiences."[158] CNN reported that Sodini made "similar complaints in his online blog, which also documents his growing rage at women for rejecting him and at the world he felt had abandoned him."[159]

In 1989, Marc Lepine murdered 14 women and injured 13 other women at the Ecole Polytechnique in Montreal, Canada. Lepine had apparently not been admitted to the university and blamed his failure on women entering and working in fields that had been previously dominated by men. At the massacre, he told the men who were present to leave, saying he wanted only women to remain. Then he shouted "You're all a bunch of feminists, and I hate feminists!" before shooting the women.[160] His suicide note read in part, "Would you note that if I commit suicide today it is not for economic reasons . . . but for political reasons. Because I have decided to send the feminists, who have always ruined my life, to their Maker . . . I have decided to put an end to those viragos."[161]

Although such expressly declared misogynistic killing sprees are relatively rare, the fear of many women who are targets of online harassment campaigns is that the mob mentality and the amped-up rhetoric might precipitate more offline real-life violence. Given these incidents, along with the rape and death threats, graphic sexual and violent messages, and instances of doxxing, it is entirely understandable that women who are being targeted would reasonably be fearful for their physical safety.

SECTION 4: CROSSING MULTIPLE PLATFORMS

A firm backhand to her whore face would provide her with a much needed attitude adjustment.[162]

I hope you never have children, your daughters would be such sluts and end up murdered in a gutter by someone like me.[163]

I'll drink your blood out of your cunt after I rip it open.[164]

CHERYL LINDSEY SEELHOFF

Cheryl Lindsey Seelhoff is one of the earliest victims of the phenomenon of gendertrolling. For her, the attacks began in July 2007. At that time, she had a feminist blog, website, and online discussion boards. At first, she began noticing that there was an uptick in the numbers of people who were reading her boards; it was a large number compared with the number who were registered users. Since she knew that sometimes the news items on her blog were used as assignments for college classes, she thought the upsurge in readers might have been due to that.

Then, the actual attacks happened all at once. She signed onto her discussion boards one day and found they had been hacked: the colors were changed to bright reddish orange and other garish hues, and her online forums were full of pornography videos and clips, including explicit, racist pornography as well as a slew of other graphic and horrifying images. The names of the discussion forums on her boards were changed, and the hackers had made themselves moderators. The hackers had also gotten the log-in information for all of the members of her discussion boards and then hacked into the members' email accounts, filling them with graphic pornography and spam.

A message was posted to her blog that began, as if in sympathy with her, "sorry this is happening to you," but then turned into a horrifying rape threat, in which the troll, in a very graphic description, threatened to stab her, creating holes in her, and then rape her in the holes.

Her blog was constantly spammed, which she couldn't keep up with, and there were "hundreds and hundreds and hundreds" of graphic rape threats made against her in various forms and on various forums.[165]

In addition to the attacks on her websites and blogs, the gendertrolls started a campaign against her on *Encyclopedia Dramatica*, an online wiki platform that documents and celebrates subversive, racist, sexist, and offensive Internet phenomena including pranks, trolling events, and raids. The attacks then spread to *Wikipedia*; Seelhoff explains that "the 4chan and Legion people went to *Wikipedia* and carried out these horrific attacks in the talk portion of the *Wikipedia* page. I've never seen anything like it. It was the most horrible, vile, racist, hideous stuff, and it was all on *Wikipedia*."[166] Although she eventually managed to get *Wikipedia* to take the offensive content down, "they didn't act very quickly. It was up there for at least several months, even longer—it was up there for a long time."[167]

They tried to dox her by taking images off her blog and website, especially pictures of her or of her with her children, and posting her real name. They also did the same to another woman who was a moderator on the discussion board with the online name "Biting Beaver." They mounted a campaign to post her and Biting Beaver's real-life names, addresses, and telephone numbers. They went searching for Biting Beaver's ex-husband, who had been abusive, and they contacted her neighbors. There were constant threats, for months. Those who publicly supported Seelhoff also got their websites or other online media attacked.

Then the DDoSing started. They hit images on her blog repeatedly in a coordinated effort, with the goal of destabilizing her website and blog so they would go down. Seelhoff and her then-partner spent hours and hours trying to combat the attacks, doing whatever they could do, changing different settings and even changing the URL. Seelhoff said that the worst of the attacks against her "lasted about six months, where it was really constant."[168]

The campaign against her was so determined and thoroughgoing, Seelhoff explains, that "wherever there was anything about me that was favorable—or was just normal—on the Internet, [the trolls] found that, and they went and did everything in their power to attack it."[169]

Seelhoff reports that "the people who took responsibility for the attacks were from 4chan, Anonymous, and a group that was then called Legion. They were all hackers. They publicly took responsibility for this. They said so in my blog and comments. They said so in emails, they posted it on *Encyclopedia Dramatica*. They posted it all over the place."[170]

Seelhoff concludes,

> Ultimately they won. They destabilized all my websites along with an innocent website that had the same name as mine. And they destabilized the whole web host system. The host said we couldn't use their system anymore, that we had to get a new web host. It didn't stop until I stopped blogging. Biting Beaver left the Internet. Everyone was too fearful to continue posting to the bulletin boards. The trolls basically won. Wherever I was on the Internet or bulletin board they attacked. They considered it a win to destroy websites, but they also seemed satisfied that I was forced to make my websites and blogs private. I still get stuff on my blog today, anytime I put anything up there, I check the comments, and there will be at least 5 or 6 hideous comments. If I went back to blogging, I believe it would come back.[171]

Seelhoff described herself at the time as "terrified, really, really scared from the really graphic rape and death threats. There were hundreds of them every day, day after day after day after day."[172] She said that the effects of the campaign against her were

> traumatic—very, very, very traumatic and scary. I was really afraid—to answer the phone, if anyone unusual was around, if anyone came down the road. I was even traumatized to even look at the computer. It was very painful. Physically, my stomach would churn. It was traumatic for as long as it continued. The really bad feelings and fears and terror went on for a couple of years. They were posting where I live. Luckily, they had a wrong phone number, but I was always afraid they would find my correct information.[173]

Another distinguishing feature of gendertrolling is that it proliferates beyond the medium or site where it began; that is, gendertrolls spread their attacks to cover a wide variety of social media and other online platforms. By contrast, generic trolling tends to remain relegated to the media or platform on which it began, such as in online video game messaging, which is a frequent site for generic trolling.

Gendertroll attack campaigns have taken place across such multiple platforms as Twitter, Storify, Tumblr, Facebook, blogs, YouTube, Google+, Vimeo, Kickstarter, Instagram, *Wikipedia*, Reddit, ask.fm, AutoAdmit, LinkedIn, dating websites, online message boards, texting, telephone calls, and email. In a 2013 report on online harassment and cyberstalking issued by Working to Halt Online Abuse, of those cases in which harassment escalated, nearly 29 percent occurred via Facebook, 25 percent by cell phone, 24 percent via text messaging, and 17 percent through Twitter and Google+, respectively. Other ways online harassment escalated were by email (16 percent), dating sites (15 percent), forged profiles (12 percent), online message boards (8 percent), and blogs, YouTube, Vimeo, and Craigslist (each 3 percent or less).[174] Although these data probably reflect gendertrolling as well as other kinds of online abuse, including cyberbullying, the pattern of using a variety of social and other media is significant.

When gendertrolls choose a target, they often make considerable effort to scan the Internet to find out which sites and media the targeted woman frequents and then attack her wherever they find her presence online. Gendertrolls have also created new websites and fake social media accounts in which they forge their target's profile in order to spread falsehoods about and otherwise attack her. In addition, they create graphic, mocking, and pornographic images and videos, which they post on a variety of sites and social media platforms. These images and videos are often reposted on other platforms and tweeted and retweeted until the abusive images and videos proliferate across the Internet. In some cases, they have harassed their target by sending her text messages on her cell phone, calling her on her home or cell phone, and even engaging in real-life encounters. Many trolls, who are often tech savvy, spend the time and effort to hack into the target's email, websites, and blogs in order to create havoc in those arenas.

An anonymous commenter identified as "Washington, DC," relates her experience of being targeted across multiple media:

> My story is a bit long and complicated, and I'm still in the court process (though three jurisdictions are now involved: Virginia, D.C., and the FBI). The case involves an individual who found me on Twitter, then created multiple email accounts and accounts on many social media platforms to stalk, harass, and threaten me.[175]

Shanley Kane, founder and CEO of *Model View Culture*, an online publication on technology, and a cultural critic and writer, has also been the target of gendertroll attacks. She explains the extensive reach of the attacks against her:

> On Friday night, the home addresses of every member of my immediate family were posted online.... People speaking up in support of me had their home addresses posted online as well, sometimes within minutes, creating a climate of fear that has functionally isolated me from most community support. I have received slurs of every variety, death and rape threats, and violent and threatening images. They have gone after my business and my family's livelihoods with slander, intimidation and attempts to cut off financial support, and tried to hack into various of my accounts and systems.

They have left pages and pages of stomach-turning comments on the front of every Internet community I am a part of and that influences my professional community and peers.[176]

Shauna James Ahern, a food blogger, sums up the extent to which the gendertrolls who harass her go to in order to proliferate their attacks:

This ridiculousness is not relegated to this space [her food blog]. There are Twitter feeds devoted to mocking my voice and what I care about. There are blogs dedicated to excoriating every post I write by writing a companion post [with the] same amount of paragraphs and sentences in ugly language. There is a forum created just for those who hate kids and the people who write about their kids online. Apparently, my section is one of the biggest. Every time I have a recipe published in a magazine or a piece written about me, there are a score of vicious comments about me. Every time. There are lots of personal attacks hidden as reviews on Amazon.[177]

Gendertrolls can be quite creative, versatile, and even ingenious in spreading their harassment across multiple media and forms of communication, using a variety of social media and websites to harass their victims. They frequently attempt to find their target's Facebook profile and then post harassing messages to her wall, where all her Facebook friends can see them, or send private messages full of abusive content. Women are also harassed on YouTube when gendertrolls, often in a coordinated campaign involving large numbers of harassers, leave hundreds, and sometimes thousands, of highly abusive posts under a video the targeted woman has posted (which results in many users closing the comments feature on their videos). Gendertrolls also go to the trouble of making multiple abusive and dishonest videos about the woman they are targeting, which are then posted widely and seen by thousands (or more) of viewers. It is also fairly common to vandalize the woman's *Wikipedia* page, if she has one, by altering it to include defamatory text about her, to insult her by saying she is a "cunt" or "whore," and to post pornographic pictures about her on the page as part of the coordinated effort to attack her online.

Blogs are also venues for harassment. Gendertrolls create fake blogs as if in the targeted woman's name, in which the trolls make outrageous statements that others believe are written by her. Threads are started on online forums with the express purpose of tracking and commenting on all her online behavior, criticizing it, and then inciting others to engage in harassing behavior against her. Reddit and 4chan are examples of sites where this kind of behavior proliferates. Entire threads and even whole topic areas are created in order to inflame others who read the site to join in the campaign against the targeted woman. Many of these threads contain not only extremely exaggerated claims, but statements that are also untrue and even slanderous. Some of the threads are devoted entirely to insulting, often in extremely graphic terms, every aspect of the woman they are targeting. This is often especially true of threads in the /b/ section of 4chan and the "men's rights" sections of Reddit. There are also numerous other sites that groups of men frequent (what is frequently referred to as the "manosphere"), where they encourage each other to harass and target women whose ideas, or sometimes mere existence as women in prominent positions, they perceive as a threat.

Twitter appears to be one of the most common ways to send harassing and abusive messages and images to targeted women. It is relatively easy to tag people when sending out a tweet, which, unless the user has blocked the sender, makes it very likely that the target will see the harassing message when she logs onto Twitter and checks her feed. Gendertrolls also create fake accounts on Twitter in the target's name so that it appears that she herself is the one sending out defamatory or outrageous tweets. Trolls will then tag her friends so they are alerted to these tweets, which the friends may think were sent out by the targeted woman. One gendertroll went so far as to create an account in the name of the recently deceased father of the woman he was targeting, Lindy West (whose story is recounted in Section 2 of this chapter), in order to taunt her with the idea that her father was ashamed of her.

Another example of creatively using online platforms to harass and stalk women online is the use of Storify, a social networking platform that lets users create narratives about topics by compiling posts taken from such social media as Twitter, Facebook, and Instagram. Storify users can add text and order the material to create a coherent story; that is, turn the information into a story so that people can read in one place all about the history of a particular topic or discussion. Storify has also been used in the service of spreading harassment and abuse. It has been used to monitor and compile everything a targeted woman has posted or written on the Internet, which can create the feeling of being stalked.

One Storify user, a man who calls himself "Elevatorgate" and who targeted Rebecca Watson (see her story in Section 6 of this chapter), has been using the platform to capture and "document" thousands of Watson's tweets. Watson says she "didn't realize the extent of his activity because she had blocked him,"[178] a common tactic that, although it protects targeted women from being exposed to the full extent of their online harassment, can leave them unaware and off guard when a harasser is becoming obsessed with them. Elevatorgate has posted over 7,000 articles on Storify, a large number of which are about the women he has been targeting in the atheist and skeptic communities, including Watson and Melody Hensley, another atheist and secular humanist activist.

One of the difficulties for the women whom Elevatorgate is "Storifying" lies in making a determination as to when his following them becomes obsessive enough to qualify as stalking and whether that signifies actual danger for the women he is obsessed with. Blogger Ana Mardoll sees Elevatorgate's activities to have crossed over the line into stalking, describing him as "obsessively compil[ing] the tweets of women he is stalking,"[179] including details about their "favorite foods, lives, and pet photos." Mardoll reports that he "would often send email notifications to many of the women whose tweets he captured."[180]

Hensley also sees Elevatorgate as obsessive. She reports that every tweet she posts has been recorded on Storify by Elevatorgate, from nearly two years ago to the time of this writing, and that she knows she is being "constantly being monitored. . . . [Elevatorgate] spends all day and all night doing this. I'm quite certain he doesn't have a job. He's definitely obsessive."[181]

Watson relates how difficult it has been for her to come to terms with the fact that there are multiple, and in some cases, massive numbers of people in the online world who occupy so much of their time obsessively stalking and targeting women and then spreading their harassment on the ever-proliferating variety of online platforms that are available to them:

> I've had to live every day knowing that there are people out there who are absolutely obsessed with me, who hate me so much that they spend hours each day blogging, tweeting, creating new social media accounts, Photoshopping my pictures, drawing pornographic images of me, making albums about how I should be murdered, and trying to get me fired from the podcast I do for free. When I'm able to find out their identities (sometimes they don't even hide them), I often find they have a history of domestic violence, stalking, or in the most recent case, "indecent liberties with a minor."[182]

It's no wonder that gendertrolled women experience an overwhelming feeling of being under siege when they find that they are being attacked in so many unexpected and surprising ways and that the gendertrolls have gone to nearly every place they frequent online (as well as some real-life places) to post harassing and abusive messages, graphically pornographic images, and rape and death threats.

SECTION 5: UNUSUAL INTENSITY

I'm going to pistol whip you over and over until you lose consciousness . . . and then burn ur flesh.[183]

what a stuck up bitch. I hope all them people who gave her money get raped and die of cancer.[184]

I will rape you when i get the chance.[185]

ANITA SARKEESIAN

Anita Sarkeesian, a media critic and blogger, began to be interested in the sexist and objectifying ways that women are represented in video games. On May 17, 2012, she began a Kickstarter campaign online to raise money for some videos she wanted to create to examine stereotypes about women in video games. In response to her fundraising campaign, gendertrolls launched an intensive, widespread, and coordinated attack against her by sending her threats of "violence, death, sexual assault and rape," trying to get Kickstarter to ban her project, attempting to hack into her various online accounts, posting her telephone number and home address on various websites and forums, and unleashing a "torrent of hate" on her YouTube channel including flagging its content as "terrorism," "hate speech," and spam.[186] She reported that she received over 5,000 comments on YouTube, most of which were negative and included derogatory comments about her appearance, threats of violence, and liberal use of the word "cunt."[187]

Trolls also vandalized her *Wikipedia* page by replacing her photo with a depiction of a woman with a man's penis in her mouth, under which they indicated that that was among her "Daily Activities." They also changed the external links on the page to reroute to pornographic websites and added racist slurs saying she was "of Jewish descent" and an "entitled nigger."[188] They wrote on the page such graphic insults as that she "holds the world record for maximum amount of sexual toys in the posterior."[189] Ultimately, Sarkeesian was able to work with *Wikipedia* to get her page changed back and locked from further changes, but in the process it was revealed that more than a dozen IP addresses were part of the efforts to vandalize the page.[190]

In addition vandalizing her *Wikipedia* page, trolls posted simulated pornographic images of Sarkeesian on various sites on the web and sent them to her Facebook page, Twitter account, and YouTube channel.[191] Sarkeesian describes the images:

> The first image depicts a woman drawn to resemble me who is tied up with a wii controller shoved in her mouth while being raped by Mario from behind. The second image is another drawing (clearly sketched to resemble me) featuring a chained nude figure on her knees with 5 penises ejaculating on her face with the words "fuck toy" written on her torso.[192]

She was also emailed pictures of herself being raped by video game characters, and attempts were made to hack into her Twitter and Google accounts.[193]

Gendertrolls perpetrated a DoS attack by overloading her website's server with so many requests to load the webpage that the server crashed, whereupon the trolls posted an image bragging that they had accomplished the attack.[194] Sarkeesian described the mob nature involved in the attacks:

> This harassment is best classified as a cyber mob attack as it's a hate campaign loosely organized through various Internet forums. Participating harassers will share these images as a way to show off and gain validation from their peers as well as to try and recruit others to join the harassment campaign.[195]

Finally, in a particularly inventive and determined act of maliciousness, a Sault Ste. Marie, Michigan, gamer identified as Ben Spurr[196] created an interactive online game called "Beat Up Anita Sarkeesian," wherein bruises and welts appeared on an image of Sarkeesian when players clicked on her face.[197] Stephanie Guthrie, a Toronto feminist, heard about the game and tweeted her support of Sarkeesian and against the game's creator, whereupon Guthrie also began to receive a slew of rape and death threats on Twitter.[198]

The onslaught of attacks and threats made to Sarkeesian occurred on a variety of online platforms including *Wikipedia*, Kickstarter, Twitter, and YouTube. Trolls also carried out their campaigns against her through attempts to hack into her email and social media accounts as well as by creating the online "Beat Up Anita Sarkeesian" game. Although the attacks were pervasive and intense, the vicious misogyny exhibited by the gendertrolls boomeranged in that she raised nearly $160,000 (from nearly 7,000 backers) to fund her video series, many times her original goal of raising $6,000.

Attacks against Sarkeesian increased with renewed energy in 2014 after she released the video of her series titled "Women as Background Decoration, Part 2." Shortly after releasing the episode, she again faced what she called a "wall of abuse."[199] In late August 2014, she tweeted, "Some very scary threats have just been made against me and my family. Contacting authorities now," and later, "I'm safe. Authorities have been notified. Staying with friends tonight."[200] She was forced to flee her home for her own and her family's safety based on the specificity and gravity of the threats leveled against her. She filed a police report with the San Francisco Police Department.[201]

Shortly thereafter, and at the same time that the Gamergate attacks began (the Gamergate story is detailed in Section 7), Sarkeesian began receiving death threats at several speaking engagements. Then, on October 14, Sarkeesian tweeted that she had to cancel her talk at Utah State University because she received specific threats by someone who said he planned to commit a massacre in the style of Marc Lepine's 1989 mass murder of female engineering students in Montreal. Sarkeesian reported that one of the threats she received claimed affiliation with Gamergate. Sarkeesian details the specific threats that were issued regarding the scheduled talk:

> The staff and faculty at Utah State University received several very specific death threats against my life and those of the students attending my lecture on the role of women in video games. The e-mails sent to USU included a list of firearms at the perpetrator's disposal. Not only did these e-mails threaten to carry out the worst school shooting in American history, but the language in the messages was also very reminiscent of, and even mentioned, previous misogynist school shootings such as the Montreal Massacre at Ecole Polytechnique committed by Marc Lépine and the UC Santa Barbara shootings committed by Elliot Rodger this past May.[202]

Although she had received death threats at prior talks that she had given, she canceled the Utah State University talk because the Utah police said they could not search people for concealed firearms before entering the event since Utah allows concealed weapons. Sarkeesian felt that this would have not allowed for reasonable safety precautions to be taken to protect both Sarkeesian and the audience. Sarkeesian explained her reasons for canceling the talk:

> I have gone ahead with events that have been threaten[ed] with bombing attacks before—three times, in fact—but each time I felt appropriate security measures were taken by law enforcement and venue security personnel. This time it was different. When I spoke with Utah police about what security measures were in place to protect the campus, I specifically requested metal detectors or pat-downs to make absolutely sure no guns were in the auditorium. Police responded by stating that they would not do any type of screening whatsoever for firearms because of Utah's concealed-carry laws. At that point I canceled the speaking event because I felt it was deeply irresponsible for me or the school to put everyone's lives at risk if they can't take precautions to prevent firearms from being present at an event at an educational institution—especially one that was just directly, clearly threatened with a mass shooting spree.[203]

The International Game Developers Association is now working with the FBI to try to head off what they see as an increase in such threats and harassment. The executive director, Kate Edwards, reported that the FBI has "noted a rise in activity," although the primary focus of their investigations into online activities has been more on cybercrime issues such as hacking.[204]

In a hopeful turn, Sarkeesian was recently included as a character in the video game TowerFall. Matt Thorson, developer of the game, said that her inclusion was a tribute to her, calling her work an "inspiration." Thorson emphasized that "it's vitally important that the cast of playable characters makes everyone feel invited to join in" and added that "this wouldn't have occurred to me if not for Anita, and feedback from players has reinforced how important it really is. We're very excited to immortalise Anita in a small way."[205]

Another feature of gendertrolling that distinguishes it from generic trolling is that it often occurs at an unusual intensity, that is, the number of harassing messages come at such a pace and are so unrelenting that the target simply can't keep up with blocking or deleting them. It is also common for women to report receiving massive quantities of harassing and abusive messages coming to them via a wide variety of online sources. Caroline Criado-Perez, the British activist and journalist whose story is detailed in Section 3, received a surge of threatening, abusive, and misogynistic messages, including rape and death threats—up to 50 rape threats and abusive tweets an hour at their peak.[206] She commented on how woefully inadequate Twitter's "report abuse" mechanism was in the face of such an onslaught.

Miri Mogilevsky, atheist/skeptic blogger, explains that she knows people are targeting her anew because the quantity of the hits she receives intensifies: "The way I know they are talking about me is I get a massive influx of hits on a particular day . . . responding to a post I have written. It's usually a minimum 50 per day, on the day that they do it, sometimes it will be more."[207]

Shanley Kane, founder and CEO of *Model View Culture*, an online publication about technology, and a cultural critic and writer, recounts the sheer volume of attacks levied at her: "I have received literally thousands of harassing, abusive, threatening and violent messages across at least half a dozen separate sites."[208]

Kim B., who was driven off the Internet during an early gendertrolling campaign that took place in 2007, reported, "I was getting, on average, one hundred negative comments daily. Invariably there were several that were violent. The onslaught of violence and hatred wore me down, exhausted me."[209]

Often the women who are harassed to such an extent become inured to its magnitude. Atheist/skeptical activist and blogger Amy Davis Roth reports that she "was subjected to daily harassment." She described a "typical day [as] Wake up. Make coffee. Block hateful messages on Twitter or other social media. . . . Make art."[210]

S. E. Smith, writer and blogger at Tiger Beatdown, writes,

> It's a good week, these days, if I only get 15–20 emails from people telling me how much they think I should die, or how much they hope I get raped, or how much they hope my cat dies or I lose my job or fall in a hole or get shot by police or any number of things people seem to think it's urgently important to tell me in their quest to get me to shut up. We are not talking about disagreements, about calls for intersectionality, about differing approaches, about political variance, about lively debate and discussion that sometimes turns acrimonious and damaging. We are talking about sustained campaigns of hate from people who believe that we are inhuman and should be silenced.[211]

Rebecca Watson, when asked how many people she would estimate were involved in harassing her, says she would "comfortably say thousands of people were involved" in attacking her.[212] She cites YouTube videos in which she was attacked that would get thousands of upvotes, a one-time vote that a user can use to indicate he or she likes or approves of a video;

thus, thousands of "likes" can be reasonably construed to indicate thousands of unique users.

Kate Smurthwaite, a British comedian and political activist, reports seeing a constant stream of abusive comments, although she believes she only sees a tiny fraction of what is out there: "I'd say in a typical week I get 10–20 abusive comments though there are undoubtedly more that I don't see on other sites."[213] She recently wrote about the sheer volume of harassment she has to contend with:

> In the last week I've received over 1,700 nasty Twitter messages. Many of these messages have been retweeted and "favourited" hundreds of times. I was going to print all the abuse out and hold it up for a photo to accompany this article. The document came out at 165 pages. To print my week's abuse I'm going to have to buy a new printer cartridge.[214]

Trista Hendren, feminist activist, author, and blogger, reported that on some days she received "more than 500 anonymous, explicitly violent comments—'I will skull-fuck your children,' for instance." Because much of her activism against rape took place on Facebook, gendertrolls used that platform to dox her, posting her home address, her children's names, and her phone number—and some did contact her by phone.[215]

Although most women who are targeted make every effort to block people who send them abusive and harassing tweets, emails, or posts, they report that, in spite of their efforts, they still receive voluminous numbers of harassing messages on a regular basis. They typically believe that they may be privy only to what amounts to the tip of the iceberg when it comes to the amount of abuse and harassment that is directed at them online. Melody Hensley, atheist/secular humanist activist, explains that she still gets abusive and harassing messages "every day now, mostly on Twitter, even though I use a blocking system (a group of people that helps block threatening messages).... The harassment has been ongoing since 2011, and I still get death threats and rapes threats daily."[216]

The effect of the widespread attacks that cross multiple social media and other online platforms, as well as crossing over into real-life venues, combined with the intensity and sheer volume of the attacks, contributes to wearing down women who might otherwise maintain the resolve to carry on in spite of the attacks.

SECTION 6: PROLONGED DURATION

> *hope you catch a sexually transmitted disease or vagina cancer, cuntwit*[217]

> *honestly, and i mean HONESTLY. . . you deserve to be raped and tortured and killed. swear id laugh if i could*[218]

> *If I lived in Boston I'd put a bullet in your brain.*[219]

REBECCA WATSON

In June 2011, Rebecca Watson, a blogger who writes on issues of atheism, secular humanism, and skepticism, was one of the presenters on a panel at an atheist conference in Dublin. She spoke about several things, including about the problems of trying to make the atheist/secular humanist community more welcoming to women. She talked about women being viewed too often by men as someone to hit on at conferences rather than being taken seriously and seen as contributors to the topics under discussion. That evening, after her talk, she joined a group of conference-goers in the hotel bar, discussing the issues about which she spoke, including misogyny and objectification of women. At around 4:00 A.M., she left the bar to retire to her room. One of the men, who had been among the group gathered at the bar, but who had not spoken to her, followed her when she left and joined her in the hotel elevator. Watson described what happened:

> As the doors closed, he said to me, "Don't take this the wrong way, but I find you very interesting. Would you like to come back to my hotel room for coffee?" I politely declined and got off the elevator when it hit my floor. . . .
>
> After all, it seemed rather obvious to me that if your goal is to get sex or even just companionship, the very worst way to go about attaining that goal is to attend a conference, listen to a woman speak for 12 hours about how uncomfortable she is being sexualized at conferences, wait for her to express a desire to go to sleep, follow her into an isolated space, and then suggest she go back to your hotel room for "coffee," which, by the way, is available at the hotel bar you just left.[220]

When she returned from the conference, Watson posted a video online in which she reported on her experiences at the conference and mentioned briefly, among many other topics, the man who propositioned her in the elevator. In the video, she highlighted the incident as an example of how not to make women feel safe at conferences, in further illustration of one of the points she had made during her talk on the panel. Although her recounting of the incident took just a little over a minute in a much longer video, and what she concluded about the incident in the video was simply "Guys, don't do that," said in an rather light-hearted and off-hand way, the resulting response to this was a several-years-long campaign of sustained, virulent hate, abuse, and rape and death threats directed at Watson (which is still ongoing as of the time of this writing).[221] Although her comments about the incident in the video were clearly light hearted in tone and brief, she sarcastically quips,

> What legions of angry atheists apparently heard [in her video] was, "Guys, I won't stop hating men until I get 2 million YouTube comments calling me a 'cunt.'" The skeptics boldly rose to the imagined challenge.[222]

Watson, in her characteristic demeanor of downplaying events and experiences that would be extremely upsetting to most people, described her typical online experience before the elevator incident: "As a woman who has opinions online, I get rape and death threats on a fairly regular basis, mixed in amongst the barrage of gendered slurs and comments about fat I am."[223] However, after she posted the video that included her comment about the elevator incident (which was thereafter dubbed "Elevatorgate"), Watson reported a dramatically increased multimedia barrage of harassment, the vast majority of which was rape threats along the lines of "I hope you get raped, you deserve to be raped."[224] In addition to the threats, the gendertrolls who targeted her conducted a multi-platform social media onslaught including the creation of multiple Twitter accounts in her name that were used to tweet offensive comments, ostensibly from her, to celebrities and to her friends. Entire blogs where her words were twisted and ridiculed were created. Thousands of harassing comments were addressed to her through YouTube, Facebook, and a variety of other social media.[225] Trolls also posted on an online forum that started in the wake of Elevatorgate, slymepit.com, "thousands of comments threatening to rape me, doing Photoshops of me, calling me a cunt."[226]

Although Watson believes that most of her attackers were men, she was also attacked by a few women. Compared with her male attackers, who tend to remain anonymous, Watson reports that the women who have participated in attacking her are more likely to use their actual names. Watson believes that, in using their real names, the women are able to gain a certain celebrity status and perhaps even cachet from the men behind the attacks. She also believes that most of her attackers are part of a loosely organized "men's rights movement" that has a significant presence online among websites such as slymepit.com, PUAHate.com, avoiceformen.com, 4chan, and Reddit. (Men's rights activism and the relevant websites are discussed in more detail in the final section of this chapter.)

Some of the threats Watson has received over the years have seemed especially credible and potentially dangerous. In 2012, a reader of her blog alerted Watson to the website of a man who had written disturbing posts about women in general and who had posted photos of her with targets on them along with specific talk of murdering her. The man created a series of posts at a band camp website, the entirety of which was about murdering Watson. Through extensive online sleuthing, Watson learned that he lived a mere three-hour drive from where she lived at that time. She contacted the police in his jurisdiction. In what is a too-typical response, they told her that there was nothing they could do except take a report so that if he did attack—or actually murder her—"they'd have a pretty good lead" on who did it.[227] Because she understandably derived little comfort from that response, she decided to contact the FBI. At first, her FBI contact appeared promising:

> The first person I spoke to was horrified by what I described to her, and she immediately forwarded my call to an agent. I gave the agent all the information I had, and he was also very understanding and professional. He told me he'd assign two agents to the case who specialize in this sort of thing, and they'd be in touch with me soon.[228]

But she never heard back from anyone at the FBI. She emailed the agents she had contacted several times—after a few days, after some weeks, and continually thereafter for a few months. She re-sent them the screenshots of the threatening posts. They never responded to her, and as far as she can tell, nothing was done by the FBI with regard to her case.[229]

In the meantime, she started to receive hundreds of harassing Tweets and Facebook messages from someone whose IP address was in the same town that the man lived in. She then engaged the services of a private detective to investigate. He found that the same man had been arrested for domestic violence, that he was the person who had vandalized Watson's *Wikipedia* page, and that he had a long history of engaging in belligerent online behavior. The detective advised Watson that it could be that this harasser would do nothing more than "rage on the Internet"; but on the other hand, it was also possible that he could follow through with his threats and that there was no reliable way to tell. The detective explained that Watson could get a restraining order, but when the harasser was informed about it, he would find out that she was the one requesting the legal restraint against him. The detective explained that a restraining order can sometimes result in harassers backing off, but it can also have the result of angering them into escalating their attacks into real-world violence, especially once they know the person who is requesting the restraining order. In the end, Watson chose not to get the restraining order.

Although, at the time of this writing, it is nearly four years out from Elevatorgate, the incident that precipitated the dramatic increase of harassment and rape and death threats against Watson, significant numbers of people are still dedicated to continuing the campaign against her. Despite the fact that the harassment and threats continue, Watson says that she receives much less of it due to having learned techniques to filter and block the harassers. She has created new social media accounts and has assiduously blocked almost all of her harassers, although they continually create new accounts, which she has to then re-block. Watson reports that, regardless of her considerable efforts to block harassers, she still receives at least one hate-filled message a day.[230]

Despite Watson's characteristic bravado when speaking and writing about her experiences, the threats and harassment she has received over the years have taken their toll on her. She reports that when the harassment campaign began, she reacted by frequently getting upset and bursting into tears, but that she has now come to realize that her ability to weather extreme levels of abuse and harassment "is my superpower—I can deal with these haters better than the average person."[231]

Although Watson is careful to emphasize she is not critical of other women's greater or lesser abilities to deal with harassment, she finds that she seems more able to slough off even the brutal and graphic threats of rape, violence, and death than a lot of other women she has met who have been the targets of gendertrolls. But she also believes that "the more I keep speaking up, the better off for everyone [because] it helps spread out the hate. The more people who speak up the better. . . . That perspective gave me the strength I needed to keep going. Today, it's water off a duck's back."[232]

Nevertheless, Watson takes anti-anxiety medications daily to quell the stress that has resulted from being gendertrolled. And, although she likes to run, she still feels she must be very cautious about running outdoors.[233]

Gendertrolling campaigns, in contrast to generic trolling, last a surprisingly long time. It is not unusual for women to be targeted for years. The intensive harassment campaign targeting Watson started in June 2011 and has continued through the time of this writing, nearly four years. This is a dramatic departure from instances of more generic trolling where trolling incidents tend to last a matter of days to weeks, to—in extreme cases—months.

Shanley Kane, cultural critic and founder of *Model View Culture*, recounts the prolonged nature of the attacks against her: "This has been my life for almost two years. I'm sad to say that part of you starts to get used to it."[234] A woman identified as "Canada" also wrote about the ongoing nature of the online attacks against her for voicing a political opinion online, which she characterized as "a simple disagreement . . . about politics." She thought the disagreement would soon be over and the man with whom she disagreed would then leave her alone. Instead, the disagreement turned into years of harassment. Her harasser found out her personal information, which he posted online, and he even contacted her employer and posted information about her employer online. He also posted false stories about her, some involving fabrications about her sexual behavior. She moved due to the harassment, she attempted suicide, and her PTSD, which was diagnosed prior to her harassment, worsened.[235]

Another woman, identified as "Massachusetts," related the story of being harassed online for over five years. She explains that while she was in college, she wrote a column on sex for her school newspaper during the end of her senior year. She says, although she was prepared to deal with "a fair amount of criticism," she was not prepared to deal with "someone going out of his/her way to ruin my life for the next five years." She reported that her harasser intensified the harassment after she obtained a job working at a high-profile consulting company, saying that "I suspect my harasser took it personally—'skanks' aren't supposed to have legitimate careers." Her harasser impersonated her online, spread lies about her on blogs created for the purpose of harassing her, and targeted her friends and boyfriends, including their families. The harasser also tried to get her fired, and when that didn't work, tried to spread rumors that she had been fired.[236]

The typically long duration of gendertrolling attacks is one of the reasons that targeted women find it so difficult to retain equanimity. Even women who can find a way to shrug off or inure themselves to the rape and death threats as well as the violent and graphic sexualized images that are sent to them and posted and reposted at great frequency across multiple online platforms can find themselves worn down from the sheer amount of time that they are subjected to attacks.

SECTION 7: PERPETRATED BY CYBERMOBS

You suck some fuckin' nerd motherfucker's dick to get that hack, you dumb cunt?![237]

You can't get rid of us. We're infinite. You're nothing but a loudmouth c*nt and we're going to show you the only thing you're good for."[238]

i hope someone slits your throat and cums down your gob[239]

GAMERGATE

The hashtag #Gamergate was coined by actor Adam Baldwin in August 2014 and has been tagged in tweets more than two million times since.[240] Although the controversy might easily have remained relegated to the world of online videogamers, video game developers, and game reviewers, perhaps because the videogaming industry is so lucrative, producing more revenue than Hollywood, the effects of Gamergate have extended far beyond videogamers. The controversy has generated reactions by large technology corporations[241] and has even been covered in mainstream media, including an interview with Anita Sarkeesian about the topic on the *Colbert Report*.

The incident that precipitated the Gamergate controversy occurred on August 16, 2014, when Eron Gjoni, the ex-boyfriend of Zoe Quinn, a video game developer, posted online a detailed and highly personal account of their relationship and subsequent breakup.[242] Quinn is a game developer who had gained some renown for a game she created called Depression Quest, which is a text-based game about the experiences of a young adult with depression. The idea of Quinn's game was met with disdain by many avid gamers who did not like that the game departed so dramatically from the more customary video game subjects and formats. Mike Pearl, *Vice* contributor, podcaster, and filmmaker, explained how the initial criticism of Quinn's game ultimately morphed into something larger: "*Depression Quest* got good reviews, despite its lack of machine guns and emphasis on exploring feelings rather than making aliens explode. . . . Some gamers even got abusive, but it apparently didn't merit mainstream headlines. Months later, though, when a blog post decried Quinn as a figure of 'corruption,' who slept her way to positive reviews for her game, it was gaming's Benghazi moment."[243]

In Gjoni's online account of their breakup, he reported that Quinn had had affairs with several other men, among whom was Nathan Grayson, a game reviewer for the videogaming website *Kotaku*. Gjoni's online tell-all spawned a slew of attacks against Quinn from people who were animated by their initial dislike of her game and latched onto the breakup story to find personal fault with her. By September 2014, the attacks against Quinn had intensified and appeared to be mostly emerging out of a variety of online forums including 4chan, Reddit, YouTube, and various IRC channels.[244] (IRC is short for "Internet Relay Chat," which is a protocol for creating online communication including discussion forums called channels.)

Although Quinn was initially the target of the massive online attacks that were the beginning of Gamergate, ostensibly because she allegedly slept with several people other than Gjoni and was therefore a "slut," the attackers soon began to change tactics as they realized that criticizing Quinn for having had various sexual relationships wouldn't gain much traction with a wider audience. They instead shifted the focus of their attacks to the idea that the ethics of journalists who cover games were in question since Quinn, a video game designer, had reportedly slept with Grayson, a reviewer of video games. Although from the content of Gjoni's post, it appears that his intentions were more to humiliate and punish Quinn for having cheated on and broken up with him, the gamers who read his account seized upon the idea, implied by Gjoni among the countless accusations he levied against her, that she had slept with Grayson in order to get positive reviews of her game. T. C. Sottek, news editor at the *Verge*, a website that covers technology, explains that "gamers came to a consensus that publicly harassing a woman over her sex life was a bad look. They quickly pivoted to focus on corruption in games journalism."[245]

Kotaku, for which Grayson was a writer, issued a statement shortly thereafter clarifying that the only mention Grayson ever made of Quinn's game Depression Quest was half a sentence long, that this mention had occurred prior to his brief relationship with her, and that he had never reviewed the game.[246] *Kotaku*'s wholesale refutation of the idea that Quinn's game received any reviews, much less favorable ones, as a result of her brief relationship with Grayson, did not, however, dampen the mob's apparent determination to continue to attack her, along with any other people who publicly supported her.

Many commentators have remarked on the irrationality of Gamergaters' obsession with the idea that Quinn obtained some kind of unfair advantage from her brief affair with Grayson in spite of all evidence to the contrary. Kyle Wagner, staff writer at Deadspin, explains,

> It's important to note that the initial claim that sparked Gamergate was not only untrue, but totally nonsensical—neither Grayson nor anyone else even reviewed the game at Kotaku, and while Grayson did write about Quinn in late March in a feature about a failed reality show, that was before they'd begun their romantic relationship.[247]

Sottek blasts the idea that concern over Quinn gaining an unfair advantage from journalists writing about her game is the real motivation behind Gamergate:

> Even Gamergate's founding claim, that games journalism is corrupt, is opportunistic horseshit from misogynists who decided to shame a woman for allegedly sleeping around because they didn't like her video game and wanted to punish her for it. Slut-shaming, gaslighting, dismissal, fallacious logic, intimidation: these are all part of the Gamergate militant's toolkit.[248]

Sottek also reported that the focus on "ethics in gamer journalism" was in fact an afterthought that was trumped up only after Gamergaters realized that harassing Quinn because she had cheated on her boyfriend didn't play well in public:

> Chat logs released soon after [Gamergate] broke reveal the movement was focused on destroying Zoë Quinn first, reforming games reporting second.[249]

Jay Hathaway, staff writer at *Gawker*, raises the point that, if ethics in gamer journalism were really a concern, it is odd that Gamergaters focused on small independent game developers rather than large game producers:

> Many #Gamergate participants truly believe that they are fighting an important fight against corruption in game journalism. But to an outside observer, it's bizarre that they identify the greatest threat as the small, independent, crowdfunded developers, and not the huge profitable game companies that advertise on game sites.[250]

Journalist Anna Merlan concludes that the motivation underlying Gamergate is misogyny and trying to drive women out of gaming:

> I think [the red herring of "ethics in gamer journalism"] is a sort of compelling way to reframe the fact this is actually attacks on women. Ethics in journalism is not what's happening in any way. It's actually men going after women in really hostile, aggressive ways. That's what Gamergate is about. It's about terrorizing women for being involved in this industry, for being involved in this hobby.[251]

Undaunted by *Kotaku*'s declaration of the facts, Gamergaters nevertheless latched onto and became impassioned by the idea that what was at stake was ethics in gamer journalism. The rallying cry "ethics in gamer journalism" proved to be an enduring rationalization for continuing their attacks on Quinn.

As a result, Quinn became the target of a concerted and widespread campaign to harass and threaten her, including inundating her page on the social networking/gaming community site Steamcommunity.com with negative reviews, hacking into her Skype account, doxxing her by publishing her home address and telephone number online, and sending her a "near-constant stream of death and rape threats."[252] In one especially detailed and specific death threat, an attacker on Tumblr posted, "Are you reading this? Of course you are. I will kill you."[253] Someone else posted in a forum discussing how to get back at Quinn, "Next time she shows up at a conference we . . . give her a crippling injury that's never going to fully heal . . . a good solid injury to the knees. I'd say a brain damage,—but we don't want to make it so she ends up too retarded to fear us."[254] Quinn felt sufficiently threatened that she contacted the police and then fled her home to rotate staying among several friends' houses so she would be harder to locate. About the attacks against her, Quinn summed up, "The Internet spent the last month spreading my personal information around, sending me threats, hacking anyone suspected of being friends with me, calling my dad and telling him I'm a whore, sending nude photos of me to colleagues, and basically giving me the 'burn the witch' treatment."[255]

Gamergate continued to escalate, and on October 10, 2014, Brianna Wu, another video game developer, software engineer, and founder of Giant Spacekatgal, a company that makes video games with female protagonists,[256] also felt sufficiently threatened that she fled her home. The day before, Wu had retweeted a photo meme called "Oppressed GamerGater," which made fun of Gamergate.[257] It was this action that triggered Gamergaters' wrath against her.

Wu was doxxed on a forum called 8chan, where gendertrolls posted her home address, phone number, and email address. Shortly thereafter, she began receiving a series of detailed threats via Twitter by a user who called himself "Death to Brianna":

> I've got a K-Bar and I'm coming to your house so I can shove it up your ugly feminist cunt

> If you have any kids, they are going to die too. I don't give a fuck. They'll grow up to be feminists anyway

> Your mutilated corpse will be on the front page of Jezebel tomorrow and there isn't jack shit you can do about it

> Guess what bitch? I now know where you li[v]e. You and Frank live at [redacted].

As Wu described it, "I was literally watching 8chan go after me in their specific chatroom for Gamergate. . . . They posted my address, and within moments I got that death threat."[258] In response, she tweeted, "And here's the part of the night where I call the police."[259]

After she was doxxed on 8chan, Wu told her husband, "We've got to get out of here." She explained, "I made the decision to leave, and law enforcement said it was reasonable. I basically just left the house. I have no idea where I'll be living this week or even next month."[260] Wu recounted that she was sobbing uncontrollably.[261] The police offered to send patrol cars by, but they also agreed that it would be wise for Wu and her husband to leave their home. The Arlington, Massachusetts, police confirmed that "the matter is now under investigation by our Criminal Investigation Bureau."[262]

Wu said that she was also attacked in other ways. Gendertrolls tried to access the financial information and assets of her company through hacking, impersonated her on Twitter, and created temporary email accounts to email journalists misinformation to try to destroy her professionally.[263] Although Wu was still not able to stay in her own home, she remains resolute that she will not be forced out of her own industry by bullies.

88   Gendertrolling

On seeing the escalation of the Gamergate attacks to Wu and others, Quinn began "monitoring the progression of this mob that sort of ended up morphing into #GamerGate. [She was] recording everything, hiding out in the IRC rooms, silently picking logs, and documenting the evolution."[264] Quinn then posted screenshots and logs from chatrooms and posts that she found on Reddit and 4chan.[265] In addition, she showed the FBI the evidence she found that showed "[r]eposting of peoples' information with incredibly elaborate rape threats and death threats. Distributing of private information, with calls to harass. There are calls for people to send naked photos of me to my colleagues—and to distribute that illegally. There's open talk of hacking, what we'd refer to as 'black-hat hacking.'"[266] ("Black-hat hacking" is a form of hacking that is unusually or especially malicious or destructive.)

The tide appeared to turn somewhat against Gamergaters based on what Quinn revealed through her online investigating. The tweets she posted were collected and dubbed #GameOverGate on Twitter.[267] As a result, an online petition was created in protest against these kinds of malicious attacks Quinn had documented, which was signed by thousands of people in the gaming industry.[268] In September 2014, 4chan founder Christopher Poole banned all Gamergate-related threats from 4chan for violating the site's rule against "no personal information/raids/calls to invasion."[269] This prompted a public exodus of Gamergaters who then moved to 8chan.

Other reactions against Gamergate included the creation of a discussion board on Reddit called "Gaming4Gamers," which promoted itself as a "community based on open-minded discussions" and "camaraderie above competition." Gaming4Gamers even received the rare honor of being promoted on Reddit's front page.[270] The website *Kotaku* also came out strongly against the targeting of women in gaming. Stephen Totilo, editor in chief for *Kotaku*, announced:

> Friday's incident [Brianna Wu's doxxing and threats causing her to flee her home] brings a different aspect of the Gamergate controversy to the fore: the targeting of women, the sense that discussion about gaming, games media ethics, and gamers will be forever contaminated by an ugliness disproportionate to the issues at hand. This is a potential new status quo that we at *Kotaku* reject. The kind of harassment that sends anyone in the gaming scene fleeing from

their homes is detestable and should be condemned no matter where one stands on anything else.[271]

The three women who were most prominently attacked by Gamergaters were Zoe Quinn, Brianna Wu, and Anita Sarkeesian, the latter of whom also received death threats when Gamergate was at its peak. Arthur Chu, culture blogger and 11-time *Jeopardy!* champion, explains the connection between Gamergate and the campaign against Sarkeesian:

> "Gamergate" itself is not particularly new. It's the same exact people as the ones who started a massive swell of harassment against Anita Sarkeesian for her Kickstarter. Before Anita had even made a single actual video criticizing sexism in games she got death and rape threats just for proposing to make videos criticizing sexism in games.[272]

In addition to Quinn, Wu, and Sarkeesian, other women have also been targeted in Gamergate-related attacks and received death threats when Gamergate was at its peak. One such woman is Jennifer Hepler, a senior writer working on the video game Dragon Age: Inquisition. Hepler received abusive phone calls, was emailed death threats, and was sent "graphic threats" about killing her children as they left school.[273] Sarkeesian described Hepler as being "attacked in many of the same ways I have been, in terms of inundating her social media and threatening her and her children."[274]

Samantha Allen, who writes about gender, sexuality, and technology and contributes to the *Daily Beast*, was also targeted in the Gamergate-related attacks. Wu describes the attacks on Allen:

> They targeted my friend Samantha Allen back in July, when she dared criticize Giant Bomb's decision to remain the only major site in videogames with a 100 percent white, straight and male employee pool.
>
> They ran through their playbook. They targeted her on Twitter, they harassed her. They researched her past. They questioned her personal relationships. They threatened her. And they have done everything possible to try to quash one of the videogame industry's most insightful and powerful voices.[275]

Wu writes about others who have also been attacked in the Gamergate onslaught:

> It's a playbook that works. They used it against Jenn Frank [a freelance writer on the games industry] until she quit. They used it against Mattie Brice [who wrote about diversity initiatives in the games industry] until she quit. They used it against Leigh Alexander [editor-at-large for Gamasutra]. They used it against Zoe Quinn. And they used it against Anita Sarkeesian who had to cancel a speaking engagement gig this week after a school shooting threat—and now they used it against me.[276]

Keith Stuart, games editor at the *Guardian*, especially laments the loss of Jenn Frank, who is, according to him,

> one of the best writers about games and games culture for the last ten years, chased from the industry thanks to a piece she wrote for the Guardian about online abuse. The irony is so bitter it burns. I commissioned that article. I edited it. I am ... devastated by Frank's understandable decision; devastated for my part in it.[277]

Of those who quit writing after the intense levels of attacks and threats, Wu writes, "They decided the personal cost was too high, and I don't know who could blame them. Every women I know in the industry is terrified she will be next."[278]

A final distinguishing characteristic of gendertrolling is that it tends to be perpetuated by cybermobs, or large to very large numbers of people—nearly all of them men—who coordinate their attacks through websites or online forums where they post about and coordinate their efforts. The sheer quantities of attackers—and their resultant ability to be exceptionally persistent due to their numbers—can easily overwhelm their target's ability to withstand such a sustained and pervasive onslaught.

Rebecca Watson, whose story is recounted in Section 6 of this chapter, is not the only target who estimates her attackers to number in the thousands. Lindy West, whose story is told in Section 2, when asked how many people she would estimate have been involved in harassing her, replied, "I would guess thousands. . . . These MRAs/PUA [Men's Rights Activists/Pick-Up Artists] communities—they are obsessed with me. There are whole message board threads about harassing me, encouraging each other to go harass me. It's a whole organized thing. And there's thousands of them."[279]

Melody Hensley, atheist/secular humanist activist, talks of even larger numbers of harassers who are dedicated to pursuing her through a variety of means in order to undermine, intimidate, and threaten her. She reports that, after voicing her public support for policies against sexual harassment at conferences held in the atheist/secular humanist communities, the number of people harassing her went from hundreds to thousands. She explains that "before I had the blocking system, I had to block 20,000 people."[280]

Cybermobs Are Mostly Men

Although many women report that a few women have been involved in the harassment campaigns aimed at them, they say that the attackers have been mostly men. Commenting about the people who perpetrate harassment of women online, Chu remarks, "But let's be honest: It's usually guys doing it."[281] Eleanor O'Hagan, journalist and columnist for the *Guardian*, also observed that the harassing "comments came mainly from men and they were always in line with existing gender stereotypes."[282]

Rebecca Solnit, writer and contributing editor at *Harper's Magazine*, explains that

> the Internet bear[s] a striking resemblance to Congress in 1850 or a gentlemen's club (minus any gentleness). It's a gated community, and as [Astra] Taylor describes today [in her book *The People's Platform: Taking Back Power and Culture in the Digital Age*], the security detail is ferocious, patrolling its borders by trolling and threatening dissident voices, and just having a female name or being identified as female is enough to become a target of hate and threats.[283]

Both Watson (her story is recounted in Section 6) and Cheryl Lindsey Seelhoff (whose story is recounted in Section 4) report that a few women were involved in the attacks against them. However, they both talked about their sense that the women served as tokens. They observed that the few women involved were given special recognition and prominence, and their real names were used (as opposed to nearly all other gendertrolls who remain anonymous), as if to attempt to convey the appearance of both women and men being equally involved in these attacks. Regardless of the few women who do join in gendertrolling campaigns, the vastly overwhelming majority of participants are men.

How Cybermobs of Gendertrolls Mobilize

If such large numbers of people are involved in gendertrolling campaigns, it begs the question as to how they are able to come together to agree to and to coordinate the attacks.

Adria Richards, technology consultant, trainer, and developer, writes about the gangs of men who targeted her and that they congregated in certain online forums in order to plan and coordinate their attacks: "This is a systemic issue, the people doing this, this is their hobby, they just move from target to target, they're like a roaming gang of some kind." Richards says she has "screen shots and screen captures of places where they were organizing these attacks" and that "they have scripts, templates."[284]

There are many websites where men (and some women) post content espousing and contributing to ideologies that foster and motivate the coordinated attacks on women who speak out online. Some of these websites are A Voice for Men (avoiceformen.com); Slymepit (slymepit.com); the now-closed Pick-up Artist Hate site (PUAHate.com); 4chan (4chan.org); 8chan (8ch.net); and Reddit (reddit.com, especially the r/bboard/ at that site, although overall users on Reddit are 84 percent male[285]).

In addition, the Southern Poverty Law Center lists other websites as part of the "manosphere," an informal network for blogs and websites that oppose women's rights and feminism, including such blogs as Boycott American Women (boycottamericanwomen.blogspot.com), Counter Feminist (counterfem.blogspot.com), and Marky Mark's Thoughts (markymarksthoughts.blogspot.com). They also list the password-protected blogs at Alcui (alcui-constant.blogspot.com) and the False Rape Society (falserapesociety.blogspot.com) and a host of websites including Men's Activism (news.mensactivism.org), RooshV (rooshv.com), SAVE Services (saveservices.org), the Spearhead (the-spearhead.com), and a now-defunct site called In Mala Fide (the author of which, Matt Forney, has since published as a book titled *Three Years of Hate: The Very Best of In Mala Fide*).[286] Other sites where similar ideologies are espoused include Viva La Manosphere (vivalamanosphere.com) and Return of Kings (returnofkings.com). Many of the men who post on or frequent these sites are considered to be part of the Men's Rights Movement, which sees men as disadvantaged by society and women and feminism to be the primary cause of men's troubles. Another group that participates in the online attacks on women are Pick-Up Artists (PUAs), men who coach other men on ways to deceive and manipulate women into having sex with them and who have a contemptuous and embittered view of women in general.

Different segments of these groups of men appear to focus their attacks on particular women. Lindy West mentioned being singled out for attack by Roosh V., who has been identified as Daryush Valizadeh and who calls himself a "pick-up artist," and his followers. Valizadeh was dubbed by the *Daily Dot* magazine as the "Web's most infamous misogynist" in February 2014.[287] West says that there are several forums on both of Roosh's sites, rooshvforum.com and Return of Kings, that are devoted to discussing "how I am fat and disgusting."[288]

Watson was targeted by the Slymepit, which has also targeted Ophelia Benson, Melody Hensley, and Amy Davis Roth, all of whom have been vocal about their support for Watson. Davis Roth points out that the various men's rights sites have some overlap among the people who frequent them. She says, for example, "Slymepit is interconnected with A Voice for Men."[289] Davis Roth reports that A Voice for Men

> has targeted my blog specifically and me individually as well as quite a few people in the audience [at the conference at which she was speaking].... It never occurred to me that I would have to hide my home address. I was never the kind of person who went around posting my home address. People found my home address because I have a home business—that's how I make my money. My business address is listed online. It was posted on a few websites, a few hate websites, and then A Voice for Men picked it up.[290]

Seelhoff was the target of a coordinated attack by the group Anonymous. She reported that her harassers came from /b/ at 4chan, Anonymous, and a group called Legion. She found that "they were giving orders as to how to destroy feminist websites. It looked like there were a couple of guys who were the leaders with many followers."[291]

During the time when Seelhoff was attacked, which was among the earliest instances of gendertrolling, Anonymous committed numerous other attacks focused on taking down feminist websites and blogs. In 2007, the same year they attacked Seelhoff, Anonymous also attacked a 19-year-old woman who made videos about the Japanese language and video games. They "hacked into her email, obtaining her personal information, and published her home address, passwords, and private medical history on various sites. [Anonymous] posted a doctored photograph of the woman atop naked bodies."[292] Under the photo, they wrote, "We will rape her at full force in her vagina, mouth, and ass." Anonymous organized a concerted effort to take down her video blog and her live journal. The group also maintained a list of feminist websites and blogs that it purports to have forced offline, taking "credit for closing more than 100 feminist websites and blogs."[293]

Seelhoff observed that since that time, Anonymous seems to have shifted its focus and the causes it champions: "In the past few years there has been an effort to rehabilitate Anonymous. . . . My sense is that there is some part of Anonymous that has tried to distance themselves from the worst people."[294] Danielle Keats Citron, author of *Hate Crimes in Cyberspace*, agrees that Anonymous has changed its mission since its early days: "In 2008 groups affiliated with Anonymous started to turn away from trolling and toward activist pursuits."[295]

Motivations of Gendertrolls

While generic trolls carry out their activities for the amusement value they derive from sowing discord or upsetting people, they don't usually have a strong belief in or conviction about the topics they pretend to espouse. Their goal is to tweak people by taking outrageous or offensive stances and then enjoy observing the reactions of shock and distress they cause. Gendertrolls, on the other hand, believe fervently in the ideas they espouse and the imagined causes behind the campaigns they carry out. They are not trolling in the conventional sense; that is, they are not doing it for the "lulz." Rather, they are committed to and passionate about the causes they believe they are defending, even if that cause is that women should not voice their opinions freely and without consequences in public venues such as the Internet. Culture blogger and *Jeopardy!* champion Arthur Chu concurs that gendertrolls are not trolls in the typical sense: "The scary thing here is how much they're *not* trolling, how desperate and how earnest they truly are, how sincerely they view themselves as a righteous minority with the world arrayed against them."[296]

The misogynist and specifically antifeminist men's rights rhetoric appears to foment and fuel many instances of men harassing women online. A woman identified as "California" writing about her online harassment recounts that, after she responded to a tweet from a comedian who frequently used the word "cunt," explaining that it is derogatory to women, he unleashed his numerous followers on her. They piled on, calling her "cunt," "bitch," and "whore" and saying that she was an example of how "feminists ruin everything."[297] Not only did this man disagree with her, but, as is characteristic of gendertrolling, he went so far as to contact and egg other people on to join in the harassment campaign against her. His expressed belief that women and feminists are somehow blameworthy appears to be at least part of the motivation fueling his harassment.

West remarked about how similar the rhetoric that misogynist gendertrolls aimed at her is to the ideas espoused by Elliot Rodger, a person who was clearly not in it for the "lulz": indeed, he was so serious about his misogynistic beliefs that he shot and killed 6 people and injured 13 in his May 23, 2014, Isla Vista, California, shooting rampage.

I don't think it's that big of a leap [from the rhetoric that contributed to Elliot Rodger's massacre to what gendertrolls write about online]. I find them really, really alarming. And the men's rights groups too, like Paul Elam, who is kind of one of the fathers of the current men's rights movement. He has written things like advocating for men to beat the shit out of women. It's really, really scary.... He wrote this post about how it's not fair that women can hit men but men can't hit women.... He claims to be very concerned for men who are being abused by their female partners.... "Next time your woman gets mad and hits you, you shouldn't just hit her back you should beat her to a pulp because then she'll learn that she can't victimize you like that." So it's all couched in this fake concern for male victims, but he uses it as an excuse to be violent toward women. It's really disturbing.[298]

David Futrelle, who blogs at We Hunted the Mammoth, a blog devoted to exposing men's rights rhetoric, thinks that the culture that spawned men's rights activists (MRAs) is borne out of a "new misogyny":

It's what I like to call the new misogyny—basically a large amorphous Internet subculture that is consumed with hating and attacking women. Some of these people call themselves men's rights activists and portray what they are doing as somehow beneficial for men. Others call themselves "men going their own way," the basic premise being that they want to live independently of women but end up talking most of the time about how terrible women are. That whole subculture is very heavily represented among gamers and on websites like Reddit....

I don't think the harassment against Sarkeesian is all done by men's rights activists, but it comes out of this subculture. And the people in this subculture share some basic obsessions.[299]

Chu elaborates on a potential motivation that he sees for the virulent attacks on women, what he calls "defensive misogyny": "The relentless attacks on the women they target as 'attention whores' bear all the earmarks of defensive misogyny, the nasty attitude of the nerdy, awkward guy who's convinced 'popular girls' are all secretly taunting him."[300] He adds that he believes that a much younger version of himself might have reacted to Gamergate in much the same way as so many others because of the numerous online forums of men sowing resentment and bitterness toward women: "If [the 23-year-old version of Chu] logged online he'd have a roar of voices from his fellow gamers feeding [his] resentment—telling him to blame his problems on 'elitist,' 'popular' voices in the hobby, on out-of-touch women who don't understand him like ... Anita Sarkeesian and Zoe Quinn."[301] Chu sees "toxic entitlement" as a motivator of much online harassment of women that emerges from gaming culture:

What is special about gaming culture . . . is that there's this kind of concentrated toxic entitlement in it that outweighs a lot of other cultures. It's hard to say exactly why. Gaming has always tended to attract people who feel particularly outcast by society, and in a perverse way has "trained" us to be desperately attached to "winning" in our little simulated realities, to being catered to and made to feel important. It's a community that, because it's been cut off from the "mainstream", has been seen as a refuge for "un-PC" entertainment aimed at straight young men, filled with unapologetic sex and violence.[302]

Futrelle sees some of the anger being demonstrated by gendertrolls as a reaction to gains that women have made toward equality:

The extent of the vitriol is something that I don't fully understand. My basic explanation, if I have one, is it's a backlash against the successes of feminism since the 90s. Feminism has made progress redefining some things that men took for granted, such as sexual harassment and date rape. So I think it's a backlash on what a lot of these guys see as restrictions on what they can say, how they can interact with women in a sexual way, and the idea that there may be consequences if they commit domestic violence. It's mostly sexual resentment, the fact that they can't get away with what guys used to be able to get away with with women, and that makes them very frustrated. Frankly I think a lot of them would prefer it if they could just go back to the way it was: Get women drunk and have sex with them. Without having the culture say, "Hey, this is date rape." And: "Your office jokes are actually sexual harassment."[303]

West adds that racism is also one of the strains running throughout the subculture of MRAs and men who harass women:

People say racist things about my fiancé, people call him the n-word and a monkey—he is African American. He doesn't get anything near what I get, but when he comes up, it's almost always racist. That's mostly from these Roosh people. There is a definite racist undercurrent to the men's rights/pick-up artist community. Which you saw in the [Elliot Rodger's] manifesto.[304]

These examples show that there are communities of men in online havens where they provoke and foster a common sense of bitterness, entitlement, and misogyny toward women. Soraya Chemaly, feminist writer, media critic, and activist, makes the important point that these groups do not exist only as a niche of online activity; they are embedded in and reflective of patriarchal ideologies that run throughout many cultures worldwide:

> [Regarding] a lot of online harassment that I see, there is an idea that it's individuals sitting in dark rooms. Unfortunately, that's not the case. In the case of women, there is no one central place, no one part of the world, no religion [where women are not targets of misogyny]. It is diffuse in the culture. However there are some very, very organized groups of MRA's that target individual people and make their lives a living hell.[305]

The ability of relatively large numbers of men to coordinate with each other to carry out gendertrolling campaigns against particular women rests on a culture-wide misogyny that has coalesced in certain sectors of online activity. It can seem surprising and even unbelievable that so many men would dedicate sometimes years of their lives to keeping up a sustained, intensive, dynamic, and unrelenting level of attacks on a particular woman online for a protracted period. However, when taking into consideration the widespread misogynistic beliefs that undergird their motivations, coupled with the creation of online forums where those beliefs are widely signal boosted, it seems less unexpected that gendertrolling campaigns are the result.

Chapter 3

Responses to Gendertrolling Campaigns

Women who experience the ongoing attacks characteristic of pervasive and persistent gendertrolling campaigns have varied reactions, as would any group of people who respond to being harassed or abused. However, a consistent message that the women I interviewed, as well as many other gendertrolled women, conveyed was a sense of respecting and honoring however a particular woman responded to the attacks on her. The women expressed a resolute conviction that there is no right way to respond to such an overwhelmingly difficult situation, and that, under that kind of prolonged duress, many different kinds of responses are warranted, reasonable, and understandable. The women I spoke to also took great pains to emphasize their sense of solidarity with other women who have experienced ongoing gendertrolling, and they refused to criticize or judge those who reacted differently than they did. In fact, the women who seemed more able than others to muster the combination of bravado, courage, and strength that allowed them not to be intimidated and to continue speaking out—even in the face of some of the harshest and most persistent harassment—were among those who were the most vocal about stressing that there is no right way to deal with that level of harassment and that each woman must honor her own needs in deciding how she should manage her response. They expressed empathy, understanding, and support to women who felt unable to stick it out and who reacted by refraining from speaking out on a specific topic or even by withdrawing from all online activities.

Lindy West (whose story is recounted in Section 2 of Chapter 2) was one of the women who has shown unusual determination and courage in the face of an extraordinary amount of harassment and abuse and who, nevertheless, expressed unwavering support for women who withdraw rather than face continued attacks:

> I want to make it really clear that I don't think my way to do it is the right way. I think women should do whatever they need to do to feel safe and comfortable and happy. The only reason I am still doing it is that I have gotten good at coping. I feel like somebody has to make these arguments and take this heat so I might as well do it since I've already been doing it.[1]

Rebecca Watson, the atheist blogger whose story is told in Section 6 of Chapter 2, has also shown tremendous courage and ability to prevail in the face of an exceptionally long-standing campaign of harassment against her. She made a similar statement:

> The last thing I would ever want is for someone to look at me and say, well, I must be defective because Rebecca can put up with this, so why can't I? I never want somebody to feel like that. There's no wrong way to react to having a shit ton of rape threats come at you from the Internet.[2]

Watson stressed that her ability to deal with her harassment was so far outside of what could be considered a typical reaction that she considers it her "superpower":

> I take a daily Lexapro and I have a Xanax for spikes. It took me a long time to figure out how to emotionally deal with this. A lot of people never get to the point where they can deal with it. I lost a lot of Skepchick [Watson's blog] contributors. I've known other people who have left the Internet for like a month, just until things quiet down, and they tell me, "I just can't deal with it." I realized eventually, even though I was getting upset occasionally and sometimes just bursting into tears, that this is like, my superpower. I can deal with these haters way better than the average person.[3]

THE INTERNET *IS* "REAL LIFE"

Another consistent theme that many of the women I interviewed echoed is to counter the too-frequent suggestion that, in response to their online harassment, they should simply eschew the Internet and online activities in favor of "real life." Nearly every woman I interviewed stressed that the

Internet *is* real life. Jill Filipovic, attorney, journalist, and political writer, explains:

> We want to believe that the Internet is different from "real life," that "virtual reality" is a separate sphere from reality-reality. But increasingly, virtual space is just as "real" as life off of the computer. We talk to our closest friends all day long on G-Chat. We engage with political allies and enemies on Twitter and in blog comment sections. We email our moms and our boyfriends. We like photos of our cousin's cute baby on Facebook. And if we're writers, we research, publish and promote our work online. My office is a corner of my apartment, and my laptop is my portal into my professional world. There's nothing "virtual" about it.[4]

As many women pointed out, increasingly, many people's professional activities are conducted on the Internet, and to ask them to stop writing or posting online would put them behind their male colleagues who are not driven off the Internet. Filipovic explains that for many women, being on the Internet is now their workplace:

> Imagine going to work and every few days having people in the hallway walk up to you and say things like, "Die, you dumb cunt" and "you deserve to be raped" and, if you're a woman of color, adding in the n-word and other racial slurs for good measure. Consider how that would impact your performance and your sense of safety. But you still love your job and your co-workers. That's how the Internet feels for many of us.[5]

Amy Davis Roth, atheist blogger and Skepchick contributor, echoed the sentiment that the Internet is real life:

> There is a false notion that online spaces are not real. That what happens online does not have an effect on the regular day-to-day life of people. As we have seen recently with the stolen photos of Jennifer Lawrence, high profile women are seen as mere objects and targets or play-things meant to be stolen, acquired and used—that if they can not handle these made up rules—that they should leave the Internet and all forms of technology behind. . . . The Internet is real life. It's time society acknowledges that cyber harassment and targeting of women is a problem. This isn't just about "trolls" . . . it's about hate crimes and terrorism directed at women using technology and we have seen one small subset of that.[6]

An anonymous online poster dubbed "California" details the ways that online harassment affects her career as an actor and her ability to participate professionally online. She explains that when a commercial that she is featured in is released on YouTube by the advertising agency, the comments on the video are "disgusting and appalling." She recounts that she and her female colleagues are threatened, their looks are criticized, and they are told they "deserve to be punched, mutilated, murdered, and raped." The harassment limits her participation in online activities that are integral to her career because she and her colleagues are "subjected to threats and aggression" by anonymous commenters.[7]

Given the increasing centrality of the Internet for business, social, and other aspects of contemporary life, to suggest that women who are harassed can solve the problem by simply not going online becomes for many women tantamount to telling them to quit their job if they are being sexually harassed at their workplace. As the Internet becomes more essential to many aspects of people's professional lives, it is an unfair burden to place on women for them to have to opt out of it in order to avoid abuse. Danielle Keats Citron, legal scholar and author of *Hate Crimes in Cyberspace*, elaborates:

> Targeted people who curtail their online activities or go offline incur serious costs. They lose advertising income generated from blogs and websites. They miss opportunities to advance their professional reputations through blogging. They cannot network effectively online if they assume pseudonyms to deflect the abuse. As technology blogger Robert Scoble explains, women who lack a robust online presence are "never going to be included in the [technology] industry."[8]

After Catherine Mayer, European editor for *Time* magazine, and several other women received bomb threats on Twitter, Mayer was counseled by the police to quit using Twitter:

> The officers were unanimous in advising me to take a break from Twitter, assuming, as many people do, that Twitter is at best a time-wasting narcotic, whose addled users tweet photographs of churches that resemble surprised chickens or post photographs of their breakfast.
> Twitter is, of course, exactly that, but it is also an interactive communication medium that, for journalists, ranks with the telephone and email as an essential tool of the trade.[9]

Mikki Kendall, writer and contributor to *XO Jane*, *Salon*, and the *Guardian*, emphasized that there is no longer a clearly distinguishable boundary between online and offline activities:

> Well, so let's back this up for a second and talk about the fact that just because someone says it online, it doesn't mean they can't find you offline, right? Even if I personally don't use Foursquare or one of the other locator services, if my friend who's with me says on Twitter or anywhere else, hey,

I'm at so and so with @Karnythia, and they talk about the restaurant name, then obviously you can find me. I write fiction as well.

Sometimes I do conventions. You can find me at a convention. You can find my name on the websites for those conventions. So I think it's really disingenuous to think that just because it's said online, it can't be taken to offline. We are all relatively easy to find if we're writing in public in the first place.[10]

Kate Smurthwaite, a British stand-up comedian and activist, writes of the effects of gendertrolling attacks against her on her career:

More problematic are the hundreds of messages disparaging my work. Quite understandably in the 21st century, the first thing a comedy promoter does when recommended an act is bang their name into Google. There's no way of distinguishing between a punter who has seen my show and not enjoyed it and a troll scrambling for new ways to ruin my afternoon. So my career is undoubtedly being detrimentally affected. Nasty comments have also appeared under basically every video of me online.[11]

ADVERSE REACTIONS

Regardless of the fact that some women manage to react with relative equanimity to the onslaught of harassment and attacks leveled at them, many, and perhaps most, women who have experienced gendertrolling report significant adverse reactions—emotional, mental, and even physical. Filipovic describes her reaction when she first discovered she was the target of an online harassment campaign:

Stuck at home and going swiftly down an online rabbit hole, I spent hours reading posts that extended beyond commenting on my rape-ability into users posting dozens of photos of me, commenting on my body, rating my physical attractiveness and listing my contact information. . . . people [who] claimed to know me in real life, or said they had at least met me, or seen me, or maybe talked to an ex boyfriend of mine. They had details about what I wore to class and what I said. I felt very suddenly like there wasn't enough oxygen in the room to fill my lungs.

The only thing I really remember when I returned to school a few days later is my head feeling detached from my body. I had a bizarre mental image of myself walking around with my skull in a fishbowl, separated from my shoulders, like a deranged skeletal astronaut. It was partly the painkillers. But it was also a mental shortcut—a short-circuit—to protect my own mind from the trauma that quickly ate away at my confidence, my intelligence and my basic sense of safety.[12]

Filipovic adds that, although it has now been many years since her harassment, it still can pack an emotional punch:

> For me, it has been almost eight years to the day since I sat at that old desktop and read through those AutoAdmit posts. I have since graduated law school. I worked as a corporate lawyer for almost four years, and now I have the privilege of writing full time and pursuing a career and a life that I love.... And yet writing about AutoAdmit, Googling the old posts to pull up the insults and the comments and the threats—essentially re-living that trauma from years ago—has my stomach in knots.[13]

The intense feelings of anxiety, upset, and even trauma that Filipovic describes are common to many women who experience gendertrolling. Caroline Criado-Perez, the British journalist and activist whose story is recounted in Section 3 of Chapter 2, described her feelings after receiving up to 50 abusive and threatening messages per hour:

> The immediate impact was that I couldn't eat or sleep.... I lost half a stone [seven pounds] in two days. I was just on an emotional edge all the time. I cried a lot. I screamed a lot. I don't know if I had a kind of breakdown. I was unable to function, unable to have normal interactions.[14]

Catholic blogger Caroline Farrow reports on some of the effects that gendertrolling had on her and her family:

> It is unsettling when someone wishes you serious harm or death, particularly when you feel that you have done nothing worse than to voice a dissenting opinion. I find it difficult to let go of the anxiety and tension and have to make a conscious effort to put it to the back of my mind so that it doesn't have an effect on my children. When my daughter cried because she was upset by mummy's distress caused by "those nasty people on your blog", I realised that I needed to be able to put this in perspective and not let their twisted objectives succeed.[15]

Many women report feeling especially adversely affected at the time when they first encountered the extreme and shocking levels of abuse and harassment aimed at them—and then becoming progressively more inured to the constant onslaught. Rosamund Urwin, journalist and columnist for the *London Evening Standard*, recounts her experiences:

> I had weaned myself off reading [the harassing comments] a few months before. That's one of the strange things about these comments though—there is something initially compulsive about reading them, even though you

know it is a damaging habit. . . . I wasn't always so thick-skinned. When I started writing comment pieces (I was a business reporter first), I naively had no clue quite how misogynistic the comments would be. The first time I was attacked, I felt both lonely and exposed. Lonely because I thought I might be the only woman suffering them . . . and exposed because I knew everyone else could see them, too.[16]

Kathy Sierra, programming instructor, game developer, and author of the now-shuttered technology blog Creating Passionate Users, described her initial reactions on receiving the horrific rape and death threats that were sent to her:

As I type this, I am supposed to be in San Diego, delivering a workshop at the ETech conference. But I'm not. I'm at home, with the doors locked, terrified. For the last four weeks, I've been getting death threat comments on this blog. But that's not what pushed me over the edge. What finally did it was some disturbing threats of violence and sex posted on two other blogs . . . blogs authored and/or owned by a group that includes prominent bloggers.[17]

As the gendertrolling campaign against her commenced in 2007, Sierra was among the earliest victims of gendertrolling campaigns. Although her blog was very prominent in her field and was once among the top 100 listed by Technorati, she has since discontinued blogging altogether in response to the attacks on her.[18]

Laurie Penny, an English journalist, author, and contributing editor at the *New Statesman*, writes about how the abuse affected her:

I'd like to say that none of this bothered me—to be one of those women who are strong enough to brush off the abuse, which is always the advice given by people who don't believe bullies and bigots can be fought. Sometimes I feel that speaking about the strength it takes just to turn on the computer, or how I've been afraid to leave my house, is an admission of weakness. Fear that it's somehow your fault for not being strong enough is, of course, what allows abusers to continue to abuse.[19]

Ashe Dryden, programming consultant, conference organizer, and advocate for diversity in technology, details some of the profound effects gendertrolling attacks had on her life:

Dealing with the effects of being a constant target for harassment, threats, and attacks requires a not insignificant amount of money and time: from putting protections in place against DDoS attacks on all my projects to trying to scrub all of my personal information from the Internet to dealing with lawyers and law enforcement to therapy, anti-anxiety and depression meds, and more. Thanks to recent events I've also been working on pulling together the money to move.

On top of that are the physical, emotional, and relationship tolls I have to pay for being a visible marginalized person demanding change. I no longer follow anyone on twitter thanks to people going after a close relative of mine who used twitter solely to send me pictures. I've lost friends and others have just disappeared without my participating on social media like I once felt able to. My relationship with my partner is strained with both of us stressing over my safety and how best to protect what little privacy I have. Even on anti-anxiety medication, I have regular anxiety attacks. I worry that my friends, aside from one woman who has been through similar situations, think I'm paranoid and over-careful, so I don't have near as many close friends as I once did.[20]

Emily May, the founder of a blog about street harassment, described how just the fact of receiving so many vicious insults, aside from the rape and death threats, devastated her:

The death threat was pretty scary.... And there have been several rape threats. But it's mostly "I want to rape you" or "Somebody should rape you." Most are not physical threats—they're more about how ugly I am, how nobody would bother raping me because I'm so fat and hideous. Once, after reading all these posts, I just sat in my living room and bawled like a 12-year-old.[21]

Shanley Kane, founder and CEO of *Model View Culture*, describes, in an untrackable post on Pastebin, her reaction to the attacks against her:

Frankly, I am devastated, depressed, vulnerable, non-functional, anxious, paranoid and isolated. I've visibly lost weight since last Thursday. My heart hurts and my body aches. I feel humiliated, exploited, and am in physical pain. I'm frightened for myself, my family, my friends, and people in my community who have supported me. I am trying to keep working but honestly, it is incredibly difficult.[22]

Another common experience that gendertrolled women encounter is being additionally targeted for admitting to having felt bothered, upset, or frightened by the harassment. Sarah Kendzior, writer, public speaker, and columnist for *Al Jazeera English*, recounted,

For the past few weeks, I have been receiving rape threats and constant harassment from people who describe themselves as leftists or communists, and apparently want to rape their way to revolution.... There are not words to describe the experience of reading an article, coming to the word "rape threats", and then seeing that the rape threat is about you—intended to debase and humiliate you for admitting you have been threatened.[23]

Some women reacted with self-blame, which is actually not a typical response to negative or abusive situations: in a vain attempt to feel they had some control over what happened to them, abused people often respond by looking to themselves to find something they had said or done that could have merited the abuse. A woman identified as "Washington" said she felt shame and some self-blame, wondering whether "it [was] crass of me to have commented on a post about hook-ups with my own satirical hook-up fantasy" and worrying whether others think she is a "whore." She says that she imagines that her reaction of self-blame is "not an uncommon reaction among first-time victims of hate-comments—to wonder what they did to deserve the negative attention."[24]

WITHDRAWING FROM OR OPTING OUT OF THE INTERNET

Understandably, many women, when confronted with the pervasive and enduring onslaught of abuse, insults, rape and death threats, and graphic images and pornography sent to them, decide to withdraw from public exposure on the Internet. An anonymous woman wrote about quitting Twitter after encountering sustained abuse: "After two days I abandoned my Twitter account. I didn't delete my profile, so I'm sure there's more that I haven't even seen, but just the thought of going back to my Twitter account makes me feel sick inside."[25]

Another anonymous commenter told how her past experiences of sexualized harassment online have induced her to be extremely cautious and circumspect about her online activities. She was first harassed when she wrote a story that she posted online, which prompted what she called a "creep" to impersonate her on various social media sites. Some time later, she created a blog where she posted stories about her life as well as commentary about current news topics. Two of the readers of her blog began posting "nasty sexual innuendos" about her on their blogs, and they started a campaign to generate negative rumors about her. She reported that one of them had previously run at least two other women bloggers off the Internet. As a result, she gave up on social media and writing online. She keeps her Facebook friends limited only to family members, and she has asked them never to tag her in Facebook pictures. She says that if she ever manages to get enough confidence to write again, she would use a male pseudonym. She laments, "It's sad and sometimes I hate myself for not being stronger, but I can't seem to get past the abuse and don't ever want to go through that again."[26]

Another woman, identified as "Massachusetts," related the story of being harassed online for over five years:

> The police simply shrugged—they don't understand and don't seem to have the bandwidth to deal with this type of jurisdictionally vague, anonymous harassment (criminal in Massachusetts). For the same reasons, a tort suit is simply not worth the effort for most lawyers. I've had to deal with it on my own, which has meant giving up personal writing and never fully participating on Facebook, Twitter, LinkedIn, etc., for fear that more innocent people I connect with will be punished simply for associating with me.[27]

Jennifer McCreight, an atheist activist and blogger, ceased blogging and stopped speaking in public because, as she said, "I wake up every morning to abusive comments, tweets, and emails about how I'm a slut, prude, ugly, fat, feminazi, retard, bitch, and cunt (just to name a few). . . . I just can't take it anymore."[28]

Feminist blogger Kelly Diels writes about speaker and technology developer Adria Richards's withdrawal from her public profile on the Internet after the harassment campaign that targeted her:

> Six months ago, Richards was at the center of a full-spectrum campaign that started with trolling—rape threats, racial threats, death threats—and culminated in a Ddos attack that shut down her company's servers. Her employer, Send Grid, capitulated to the mob and fired her. Since then, "for safety reasons," Richards has "been lying low."[29]

Marcela Kunova, a digital journalist, blogger, and photographer, reports that journalist Linda Grant, who was a feature writer for the British newspaper the *Guardian*, ceased writing for that online publication due to harassment and intimidation:

> The worst thing is that the strategy of harassing and intimidating female journalists, bloggers and other female public figures, was often sucessful [sic]. Some journalists, like Linda Grant, admits she stopped writing her regular column for the Guardian, because of violent threats. Some bloggers think twice before publishing a post. And even in their offline life, women are often afraid to speak up for themselves for fear of being insulted, belittled and harassed.[30]

Brianna Wu, video game developer who was targeted in Gamergate, cites several women she knows who have been driven out of the technology industry by gendertrolling:

We've lost too many women to this lunatic mob. Good women the industry was lucky to have, such as Jenn Frank, Mattie Brice and my friend Samantha Allen, one of the most insightful critics in games media.[31]

Wu thinks that many more women may have dropped out of technology by witnessing the targeting of women during Gamergate:

During the reign of terror of Gamergate, I have had hundreds of conversations with other women. We're exhausted, we're terrified we'll be next, we're all thinking of quitting.

I have a folder on my hard drive with letters from dozens and dozens of women who've abandoned their dream of becoming game developers due to Gamergate, some as young as 12.[32]

Sierra withdrew from most of her online and technology-related activities, ending her blog, cutting out nearly all speaking engagements, and rarely appearing in technology forums online or events offline. She explains her reasons:

I do not want to be part of a culture—the Blogosphere—where this is considered acceptable. Where the price for being a blogger is kevlar-coated skin and daughters who are tough enough to not have their "widdy biddy sensibilities offended" when they see their own mother Photoshopped into nothing more than an objectified sexual orifice, possibly suffocated as part of some sexual fetish. (And of course all coming on the heels of more explicit threats).[33]

Even seven years after she withdrew from her online activities and abandoned her very successful technology career, Sierra still asserts that she was under too much danger to continue: "I had no desire then to find out what comes after doxxing, especially not with a family, and I had every reason to believe this would continue to escalate if I didn't, well, stop [writing]."[34]

Anita Sarkeesian, in an interview with Amy Goodman on *Democracy Now*, explains that online harassment isn't relegated only to the gaming industry:

Online harassment, especially gendered online harassment is an epidemic. Women are being driven out, they are being driven offline. This isn't just in gaming. This is happening across the board online, especially with women who participate in or work in male-dominated industries. So the harassment actually has a very real effect on us as a society in terms of making this space unwelcoming for women. But it also has a chilling effect, so women who are watching this happen, who are watching me get terrorized for two years, are going to question whether they actually want to be involved, whether they want to speak up, whether they want to participate.[35]

Liz Ryerson, video game designer and critic, talks about the effects that seeing other women harassed has on those who are observing it:

a lot of us look to someone like Zoe Quinn or Anita Sarkeesian and the image of more cultural visibility is not exactly very appealing. living with no privacy is not appealing. living in fear for your personal safety all the time for doing what you want to do is not appealing. i have my whole life ahead of me. i'm still working through tons of issues with depression and anxiety. i don't want that to be ruined by a few people who can't get a fucking life and leave me alone.[36]

Ryerson quotes Lana Polansky, a writer, designer, and critic who focuses on digital art, who eschews success if the costs are so high: "Lana Polansky (@LanaTheGun101) on twitter: like why, as a woman, would i even WANT success in this industry where bitter nerds are constantly trying to tear me down and ruin my life?"[37]

Soraya Chemaly, freelance writer, media critic, and activist, points out the irony of losing so many women's voices in defense of "free speech," which many people so often cite as the reason nothing can be done to curtail the harassment of women on the Internet:

"I've spoken to many women who simply stopped engaging.... They don't support other people online because they don't want to be targeted, they've stopped writing about certain topics, they silence themselves—which is of course the issue.... I'm happy to talk about free speech, it's very dear to me ... but the free speech we have to take care of first is the speech that is already lost," because women are being intimidated off the Internet, out of public life and into silence.[38]

CURTAILING SPEECH OR SELF-CENSORSHIP

Other women choose to remain online, but, after observing what happens to the more outspoken women who are targeted, they decide to tone down their opinions or avoid certain topics. Eleanor O'Hagan, journalist and columnist for the *Guardian*, explains her strategy to try to avoid online abuse:

> On the whole, I've managed to avoid the worst threats and misogyny that other women writers endure . . . because, very early on, I became conscious of how my opinions would be received and began watering them down, or not expressing them at all. I noticed that making feminist arguments led to more abuse and, as a result, I rarely wrote about feminism at all.[39]

Another anonymous commenter believes that, because she works in the competitive, male-dominated field of IT security, she would be attacked much more heavily than she has been if she blogs the way she would like. She also believes that she would likely be attacked by people with whom she works, or possibly, by people from whom she may be seeking jobs in the future. She is therefore purposely very neutral in commenting online. Although this has kept her safe from harassment, she believes that "this has cost my work. I have no online presence to prove my chops. But I will not put myself through that. It infuriates me, but I will not put my sanity or physical safety at risk."[40] She adds that part of the reason she feels she must be especially protective of herself is that she is a survivor of childhood sexual abuse. Certainly, many, many women have histories of various kinds of abuse, including childhood sexual abuse, incest, rape, or domestic violence, and those women, who represent a sizeable proportion of women, must be especially guarded against anything that could trigger a trauma reaction.

Another woman, posting anonymously, explained that, although what she is writing about on her blog has been well received and she has a growing readership, she is reluctant to do anything to bring more traffic to her site.

> This year I started a blog where I do a feminist analysis of the British sci-fi show Doctor Who. My audience grew rather quickly, and so far most of the responses to my work have been positive. Of course, not all of them have been. So far, the worst harassment I've received is swearing and name calling: "Cunt," "Fuck you bitch," and "She's got daddy issues" (my parents got a kick out of that one). So as odd as it seems, I count myself as one of the lucky ones. But I'm constantly worried about what comes next.
>
> I want to expand my audience, but I hesitate to do so because even if I bring in a few thousand more followers that love my work, I could get the attention of that one person who can make my life a living hell. I've seen it happen to other women commenting on pop culture. The harassment of high-profile women on the Internet has devastating ripple effects, and I wonder how many other young women are silencing themselves before they've even received any harassment or abuse because they've seen what happens to the women who do speak up on the Internet.[41]

Another woman, identified as "Europe," explains how fear of being harassed structures her online activities:

> I will not share a story of harassment, but a story of fear: the very fear of harassment already keeps me from being less active online than I would like to be. It is a conscious decision not to act on my potential.
>
> Let me add why this fear is so powerful: I have children. And whereas I can imagine dealing with rape/death threats to myself, I couldn't bear my children being targeted by even one single threat.[42]

IGNORING OR BECOMING INURED

Many other women have responded to gendertrolling campaigns against them by valiantly attempting to do what is so often recommended by people who haven't experienced gendertrolling: try to ignore or slough off the constant and ongoing threats and abuse directed at them. Dawn Foster, a writer and editor on the topic of sustainable housing in England, found the best way for her to deal with gendertrolling was to ignore it:

> Occasionally, I'd respond to emails casually, to show the sender hadn't affected me in any way. Their responses usually disintegrated into unhinged ranting, away from discussing how much they hated me and into their hatred of women in general. . . . In the end, I discovered the best way to combat the abuse was to ignore it. If someone writes a derailing comment, delete it. Someone wishes rape upon you on Twitter, block them. Someone emails you self-righteous bile, don't reply: forward it on to your friends to amuse them during their coffee break.[43]

Indeed, some women have been so successful in inuring themselves that they report instances of harassment that others find horrifying with relative sangfroid. Smurthwaite explains, "At first it really upset me, but much less so now. My friends are always surprised with the casualness with which I can mention threats of gang rape."[44]

Several people pointed out negative aspects of women becoming inured to high levels of threats and harassment. A blogger with the pseudonym Dr. Nerdlove, who writes a column about "nerds" and romance, highlights the problem of such harassment becoming normalized. Referring to the harassment of Janelle Asselin, an academic researcher on comics and editor of several DC Comics titles who was targeted for a harassment campaign after she criticized the cover of a comic book, Dr. Nerdlove writes:

> ... this isn't about whether or not Asselin is legitimately afraid for her personal safety—while not ignoring that these are threats from people who know what she looks like, where she works and where she lives—or if these threats are at all credible. It's about the fact that this is so common place, that women get *so many threats that it stops bothering them.* . . . I want to reiterate that so that it sinks in: women getting so many anonymous, sexually violent threats that it just becomes *normal to them.*[45]

Filipovic discusses another drawback of becoming accustomed to and therefore inured to the abuse:

> I know how quickly the lines between the "real" and the virtual can blur. Before I discovered the AutoAdmit threads, I had already been blogging about feminism for a little while, and rape and murder threats weren't new. It remains standard for people to leave comments like, "Here, babycakes, let me give you some roofies and fuck you up the ass, in the ear and up your nose until you weep and bleed" on my site. For the first year or two they shook me up. Then I learned how to roll my eyes, copy and paste them into a dedicated folder and hit the delete key. I did what all the male bloggers told me to do: I ignored the bullies, I grew such thick skin that now I worry about my lack of a fight-or-flight fear reflex, my ability to eat whatever shit is put in front of my face, how in real-life arguments with loved ones and moments of trauma I go stone-cold and it's almost like my heart shuts off. But I bucked up. I knew how to be tough on the Internet.[46]

EFFECTS ON WOMEN'S OFFLINE LIVES

While responses to online abuse and threats vary, from the perhaps less dramatic reactions such as withdrawal, self-censorship, or attempts to ignore the attacks, some women's lives have been more profoundly disrupted by gendertrolling. Some women have become so frightened and alarmed about the specificity and credibility of the online threats made against them and their families that they have resorted to making significant life changes, or even moving their domicile entirely, to try to ensure their safety.

Dryden rarely ventures out, and when she does, she does not leave her own home unaccompanied. She relates the effects of online stalking and harassment on her life:

> 4 months ago I filed a police report against a man who had been stalking me for months and had threatened to rape and murder me. This man lives in the same small city that I reside in. The stalker erroneously received the

police report I filed against him and chose to further harm me by posting it online—in doing so, sharing my home address and phone number. . . .

Because of this man, I've stopped leaving my house alone. I now rarely leave home at all. I've had to notify friends, family, and neighbors to look out for suspicious people asking about me. I'm terrified every time I receive a phone call I don't recognize.[47]

Kane describes significant real-life effects since the gendertrolling campaign against her became increasingly menacing. She writes that she no longer makes public appearances or speaks at public events. She is careful not to let anyone know where she is or where she lives, and she doesn't have friends over, except a few very close ones, in order ensure that her address is confidential. She finds that people are reluctant to support her because they are afraid they will be targeted as well. She adds that she spends "an enormous amount of money and time securing my safety."[48]

Many women have felt the threats to be sufficiently dire to leave their homes temporarily or even move to a new residence in order to ensure their physical safety. The women who were most targeted in the Gamergate campaign, Zoe Quinn, Brianna Wu, and Anita Sarkeesian, fled their homes for safety after the threats against them became credible. Quinn began couch surfing among friends in order to elude anyone who might have been induced to personally target her by the release of her address online. Wu and her husband left their home after an online harasser said he was going to rape and kill her.[49] When a gendertroll posted the location of Sarkeesian's apartment and threatened to kill her parents, she fled her home to stay with friends.[50]

S. E. Smith, blogger at Tiger Beatdown, is in the process of moving and feels sufficiently threatened to be taking other significant real-life precautions:

> It took a few years to reach this point, but I finally have, the point where I do have concerns about my physical safety, and have had to reevaluate certain aspects of my life and work. I've gotten those emails that send a long chill down my spine and create a surging feeling of rage, mixed with helplessness. People have sent me my social security number, information about my family members, identifying details that make it very clear they know exactly how to find me. They have politely provided details of exactly what they'd like to do to me and my family, they send me creepy things in the mail.
>
> "I'm glad your stupid cat died," someone wrote me last October. "You're next, bitch," and followed up with my street address. . . .
>
> I spent the remaining week almost entirely at the new house [where she is moving], working on the house during the day and slinking home late at

night, leaving the lights off to make it look like I wasn't home, leaving my distinctive and highly identifiable car parked at a distant location.[51]

Sierra felt her only safe option was to move after she received credible rape and death threats in 2007.[52] Watson reported that Davis Roth, colleague and fellow blogger at Skepchick, was induced to move to safeguard where she lived when her home address was posted on a forum "dedicated to hating feminist skeptics."[53] Mikki Kendall, writer and contributor to *XO Jane*, *Salon*, and the *Guardian*, likewise felt she had to move after a photo of her and her children that was taken where they live was posted online:

> I've actually gotten rape threats. I've gotten death threats. . . . Someone sent me a picture of me and my kids walking across the parking lot of the building we were living in and threatened to come see us. We had to move. I had to actually move a few years ago. And it was horrible. And I've sort of gotten, in the wake of that experience—of an actual stalking—I've sort of gotten this sense of when I have to pay attention to the threats and when the threats are such that I can make fun of them.[54]

Reactions and responses to gendertrolling campaigns have varied from woman to woman. Within one woman's experience, emotions can run from shocked and horrified initially, to inured and defiant later on. Many women report experiencing high levels of anxiety and upset, to the point of having to take anti-anxiety medication and even incurring symptoms of PTSD. Gendertrolling harassment campaigns have induced many women to sharply curtail the topics about which they write, to undertake measures to avoid increasing the number of readers of their online writing, or to withdraw from online activity partially or entirely. Other women become inured to the abuse, although they often still report experiencing significant anxiety. In many cases, women who have received specific and credible threats have made a variety of not insignificant changes in their lives and some have even fled their homes or moved to a new home in order to ensure their physical safety.

Chapter 4

Fighting Back

Although many women's reactions to the combination of sustained and prolonged attacks and abuse that typify gendertrolling are understandably negative and leave the targeted women reeling, others, after initial feelings of shock and distress, have rallied to take steps to fight back against the abuse.

APPEAL TO AUTHORITIES FOR HELP

One way women have attempted to fight back is to seek help from the police or other law enforcement authorities. Women have tended to appeal to law enforcement when they felt that the rape and death threats crossed over from being purely virtual into becoming a potential real-life danger to their health and safety. Notably, this point often represents an extraordinary level of threat since the women have, in most cases, been the recipients of ongoing and continual threats and harassment for quite some time.

Unfortunately, women who do seek help from law enforcement often find that the police have not been trained with regard to online harassment and threats, that they don't understand online social media, and that they tend not to take even credible and specific rape and death threats seriously.

An anonymous woman identified as "Canada" explained that when she attempted to alert the police to the threats made against her online, they told her to get off the Internet. Because she is a computer programmer, getting off the Internet is not a viable option for her. In addition, when she went to the doctor to get medication to help her deal with the stress of receiving the threats, the doctor likewise advised her to get off the Internet. When she tried to explain that she has to be on the Internet because of her profession, she was advised to retrain for another career. She found the experience of trying to get help from the police particularly frustrating because when she contacted the police in her jurisdiction, they told her to contact the police department in the harasser's jurisdiction; when she contacted them, they referred her back to the police in her own jurisdiction. She described it as "a very exhausting and stressful situation."[1]

Another commenter, identified as "New York," told how her attempts to seek help from the police were not taken seriously:

> As a feminist and abortion rights activist, I've been harassed on Twitter relentlessly, but one troll in particular has started to stalk me and send me death threats (and now contacts me via email). I wrote about my experience for *The Daily Beast* about how neither Twitter nor the New York Police Department took my reports seriously. This man who stalks me littered my article with comments and he's now like a phantom limb. I really can feel him wherever I go.[2]

A commenter identified as "Texas" tells of her experiences of the police dismissing the threats against her. She was targeted by a man who told her he was going to rape her and continued sending her threats over a three-month period. In addition, he harassed her family, making fabricated claims that her father had hired him as a male escort and that her father had physically beaten him. He posted negative reviews of her employers and called them at home to say she had been rude to him in their store, despite the fact that her employers offered no public services and did not have a store. When she tried to file a police report, the police seemed uninterested, even though she showed them the physical threats that he had made, explained that his IP address revealed that he was located close to her home, and told them that his name from his residential phone had appeared on her home phone caller ID. She reported, "They did nothing. They didn't even file a report. They wouldn't even give me the paper trail I would need."[3]

Journalist Anna Merlan had a similar experience attempting to obtain help from the police. The police officer who responded to her call explained to her, "I don't want to take the report and have it get pushed aside.... It's stalking and aggravated harassment. But with an unknown perpetrator, we'd have to close it right away." He also told her, "This is, at most, harassment.... It doesn't take a genius to figure this out. It's more bark than bite. And anyway, these are Canadian phone numbers and we can't trace them." Merlan says that the numbers he was referring to were links in a chat, which, according to her, "did sort of look like phone numbers, [only] in that they were strings of numbers."[4]

Amy Davis Roth, atheist/skeptic blogger, recounts her unsuccessful attempts at getting help, first from the police and then from the FBI:

> In one case, I went to the authorities too because I was being harassed by a stalker from another country. He was threatening me so I went to my local police, who then told me to go to the FBI. But they don't do anything.... So what I was told is that until someone actually comes to my door, or someone actually comes to my house or confronts me physically, there is no recourse that I can take. So you have to sort of play this Russian roulette game where you're just waiting to see which person is actually going to follow through on a threat. And it's frightening and it's sort of like what we've seen recently with the killing spree with [Elliot] Rodger, who decided he hated women and clearly has left a misogynist trail all over the Internet. So until someone actually acts on it, they're not considered a threat.... I feel like we're just expected to be quiet and behave and just wait until the abusers come get us before we can actually do anything and often times that is too late.[5]

Rebecca Watson (whose story is detailed in Section 6 of Chapter 2) tells about her first attempt at obtaining help from the police when she was sent what she considered to be a serious and credible threat:

> The first [serious threat] came back in 2005 when I lived in Boston and had just launched Skepchick.... I received a brief email from a man calling me a cunt. I responded with a chipper "Thanks for taking the time to write!" He responded with, "If I lived in Boston I'd put a bullet in your brain."
> That escalated quickly.
> I checked his IP address and found he was most likely writing from North Carolina. I called the Boston police and described the exchange. They told me there wasn't much they could do because he apparently lived in another state. They offered to take down a report, but admitted that nothing would come of it unless someone one day put a bullet in my brain, at which point they'd have a pretty good lead.[6]

Several years later, Watson again attempted to report a threat that she considered, out of the countless ones that she receives, to be especially credible:

> The last one I reported was last year. A Skepchick reader happened across the website of a man who had written disturbing things about murdering women in general and me in particular, including photos of me with targets on them. The reader alerted the other Skepchicks, who compiled as much

information as they could on the person, including his real name, age, and location (about a 3-hour drive from me). Let's call him "Rick."

Because I knew what town "Rick" lived in, I called his local police department. They told me there was nothing they could do and that I'd have to make a report with my local police department. So I called my local police department and the operator transferred me to a detective, but I got a busy signal. I called back and the operator sent me to another line, which rang and rang for ten minutes before I hung up. I called back and finally got through to someone who told me that there was nothing they could do but take a report in case one day "Rick" followed through on his threats, at which point they'd have a pretty good lead.[7]

After several attempts at obtaining help or protection from the police, Watson concluded that contacting the police for online threats is fruitless:

At the time, I assumed my local police department was the exception, but as the years passed I learned that they're actually the rule. I've lived in several different cities since then and received several frightening threats, and never have I met a single helpful cop who even made an attempt to help me feel safe.[8]

Watson then tried contacting the FBI for the latest threat, thinking that perhaps they might be more responsive. She found them to be initially more cooperative. An agent agreed that the threat was credible; however, she did not contact Watson again despite numerous attempts on Watson's part to follow up. Finally, Watson informed the agent that she would be giving a public talk only an hour from where "Rick" lived. The agent told her, "You take whatever precautions you need to take," and Watson never heard from her again.

Watson reports that "Around this time, I started receiving hundreds of harassing Tweets and Facebook messages from a pseudonym using an IP address that came from 'Rick's' home town."[9] She hired a private investigator when the police and the FBI failed to take seriously the death threats made against her. Although a prior domestic violence arrest indicated that the harasser, who was making clear statements online about his intentions to murder Watson, had a history of committing violence against women, the private investigator advised Watson against a protective order because it might further anger him and prod him into actually committing violence.[10]

Davis Roth, echoing the sentiments of many other women, felt that the police were just not aware of, trained for, or able to understand the phenomenon of online threats: "It seems to me at this point in time law enforcement (and I'm not blaming them) . . . just aren't equipped to handle what's happening online or they don't understand it."[11] Davis Roth, like several other women, was advised by the police against obtaining a restraining order because they believed that they were often not effective:

> Another thing that [the police] tell us is that you can file a restraining order. So if I wanted to file a restraining order against my harassers, I could do that, but all that happens is that the police take a restraining order to that person's house, and they tell you, "we don't recommend that you do this because it's probably gonna just piss them off and then they are more likely to be aggressive." So it's like victim blaming, it's put on us, there really no recourse at this time for us to protect ourselves from these threats until someone actually does something. So what do you do? The police actually tell us things like "get a gun."[12]

There have been a few instances where police intervention was effective, such as in the case of an anonymous woman identified as "Washington," who had a job at a small Internet service provider. People created Photoshopped images of her head grafted onto pornography; rap lyrics were written about her that described her as a "breeder" and a "whore." One of the customers at the small Internet service provider where she worked began stalking her and her roommate, posting announcements about her physical whereabouts such as where she parked at school or that he had seen her coming out of a particular building. She contacted the sex crimes unit of the police. Since she had records in her company's service logs of his activities, she gave them access to all of the data that showed he was stalking her. She recounted that the police were very helpful. They contacted the stalker and told him that she had a solid case against him, but that they would not go forward with prosecuting him if he left her alone. She reports that, to her surprise, he did cease stalking her after that, but that she does worry that he may still be stalking others.[13]

Nevertheless, most women report that their attempts at getting law enforcement to enforce laws against making credible threats of violence against them are not successful. It appears that much of the problem is attributable to the fact that the Internet is a relatively new technology, and therefore, many law enforcement personnel are not familiar with the potential ramifications of online speech and behavior. In addition, many people, especially those whose occupations do not involve extensive use of computers and the Internet, such as the police, still see the Internet as a purely virtual medium, the effects of which do not cross over into real life. Because law enforcement tends to envision the Internet as not real, they don't have a sense that online threats are real and are therefore a crime in the same way that offline threats are. They also tend not to be familiar with the potential dangers that online threats and doxxing can have, such as the fact that there are many instances in which gendertrolls have been emboldened enough to locate and contact targeted women in public venues as well as at their homes.

Another problem that women encountered when attempting to get help from law enforcement is lack of training and knowledge about online platforms that gendertrolls use to target women. Catherine Mayer, the European editor for *Time* magazine who was among those targeted for bomb threats in England, explains that when she contacted the police, they lacked the knowledge and tools to effectively investigate the threats. She reported that the officers did not use nor seem to understand why anyone would wish to use Twitter, with one officer mistaking the Twitter handle of the person making the threat for a sort of code.[14]

Amanda Hess, *Slate* contributor and freelance writer, also encountered officers who didn't know what Twitter was, which contributed to the police not taking online threats against her seriously:

> Well, threats of physical violence, whether they are carried out in person or online are already illegal. They—it's a criminal act, but the problem is that there is not a lot of movement to even investigate these crimes. So, for example, when someone this summer threatened to rape and kill me, when I interfaced with the police about it—first of all, they had no idea what Twitter was, which was the platform where the threats came over.[15]

Kathy Sierra, the technology blogger who was driven off blogging and sharply curtailed her online presence as a result of being gendertrolled, sums up the woeful inadequacy of appealing to law enforcement for help with the threats that accompany gendertrolling campaigns: "You're probably more likely to win the lottery than to get any law enforcement agency in the United States to take action when you are harassed online, no matter how viscously and explicitly. Local agencies lack the resources, federal agencies won't bother."[16]

SHOWING DEFIANCE

Although most women's attempts to fight back against gendertrolling by obtaining enforcement of the laws against threats of violence were rarely effective, some women had more success in fighting back through refusing to be silenced and remaining defiant in the face of gendertrolling campaigns against them. Many women report that, although they initially reacted with distress and fear and were reeling from the shocking level of the attacks against them, they ultimately summoned up their strength and were able to demonstrate courage and bravado in the face of their attackers. This communicated the powerful message that even shocking levels of abuse and threats were not able to intimidate them and that they refuse to be silenced.

Shauna James Ahern, chef and food blogger at Gluten Free Girl, talks about her devastation when the gendertrolls who targeted her impersonated her infant daughter, but, regardless, she vowed to keep writing and not let the trolls stop her:

> There was also one [message] written in the voice of our daughter. Our 10-month-old daughter. And it was repeatedly making fun of the shape of her head.
>
> Seriously, who writes a Twitter feed to mock the skull of a 10-month-old?
>
> After we found that one, Danny [Ahern's husband] and I froze. We didn't want our lives public anymore. I thought about taking down this blog. Finding a new job. I made all the photographs of [her daughter] private. I wouldn't write about her at all. For a time, I didn't want to write about our lives. I could make gluten-free cookies and not say a thing about us. Put up bread and everyone would be happy. I tried this for awhile.
>
> And then I felt so stifled and itchy that I knew I couldn't do this anymore. We got through [her daughter's] surgery and realized that I had given in. I didn't want to let these people win.
>
> I started writing our stories again. I haven't stopped since....
>
> I am tired of not talking about this. I'm tired of keeping this inside, tightening my lips, and deleting. It doesn't feel honest to not talk about this.[17]

Lindy West, feminist blogger and activist whose story is detailed in Section 2 of Chapter 2, explains that she derives personal empowerment, both for herself and—she hopes—for others, from standing strong in the face of the long-standing campaign against her and from refusing to be silenced:

> I talk back because the expectation is that when you tell a woman to shut up, she should shut up.... I talk back because it's fun, sometimes, to rip an abusive dummy to shreds with my friends. I talk back because my mental health is my priority—not some troll's personal satisfaction. I talk back because it emboldens other women to talk back online and in real life, and I talk back because women have told me that my responses give them a script for dealing with monsters in their own lives.[18]

Iram Ramzan, a British Muslim reporter and freelance journalist who was the victim of extensive online harassment, echoes this sense of empowerment through defiance:

My message to these people, if you are reading this, is that you will never silence me. I have an opinion, a mind and a voice and I will be damned if I am going to let cowards hiding behind their computer screens scare and bully me into silence and submission.[19]

Brianna Wu, a video game developer who was targeted in Gamergate, embraced her strength and defiance in the face of serious rape and death threats:

> They threatened the wrong woman this time. I am the Godzilla of bitches. I have a backbone of pure adamantium, and I'm sick of seeing them abuse my friends.
>
> The misogynists and the bullies and the sadist trolls of patriarchal gaming culture threatened to murder me and rape my corpse, and I did not back down. They tried to target my company's financial assets and I did not back down. They tried to impersonate me on Twitter in an attempt to professionally discredit me and I did not back down.
>
> The *BBC* called me "Defiant," in a caption. I plan to frame and put it on my wall.[20]

Shanley Kane, cultural critic and founder and CEO of *Model View Culture*, after detailing extensive online harassment including doxxing and targeting of her family members and supporters, remained resolute on continuing her work even, remarkably, in the immediate aftermath of the ramping up of attacks on her:

> I'm not stopping, I am not going away, and I will continue, even if it happens a little slower or a little later than I planned. Changing tech is my life's work. I'm only 28, so you'll probably have to deal with it for at least the next few decades. This is a set-back for my health and my ability to work, but I'm here for the long-term.[21]

RAISING AWARENESS AND ACTIVIST CAMPAIGNS

Finally, several women have enacted a kind of "turn into the skid" move, in which, rather than hiding the graphic and horrific insults and threats they were sent, they display, in lurid detail, exactly what they have been subjected to, so that other people can be made aware of what women who are gendertrolled have been facing. This move is especially powerful because it flies in the face of any sense of shame that gendertrolls may be trying to elicit in the people they target, especially because so many of the insults, abuse, and harassment are sexualized in a particularly ugly way and are personally insulting of the women they target. Most people have a hard enough time even reading the kinds of abuse aimed at them, let alone broadcasting them to the broader public, which is why this tactic is so powerful. This kind of move affirms that the shame properly belongs to those who generate the abuse and not on the recipients of the abuse.

An anonymous commenter identified as "California" recounted trying to turn the negative into something more positive:

> Harassment changed the way I wrote and shared on my blog for a little while—but I also took it as a challenge, to absorb the nasty and transmute it into something useful. We call this art, no? The silver lining is that this kind of trolling rallies one's tribe. I was able to connect with a number of other feminist bloggers who were also harassed.[22]

Soraya Chemaly, feminist writer, media critic, and activist, points out the importance of trying to increase awareness of, rather than trying to ignore, gendertrolling harassment. Chemaly also endorses a Twitter campaign, #silentnomore, which was started in 2013 by Caroline Criado-Perez, the British activist who campaigned for a woman's face on a British banknote. The campaign encouraged other women to speak out against the online harassment they have experienced.

> While I understand "don't feed the trolls" and "don't read the comments" advice, I think that it [is] crucially important that women who are experiencing this online harassment make people aware of it. So does Caroline Criado Perez, who today wrote about a new hashtag, #silentnomore, which she started to encourage women to speak out about their experiences and confront pervasive troll culture. Studies show that confronting sexism works.[23]

In another Twitter campaign aimed at bringing the abuse and harassment to light rather than hiding it, Nancy Miller, editor of *Fast Company*, urged bloggers to retweet the harassment and threats they receive—including the harassers' names and employers—tagged with the hashtag #ThreatoftheDay.[24]

Other women have come up with some inventive ways of trying to counteract the effects of the abuse by highlighting how horrific the content of the harassment is while at the same time defusing it by using humor or creativity in their method of presentation. Jill Filipovic, feminist blogger, author, and lawyer, turned the abuse and harassment she and other women had been receiving into an ongoing contest on the blog Feministe, which they called "Feministe's Next Top Troll." Emulating television competition reality shows, the contest has "seasons," and people got to vote for the harassment incident they believe qualified as the worst incident, which then "won" the contest.[25]

Miri Mogilevsky, atheist/skeptic blogger who was harassed in part for her support of Watson, created an anti-trolling day Facebook event, in which she encouraged others to bombard people with what they appreciated about them, as a kind of antidote to the persistent abuse and insults that the bloggers were receiving. Mogilevsky reported that the event was successful, especially because "it was nice to get [the supportive comments] and to make them."[26]

Watson created an online "Page o' Hate," where she has posted many of the abusive and insulting things that have been sent to her, noting that "this is a very small portion of the hate" she has received and doesn't include "entire blogs devoted to me, videos people have made about me, or actual, credible threats that have been reported to authorities." She explained that she has also "blocked most of the haters and so these days I only see a small trickle of what gets thrown at me."[27]

Anita Sarkeesian, in an attempt to "effectively communicate just how bad this sustained intimidation campaign really is," posted on her Tumblr page just one weeks' worth of hateful, abusive, and threatening tweets directed at her, which numbered over 150.[28]

Lindy West, whose story is recounted in Section 2 of Chapter 2, responded to the gendertrolling campaign against her by creating a video in which she read out loud, with an extremely flat affect, some of the harassing comments, insults, and threats she had received. The matter-of-fact tone with which she read the comments highlighted their cruelty and senselessness. She recounts the effectiveness of this approach:

> I compiled a ton of the comments that I have gotten—and we made a video. This is probably the thing I am most proud of in my career. It was really effective. We made a video, it's just me looking into the camera reading like 5 straight minutes of these horrible comments out loud. And then I posted it on Jezebel [in a post titled] "If Comedy Has No Lady Problem Why Am I Getting So Many Rape Threats?" It just dismantled their whole side of the argument. It was really, really effective and really satisfying because . . . the way [the harassers] tried to convince me that comedy didn't have a misogyny problem was with this avalanche of violent misogyny. I thought of it like an art piece.[29]

West subsequently was featured on the popular podcast *This American Life* to tell the story of confronting one of the particularly vicious trolls who created false accounts in the name of her recently deceased father, from which he harassed her and attempted to make her feel that her father was ashamed of her. Her poignant and touching story ended, in what is a highly unusual outcome, with her communicating openly with the man who did this and with him sincerely apologizing to her.[30]

Blogger Chelsea Woolley also created a video, called "That's Just Mean," in which six men between the ages of 18 and 25 read some vulgar and cruel tweets that were sent to women. The video shows the young men becoming increasingly uncomfortable as they are confronted with the vicious cruelty of the tweets. One of the tweets reads, "I just found out that a girl I know gets passed around at parties like a hacky sack #whore."[31] It is especially gratifying, and even heartening, to see the looks of upset and horror on the young men's faces in the video as they begin to realize the kinds of abuse that women are subjected to online.

Finally, in an especially creative and imaginative response, Davis Roth used the harassment aimed against her and other women bloggers in her online community to create an art installation that features an office space, complete with typical office furnishings, on which are inscribed the words of online abuse and harassment that women have received. Davis Roth describes the space she created:

> I am building a free standing 8ft by 8ft office space.... The room is intended to be an average office that a woman would work in. It is simply a normal office space, with a door, desk, chair and a computer and other small objects that one might have in a workspace, but this particular room has been transformed to clearly show the viewer what it can feel like to be targeted in your place of work, over multiple years with aggressive online stalking and harassment.
>
> The room and its objects are blanketed with actual messages sent to, or publicly posted about the women who have contributed to the exhibit.[32]

She describes the intent of the installation:

> This particular room has been transformed to clearly show the viewer what it can feel like to be targeted in your place of work, over multiple years with aggressive online stalking and harassment.... I have been told by a lot of people to just "turn off the computer" or to "walk away" when I bring up the topic of online harassment directed at women. The people who say these things to me haven't experienced the misogynistic, targeted attacks that certain women receive online. I created this installation to educate the public that the harassment and attacks are a serious problem, online life is real, and we as a society need to address these issues.[33]

One goal of this art installation of online harassment is to help people understand how it feels to be bombarded by this kind of harassment and abuse in one's workplace, which is why the installation was created in the form of an office. Davis Roth explains:

> People don't really understand it unless it's happened to them. You don't know what it's like to wake up at 7 am, sit down on your computer, and the first thing you read is that "you're a horrible cunt that I want to rape with a beer bottle." Unless that's happened to you, you can't understand how much . . . it affects your everyday life.[34]

All of the messages pasted onto the office furniture and other effects are actual messages that were sent to or publicly posted about gendertrolled women. Davis Roth explains that the installation is meant to "put you, the viewer, in *their* [the harassed women's] *shoes* if only for a moment. See what it is like to be obsessively judged based on 'fuck-ability', 'rape-ability', as an object, or alternatively as what seems to be a target in a socially accepted (or otherwise ignored) game of online stalking, harassment and silencing techniques."[35]

The variety of methods that women have employed to counter their online harassment highlights their strength, resilience, inventiveness, and creativity, even in the face of coordinated campaigns of intense, prolonged, and pervasive online harassment. Some women have attempted to fight back by reaching out to the police or the FBI to obtain enforcement of existing laws against threats of violence, with very limited success. Many women have fought back by resolving to stand strong and resolute in the face of the attacks on them and by remaining determined not to be silenced regardless of the threats they receive. Other women have even begun raising public awareness about online harassment against women by showcasing their abuse through Twitter campaigns, online postings, videos, and even an art installation.

Part II

GENDERTROLLING IN HISTORICAL AND SOCIAL CONTEXT

Chapter 5

Gendertrolling: It's Not about the Internet

Many people lament the notion that there is something inherent in the Internet as a new technology that has resulted in the kinds of virulent and sustained attacks on women that are typical of gendertrolling. There are indeed some aspects of the Internet, such as anonymity and the ability to reach large numbers of people at little-to-no cost or effort, that uniquely shape the way gendertrolling attacks are carried out and may even exacerbate the virulence of the attacks. As Amanda Marcotte, author and blogger, explains, gendertrolling has been brilliantly adapted to take advantage of the new technological features of the Internet:

> The Internet doesn't create the urge to harass women, and it probably doesn't even magnify it. What it does is it makes harassment more *efficient* and *personal*, all at the same time. A man who likes to abuse and harass women is limited by physical proximity, time restraints, and legal considerations in the real world.... Online, however, a man who enjoys harassing women can attack dozens in a very short period of time. He can recruit his friends to make the attacks more intense and has a lot more avenues for attack, going through email, Facebook, Twitter, and blog comments. It's harder for women to just walk away from your cat-calling online; they have to actively block the harasser.[1]

However, the systematic and persistent attacks on women that are characteristic of gendertrolling are not a uniquely idiosyncratic behavior pattern that emerged with the advent of the Internet, nor is gendertrolling an inevitable result of the particularities of the Internet. To the contrary, there is a long historical precedence for the quality and tenor of these kinds of attacks on women, and gendertrolling merely reflects the shift from offline to online of these long-standing patterns of misogyny. Marcotte sums up this perspective eloquently:

> By focusing the discussion so much on the Internet and the newness of this kind of harassment, we run the risk of taking an overly reductive view of the problem. While Internet harassment is, relatively speaking, a novel and often overwhelming problem, it is hardly a unique problem in the world. It needs to be seen for what it is, an extension of the constant drumbeat of harassment and violence that women around the world face—and have always faced—for no other reason than they are women. Women are abused on the streets, in our workplaces, and in our homes. That we are also abused online shouldn't be surprising at all. The Internet presents new challenges, but the problem of misogyny is the same as it ever was.[2]

As Marcotte points out, gendertrolling, rather than being a new and unprecedented phenomenon, is a reflection and embodiment of long-standing cultural patterns of misogyny—both beliefs and practices. Dale Spender, an Australian scholar who has worked on revealing the ways that women's voices have been silenced throughout U.S. and European history, explains that harassment is an age-old method of preventing women from being full participants in public discourse as well as from fully occupying public spaces. After an extensive review of European women who have tried to contribute their ideas to the discourse of their times, Spender concludes that "[b]y such harassment, women are kept in their place, and men's claim to ownership of the realm of ideas and creativity is upheld."[3]

As an online adaptation of widespread cultural misogyny, gendertrolling has much in common with other offline misogynistic behaviors, and it can be squarely situated within the broader pattern of harassment and abuse of women that has a long historical precedent. The overall commonality that gendertrolling shares with other kinds of misogynistic behaviors, both on- and offline, is that they all manifest as a systematic pattern of harassment that works in an overly coincidentally singular direction to inhibit and shame women from fully participating in public spaces. The net effect of this pattern of harassment is to keep women subordinated economically, socially, and politically.

GATEKEEPING

One way that gendertrolling functions to subordinate women is through gatekeeping, that is, effectively shutting women out of professional, social, or political opportunities. Although, the (mostly) men who wage gendertrolling attacks against (mostly) women do not expressly articulate that their behavior is motivated out of a desire to gatekeep, there is a long history of men harassing and denigrating women as a means of trying to drive them out as potential competitors. Gendertrolling behaviors fit so seamlessly within that tradition that it seems—at a minimum—highly probable that the underlying motivation behind them is similar.

Moreover, gendertrolling has the same effect as other historical patterns of gatekeeping of women—it drives women out of public spaces, or, at least, hinders them from receiving recognition and respect in the public sphere. Its effects culminate in preventing women from being seen as experts, from being looked to as authorities on traditionally male-dominated topics, and even from gaining equal access to jobs in male-dominated fields.

A History of Shutting Women Out of Public Discourse

Mary Astell, who wrote during the turn of the 17th century, wrote about the very hostile reception that women were met with at that time when they attempted to write. She concluded that men were trying to prevent women from having access to writing, explaining that it appeared to her that men, "having possession of the pen, thought they also had the best right to it."[4] Spender concurs with Astell's assessment and explains that, during the 17th century—the time Astell was writing—gatekeeping was a motivating force behind men's harassment of women's writing. Spender elaborates:

> [Men] were hostile to women's entry to the literary ranks and consistently engaged in harassing behavior which was designed to discourage and disparage women, and to force them to retire. For, after all, this was not just a theoretical debate about whether a woman writer could reach the standards men had deemed appropriate for themselves, it was on many occasions a practical matter of livelihood, with women competing for "men's" jobs.[5]

The pseudonymous author of a 1739 treatise called *Woman Not Inferior to Man*, "Sophia, a Person of Quality," describes why she thinks men so adamantly resisted women's attempts to gain an equal education:

> Why are [men] so industrious to debar us that learning we have an equal right to with themselves? . . . for fear of our sharing with them in those public offices they fill so miserably. . . . The same sordid selfishness which urged them to engross all power and dignity to themselves, prompted them to shut up from us knowledge *which would have made us their competitors*.[6] [italics added]

Laurie Penny, British journalist, author, and a contributing editor at the *New Statesman*, points out that Mary Wollstonecraft, who wrote in the late 18th century, was insulted for speaking out publicly as a woman: "The implication that a woman must be sexually appealing to be taken seriously as a thinker did not start with the Internet: it's a charge that has been used to shame and dismiss women's ideas since long before Mary Wollstonecraft was called 'a hyena in petticoats.'"[7]

Spender sums up the findings of her lengthy book, *Women of Ideas and What Men Have Done to Them*, which details the history of suppressing European women's contributions to public discourse:

> We have three hundred years of evidence that men *do* discredit and bury women's work on the basis of their sex, and the question I ask myself repeatedly is how much more evidence do we need before we defiantly assert that men's treatment of women's intellectual and creative contributions is consistent and systematic and constitutes sexual harassment, where by women are treated on the basis of their sex and not their work?[8]

The underlying motive for past harassment, abuse, and threats against women for speaking out in public fora can be plainly seen, at least based on the historical record, to have been gatekeeping. This is the case despite the fact that such a motive may not have been explicitly stated by (or even perhaps in the conscious awareness of) many, if not most, of those who were involved in condemning women for appearing or speaking publicly.

More contemporary behaviors, such as, for example, sexual harassment in the workplace, can likewise be seen to continue the historical tradition of discouraging and inhibiting women from competing with men for employment. Another contemporary patterned behavior, harassment of women on the street, serves to imbue women with a sense of potential danger when they venture out of their homes, making them fearful and thus rendering them less likely to occupy certain public spaces. The advice by many as to how women can keep safe from being raped is often not to go out alone or after dark, which is another restriction on women's ability to fully participate in public spaces as freely as men. Indeed, many contemporary sexist and threatening behaviors that target women function in a manner that keeps women from full participation in public life.

Gendertrolling as Gatekeeping

The pattern of intimidating and threatening behavior holds for online harassment of women: regardless of the ultimately unknowable motivations on the part of perpetrators (even perhaps to themselves), the *effect* of gendertrolling is to inhibit women from pursuing interests, and even careers, in what have been male-dominated arenas, many of which have now moved online. Given the history of the multitude of ways women have been harassed when attempting to freely enter or speak in public venues and to participate in public discourse in general—and the very similar pattern that gendertrolling takes—the idea that gendertrolling happens for any other reason seems highly improbable. Thus, I am arguing that gendertrolling is a kind of mass cultural response to women asserting themselves into previously male-dominated areas and that it functions to impede and penalize women for fully occupying places of authority online and from publicly promoting equality for women.

Regardless of the stated intentions of the perpetrators, in actual fact, the extreme levels of online abuse and harassment do dissuade many, many women from pursuing or continuing careers, or even interests, online, especially in such male-dominated fields as technology and video gaming. A woman identified as "Maryland" in an article about online harassment writes about her experiences being sexually harassed online as a young girl, which caused her to renounce her early interest in computers and computer science:

> When I was 12, I had just gotten very excited about coding. I coded a Star Wars fan site on Geocities using HTML from scratch, and I opened an AOL Instant Messenger account. I learned HTML tags and Javascript. I was enthusiastic; it was my new obsession. . . . One day, I got a message from a user I didn't know. . . . I asked if I knew the person. He responded by asking me how old I was. I replied something along the lines of not giving that information out to strangers. He replied by calling me a whole litany of obscene names, beginning with the c-word and followed by a number of gendered insults that I had never heard before. My heart was racing, my palms were sweaty, and I blocked him immediately. I was terrified. I wondered if I should tell my parents. I decided he was one psycho and couldn't know anything about my real identity, so I didn't. I convinced myself not to worry, but I started to withdraw.
>
> It wasn't the last time. I would go on to receive these kinds of insults and threats in most of the places I frequented: Xanga, Reddit, Digg, various MMORPGs [Massively Multiplayer Online Role-Playing Games]. I knew I wasn't welcome. I stopped making websites. I stopped playing games. I didn't pursue computer science like I thought I would.[9]

Indeed, many women who are the victims of extensive gendertrolling campaigns see their harassment as having a gatekeeping effect. Chris Kover, a journalist who writes for *Vice News*, an international news organization, concludes that gatekeeping is part of the function of the virulent online abuse of women: "The other thing is women starting to move into these areas that these guys have just decided that they want to claim for men. They don't want women to come into gaming and tell them not to call women whores when they are playing Call of Duty."[10]

Brianna Wu, one of those who was forced to flee her home due to the threats leveled against her as part of Gamergate, also sees that exclusion of women from the male-dominated arena of video gaming is a key motivation behind the harassment campaigns:

> Gamergate is basically a group of boys that don't want girls in their videogame clubhouse. Only, instead of throwing rocks, they threaten to rape you. And, if that doesn't work, they'll secretly record your conversations and release the lurid details of your sex life in a public circus. From seeing the #gamergate mobs plan this on 8chan.co, it seems like they're having a lot of fun.[11]

Wu told the *Washington Post* that she and other gamers have heard numerous stories about young girls who have been driven out of gaming and game developing:

> My friend Quinn told me about a folder on her computer called, "The Ones We've Lost." They are the letters she's gotten from young girls who dream of being game developers, but are terrified of the environment they see. I nearly broke into tears as I told her I had a folder filled with the same. The truth is, even if we stopped Gamergate tomorrow, it will have already come at too high a cost.[12]

Kathy Sierra, the programming instructor and game developer who was harassed and threatened to the point that she quit her highly popular blog on technology and moved for the safety of her family, believes that gendertrolls harass women whom they see as competing with men for jobs:

> A particularly robust troll-crafted hot button meme today is that some women are out to destroy video games. . . . Another is that they are taking jobs from men. Men who are, I mean obviously, more deserving.[13]

David Futrelle, blogger at We Hunted the Mammoth, a feminist blog that tracks and exposes men's rights activists (MRAs), sums up the attitudes that he sees within the online communities of MRAs, many of whom participate in gendertrolling and on whose websites gendertrolls often coordinate their attacks:

> They define certain cultural spaces as being properly male only and then go after women—women in general but often individual women—who they

see as interlopers invading what they feel should be their safe space. You see this in general discussions about women and tech and women going into STEM fields. But also in other fields like atheist activism. For whatever reason that seems to draw a lot of very misogynistic guys too.[14]

SILENCING WOMEN

In addition to gatekeeping, gendertrolling silences women from speaking out or having opinions online about a wide variety of topics, but especially when advocating for women's full equality. Speech is a powerful tool in shaping public discourse and perceptions, and it can lead to shifts in cultural values and priorities. Those who wish to maintain the status quo on, for example, male dominance, are fiercely motivated to resort to using whatever methods they can, no matter how nefarious, to silence speech that undermines their privileged positions.

A History of Silencing Women

There is a long historical precedent in Western, English-speaking history of silencing women that undermines the potential for women to raise awareness about the conditions under which they have lived. Classicist Mary Beard (who has been the victim of gendertrolling attacks) reviewed some historical incidents of silencing women, the earliest of which she found described in the *Odyssey*, written around the eighth century BCE. Beard recounts an incident when Penelope comes "down from her private quarters into the great hall, to find a bard performing to throngs of her suitors," she asks him to sing a different song. Telemachus, the son of Odysseus and Penelope, replies to her "'speech will be the business of men, all men, and of me most of all; for mine is the power in this household.'"[15] Beard also describes an example from the fourth century BCE: "In the early fourth century BC Aristophanes devoted a whole comedy to the 'hilarious' fantasy that women might take over running the state. Part of the joke was that women couldn't speak properly in public—or rather, they couldn't adapt their private speech (which in this case was largely fixated on sex) to the lofty idiom of male politics."[16]

In another historical example of women being prohibited from speech, there is a passage in the Bible that admonishes women against speaking in church, a prominent public space in the first century: "Let your women keep silence in the churches: for it is not permitted unto them to speak; but they are commanded to be under obedience, as also saith the law."[17]

Barbara Miller Solomon, scholar and professor of history, writes about a later example, regarding Priscilla Mason, salutatorian of the 1793 graduating class of the Philadelphia Young Ladies Academy, the first all-female academy in the United States. Solomon quotes from Mason's salutatorian speech in which she protests against the prohibition of women's speech in public venues: "They have denied women a liberal education and now if she should prove capable of speaking, where could we speak? The Church, the Bar, the Senate are closed against us."[18] Solomon explains that at the time, "While men were expected to declaim as preparation for public life, religious precepts held that women should remain silent in church and in mixed company."[19]

In 1840, at the World's Anti-slavery Convention held in London, women were seen as unfit to speak in public when the credentials committee decided that women were "constitutionally unfit for public and business meetings."[20] Historian Jone Johnson Lewis explains that at the convention, "The women were relegated to a segregated women's section which was separated from the main floor by a curtain; the men were permitted to speak, the women were not."[21] In yet another example of women being proscribed from public speaking, Lucy Stone, U.S. abolitionist and suffragist, was asked to write a commencement speech for her 1847 graduation ceremony while attending Oberlin College. However, when she found that she was to be barred from reading her own speech and that a man would have read it in her stead, she "refused to write a commencement speech or to participate" at the commencement.[22] Finally, it is documented that, in the 19th century, U.S. schoolchildren were taught in public schools to support laws against women speaking in public, voting, owning property, and holding political office.[23]

Spender sums up the historical perspective on how women who attempted to speak publicly or to voice their opinions in writing were treated: "It becomes immediately obvious that [women throughout the history of English-speaking countries who adopted a 'woman's perspective' in their writing] were ridiculed, belittled and abused, in short sexually harassed—condemned more often as women rather than responded to as writers or thinkers."[24] Spender adds that the ideas and contributions of women who, in spite of the prohibitions against them, did manage to speak publicly or have their writing published were ultimately dismissed and overlooked in the historical record, so that if their voices were not silenced at the time in which they lived, they eventually were. Spender sums up: "My study of Wollstonecraft revealed that long before her time women had been generating ideas and men had been erasing them."[25]

Gendertrolling as Silencing Women

Gendertrolling is likewise about silencing women from voicing their opinions on the Internet, as many women have come to believe after their experiences. Cindy Tekobbe, a scholar who studies digital media, explains:

> If you look at women online in general, women who speak out on Twitter about women's issues, or even if you see articles on newspapers or websites or possibly even your website, where women's issues are discussed, you'll see trolling—trolling is a word we use to describe negative comments that are ad hominem attacks on the women in question.... It's particularly vicious right now in women in video games because these threats are specific. They are ... rape threats and death threats, they give times and places. They engage in what we call doxxing, which is revealing ... private information about these women in a public forum, like their credit card numbers, like their addresses. The threats are specific and pretty ugly.... The trolls will tell you that they are doing it as free speech, that it's fun, that it's amusing to them, *but really these threats tend to drive women out of public spaces and discourage them from speaking about women's issues in public.*[26] [italics added]

Shanley Kane, cultural critic and founder of *Model View Culture*, dismisses the wildly free-ranging rationalizations given for the virulent online attacks on her and powerfully articulates her belief that men are trying to silence her outspoken writings about technology culture instead:

> While many are eager to claim that I am actually being abused because I'm crazy, a liar, a fraud, a troll, a hypocrite, a neo-Nazi, a whore, because I've had kinky sex, because I dated an abuser, because I'm mean to men on Twitter, because I swear a lot, because I'm a "blogger" that contributes nothing to the field: I am being targeted because of my work speaking up against tech culture....
>
> This work is what people are desperate to stop, by any means including trying to get my family killed by SWATing, trying to convince me to kill myself, terrorizing my supporters, stalking me (I have had multiple men stalk me for 6–14 months at a time), hacking my computers and accounts, "exposing" my sex life, cutting off my funding, belittling and erasing my writing, plagiarizing my content, sending constant rape and death threats, and ceaselessly holding me up for abuse to hate groups.[27]

Eleanor O'Hagan, journalist and columnist for the *Guardian*, concurs:

> To me, misogynistic abuse is an attempt to silence women. Traditionally, men have been the ones who influence the direction of society: I think there

is still a sense that it's not women's place to be involved in politics. That's why the abuse women writers experience is really pernicious and needs to stop. Women will never achieve equality so long as they're being intimidated out of the picture.[28]

Marcotte also agrees that harassment of women online is done to coerce women into silence and submission: "It's all just a new way of expressing a very old—indeed, an ancient—sentiment, that a woman's place is to be silent, submissive, and servile to men and that any women who disagree are to be put down with violence."[29]

An anonymous blogger, quoted in a *New Statesman* article about online harassment of women, also sees gendertrolling as a way to attempt to intimidate or silence feminists or, at a minimum, to induce them to be overly cautious in their writing:

> I would say the misogynistic abuse that a number of women bloggers and writers have received functions as a form of censorship and warning to the ones not currently experiencing it to watch what we say.
>
> As feminists, we know that there's at least something about us or something we want to say that will incur the wrath of misogynists. We're constantly ducking and diving, choosing our words carefully and having to walk the tightrope of being completely true to our beliefs, regardless of whether they happen to please other feminists or (conversely) the sexist majority, but also making sure we don't prompt misogynists to attack us because of an ill-chosen word or two.
>
> We feel like our arguments have to be tight at all times and that we'd better not type out anything less than reasonable (in anger) because the punishment we receive is likely to be disproportionate to the intellectual crime.[30]

Freelance journalist and blogger Marcela Kunova also sees the trolling and threats against women as a way to suppress women from speaking publicly:

> Virtually every woman who publicly contributes to a political debate is subjected to virulent and largely anonymous online invective, or "trolling." But it is far more than simply readers' feedback. Trolling is intended to make women shut up—and to remind them their primary purpose is to be there for male sexual pleasure. Or not to be in public life at all. It now seems to be an established act: women who speak publicly get threatened with rape, physical violence, harming their relatives and murder.... Many are stalked and get their home addresses published."[31]

Atheist activist Melody Hensley, although she was harassed extensively by fellow atheists, found that the harassment of women online was not limited to specific communities as she had originally thought and therefore concluded that online harassment was more about silencing women in general rather than about a particular topic of conversation:

> The worst of it came when I realized that it wasn't just about the atheist community. It's about men wanting to silence women. It doesn't matter if you're from the atheist or skeptic community. You could be a journalist. You could be a professional feminist. It doesn't matter. A woman in a position of power or a woman with a voice. I've talked to many women in different professions. These men will try to silence you. They will do that by doing anything possible to try to get you off the Internet.[32]

Lindy West, feminist performer, editor, and writer, also believes that harassing women online is a tactic to try to silence women in order to preserve male-dominated spaces online:

> There's a reason why the most violent, sexually explicit, long-term abuse is reserved for people who agitate for diversity in traditionally white-male-dominated spaces: video games, comedy, atheism. Internet trolls (or, more accurately, the agitators who whip them into a frenzy) want to control who gets to talk, because their dominance is threatened by what's being said. We really have no way to gauge how many voices have already been silenced, and how many will be too afraid to ever speak up in the first place.[33]

Finally, Mary Beard comes to a similar conclusion: that the harassment against her and other women was about silencing women and points out the irony of advising women to keep silent in the face of abuse as a strategy for combating their harassment:

> A significant subsection [of online abuse and harassment] is directed at silencing the woman—"Shut up you bitch" is a fairly common refrain. Or it promises to remove the capacity of the woman to speak. "I'm going to cut off your head and rape it" was one tweet I got. . . . Ironically the well-meaning solution often recommended when women are on the receiving end of this stuff turns out to bring about the very result the abusers want: namely, their silence. "Don't call the abusers out. Don't give them any attention; that's what they want. Just keep mum," you're told, which amounts to leaving the bullies in unchallenged occupation of the playground.[34]

Gendertrolling, then, follows in the long historical tradition of attempting to control women's access to public and professional spaces, using abuse, harassment, and threats in an effort to silence women's speech and to intimidate women from fully participating in public discourse. Despite the plethora of justifications and rationalizations that gendertrolls give for their reprehensible behavior, the bottom line is that they are targeting and threatening women in order to try to silence them.

WOMEN ATTACKED NOT FOR THEIR IDEAS, BUT FOR BEING FEMALE

When women are gendertrolled, they are criticized and harassed not for *what* they are writing, but because *it is women who are doing the writing*. Many women who have been attacked online emphasize that they are not objecting to criticism about their writing or about their ideas in general—they maintain that even very negative responses are not the problem. The problem is that it is not the quality of their ideas so much as the mere fact that it is women who dare to have them that inspires the attacks. Summing up the erasure of women in European history, Spender establishes that this, too, has historical precedent: "[i]t is this treatment of a women's contribution where the judgments are made on the basis of her *sex*, and not her *work*, that I am describing as harassment."[35]

Eleanor O'Hagan concurs with the sentiment that it is not even "outright nastiness" that she objects to as much as the attacks that attempt to diminish her for simply being female:

> When you start writing, nobody warns you about the abuse you'll receive. For me, it began almost instantly: not outright nastiness, though I have had my fair share of that, too, but attempts to discredit me. The comments came mainly from men and they were always in line with existing gender stereotypes. Instead of engaging with my opinions, commenters would make me out to be a hysteric, a "silly little girl" or a whinger. I remember some commenters telling me to stop going on. It was like they saw me as a sort of nagging fishwife, not a political commentator.[36]

Dawn Foster, a British writer and editor, described how the topic she discusses gets sidelined by insults directed at her for being a woman: "Occasionally, I'd respond to emails casually, to show the sender hadn't affected me in any way. Their responses usually disintegrated into unhinged ranting, away from discussing how much they hated me and into their hatred of women in general."[37]

When Mary Beard was gendertrolled, she remarked on how little people cared about what she had to say when she went on a television program called *Meet the Romans* and how much they remarked on her appearance, specifically her age and her gray hair, instead:

Grey is obviously something most women on TV don't do.... I think most people tuned into Meet the Romans because they wanted to learn about the Romans. And what I had to say was important. Grey is my hair colour. I really can't see why I should change it. There clearly is a view of female normative beauty but more women of 58 do look like me than like Victoria Beckham.[38]

Natalie Dzerins, author of the feminist blog Forty Shades of Grey, even expressed dismay at not having what she felt would be a privilege, that of having her arguments taken on and challenged on the basis of her ideas, rather than simply being insulted:

And if the best argument someone can come up with against something I've written is to call me fat, I'll consider that a win. If they could actually prove what I say to be incorrect, I'm sure they would have. I do sometimes wish that I were a man though, so that if I were to get abuse, it would be for my ideas, not for having the gall to have them in the first place.[39]

The fact that women's opinions and arguments are not taken on, challenged, or discussed by others, but rather that women are insulted for their looks or for simply being women has a greater effect than simply offending the women involved. Through this practice, women's ideas are not taken seriously or are sidelined and ignored, with the result that women's intellectual contributions to public discourse are disregarded, dismissed, and erased.

Men Are Treated Differently Online

While all types of harassment certainly happen to a great variety of people on the Internet, including men of course, it is women who are the primary targets of gendertrolling campaigns. Many people have commented that they find men's harassment to be of a different nature and tenor than the kind of enduring, pervasive, sexualized, rape-and-death threat campaigns that happen to women. Dawn Foster reports that "speaking to friends who also blogged, but were men, I learned this type of abuse wasn't common, unless you were a woman."[40] Iram Ramzan, a self-identified progressive Muslim woman, journalism student, and blogger, highlights that attacks on women are particularly sexualized: "Of course, men, too, come under attack.... But when you are a woman, it is easier to be attacked. Men are not labelled as whores who sleep around. That delightful label is reserved for us females alone."[41]

Many men report that they write articles or posts online that are similar to what women are writing, but they observe that women are treated very differently for similar opinions. Robert Scoble, author of the technology blog Scobleizer, commented on this phenomenon after Kathy Sierra got harassed and driven offline in 2007: "It's this culture of attacking women that has especially got to stop. . . . Whenever I post a video of a female technologist there invariably are snide remarks about body parts and other things that simply wouldn't happen if the interviewee were a man."[42]

Blogger David Allen Green observed that the abuse he received was of a different magnitude and tenor than what women he knew had received: "In three years of blogging and tweeting about highly controversial political topics, I have never once had any of the gender-based abuse that, say, Cath Elliot, Penny Red or Ellie Gellard routinely receive."[43]

Ben Atherton-Zeman, spokesperson for National Organization for Men Against Sexism and public speaker on issues of violence prevention, describes having a very different reception to his writing about feminism than women get:

> When I write about feminism and men's violence against women, I often receive supportive comments. While some of the praise is earned, much of it gives me a lot of credit for doing very little.
>
> When women write about those same topics, it's a different story. We men threaten women bloggers and writers with rape and murder. We call women "man-haters," verbally abuse them, hack into their email accounts and stalk them. We alter photos of women, putting cuts and bruises on their faces. Then we excuse ourselves, saying we were "just joking—can't you feminists take a joke?"[44]

John Scalzi, a science fiction writer and blogger who receives numerous comments on his popular blog, was asked by a fellow blogger whether he gets the same kind of comments she gets and whether he thought the comments she receives were related to gender. He responded,

> The short answer: No I don't get those, and yes, I think it's substantially gender-related.
>
> The longer answer: I do of course get hate mail and obnoxious comments. . . .
>
> What I don't have, however, is the sort of chronic and habitual stream of abuse this blogger describes. . . . What I don't receive, other than exceptionally rarely, is what I consider to be actual abusive commenting, where the intent is to hurt me, from people who are genuinely hateful.[45]

Scalzi elaborates on the differences he observes between the kinds of comments women and men get on their blogs:

Gendertrolling: It's Not about the Internet 145

Talking to women bloggers and writers, they are quite likely to get abusive comments and e-mail, and receive more of it not only than what I get personally (which isn't difficult) but more than what men bloggers and writers typically get. I think bloggers who focus on certain subjects (politics, sexuality, etc) will get more abusive responses than ones who write primarily on other topics, but even in those fields, women seem more of a target for abusive people than the men are. And even women writing on non-controversial topics get smacked with this crap. I know knitting bloggers who have some amazingly hateful comments directed at them. They're blogging about knitting, for Christ's sake.[46]

Even though much of the harassment people receive online also relates to race and racist abuse, some people have observed that men of color don't seem to be subjected to the same levels of racist harassment and threats as women of color. Miri Mogilevsky, atheist blogger, relates the experiences of bloggers at Free Thought Blogs:

Our only prominent blogger of color [at Free Thought Blogs] ... didn't seem to get threats, not even about his race. I'm sure he got racist comments from people, but I don't think it was from this same kind of group of trolls. ... [He] got ... trolls, but when I saw the stuff they were saying to him, it was mostly just annoying disagreement, just annoying kinds of stuff. Maybe he did get threats, but he didn't talk about it if he did.[47]

Feminista Jones, the activist whose story is recounted in Section 1 of Chapter 2, observed that black men were accorded more respect online than black women:

A guy would step in and [the harassers] would change their tone, even if it was a black man. They would change their tone in the way in which they were talking to them, because there was still this respect, I guess. ... It's just like, "Oh this is a man. I can't speak to him in the same kind of way."[48]

Several black women have adopted white male identities online in order to see if there is a difference in the way they are treated when seen as white men. Astra Taylor, Canadian-American documentary filmmaker, writer, activist, and musician, recounts the experiences of Jamie Nesbitt Golden, podcaster and contributor to the XO Jane blog,

Over the last few months, a number of black women with substantial social media presences conducted an informal experiment of their own. Fed up with the fire hose of animosity aimed at them, Jamie Nesbitt Golden and others adopted masculine Twitter avatars. Golden replaced her photo with that of a hip, bearded, young white man, though she kept her bio and continued to communicate in her own voice. "The number of snarky, condescending tweets dropped off considerably, and discussions on race and gender were less volatile," Golden wrote, marveling at how simply changing a photo transformed reactions to her. "Once I went back to Black, it was back to business as usual."[49]

In another case, Sydette Harry, a cultural critic and contributor to *Dissent* and *Salon*, said that she sometimes switches her online avatar to a nonhuman image that doesn't reveal that she is a woman of color when she wants to avoid harassment. She did find that when she use an image of a white man as her avatar, "the harassing and racist tweets virtually stopped."[50] Harry reported that

> As a white man, that was the most fun I had online in terms of actually getting to talk to people and not be insulted by them. . . . People thought I was wrong, people thought I was ridiculous but nobody thought I was stupid. I received fewer slurs and people were a lot more interested in my thought process than when I was anything else.[51]

It is impossible to tease out the relative proportion and kinds of harassment women of color receive by virtue of being women versus being of color. Indeed, there is much literature on intersectional theory that argues that these oppressions can never be taken apart and viewed separately, that they have multiply reinforcing effects on each other that result in an entirely unique amalgam. However, in these experiments, it is clear that there is a dramatic difference between having an online presence as a woman of color compared with that of a white man.

Finally, Jane Fae, a transgender woman who blogs on information technology issues, wrote of her experiences as having blogged first as a man, and subsequently, as a woman:

> So I am in the fairly unique position of having written under both genders—and having sight of my email postbag as male and female. There *is* a marked difference. In fact, when I first started to notice the difference, I was quite shocked.
>
> First off, even the nice comments seem, at some level, to be more personal. I won't say I never got strongly dissenting views before I transitioned: but there was usually, mostly, some appeal to the rational argument underlying. Not so much any more, as many of those critical of what I have to say seem far readier to reach for the personal attack: the implication that I only say what I say because I am a woman. Or, as one politely put it, "an ugly woman".[52]

Men Can Be Gendertrolled for Defending Women

The instances in which men are most likely to be targeted by the virulent and sustained attacks that qualify as gendertrolling, including menacing threats and doxxing, most often occur when they have publicly supported women who are being gendertrolled. For example, Phil Fish, an independent video game designer who showed support for Zoe Quinn during the Gamergate attacks, was doxxed and forced to leave Twitter. His website was hacked, and personal details and documents relating to his company, Polytron, were exposed in a hack, which led to him selling the business and leaving the gaming industry.[53] In another case, Tim Schafer, a computer game designer, posted a link to Anita Sarkeesian's video about the way women are portrayed in videogames. Shortly thereafter, his video game production company, Double Fine Productions, was put on a list by Gamergaters to boycott.[54]

Atherton-Zeman concurs that men are attacked more harshly online when they publicly support women's issues and gave the example of Jamie Kilstein, a comedian who was especially targeted for speaking out against rape culture:

> When men are harassed online, it's often because they are speaking out against rape culture. Comedian Jamie Kilstein reports receiving a few combative emails after questioning God's existence or challenging Glenn Beck—but he received "thousands" after challenging rape culture.[55]

GENDERTROLLING HAPPENS TO WOMEN BECAUSE THEY ARE WOMEN

Although cyberharassment and generic trolling happen to a wide variety and number of people on the Internet, gendertrolling happens to women *because they are women*. Brianna Wu, one of the women who was targeted in Gamergate, believes that the entirety of Gamergate would not have started had the precipitating incident not been about a woman, in other words, had it involved a *woman* blogging about how her *male partner* had cheated on her instead of the other way around:

> [Gamergate] started two months ago, when my friend Zoe Quinn dated Eron Gjoni. Their relationship ended, as relationships sometimes do. Only, rather than get drunk and play Madden, Eron decided to secretly record everything Zoe said, and released it on a blog he titled "The Zoe Report," in an attempt to destroy her professionally.
>
> If Zoe had been a man, the blog would have been laughed off as the work of a jilted lover.[56]

A lot of reasons are given for gendertrolling attacks, other than that women are targeted for simply being women: if the woman would have not talked about whatever topic she talked about or if she been more attractive, less attractive, not fat, not old, or somehow different in some other respect, she would not have been harassed. Or, harassed women deserve virulent attacks because what they wrote is particularly poorly thought out, written, or articulated. Or women are harassed and threatened because of some particular content they have posted or due to their having a specific opinion (in spite of the fact that, as we have seen, women who post online on a wide variety of topics, as well as women whose opinions run a very wide gamut, have been gendertrolled). Or, if all else fails, the harassed women are said to be too sensitive, or they are told it's not that bad, that men get harassed just as badly, or that women don't know how to take a joke.

Ultimately, gendertrolling, whether it occurs for the purposes of gatekeeping or silencing women—or for some other unfathomable reason—limits women's equality and opportunities online. Amanda Hess, freelance writer and contributor to *Slate*, writes about the intimidating effects that the chronic rape and death threats that are characteristic of gendertrolling have on women's equality, regardless of whether they are actually carried out:

> I think whether or not a threat escalates into an actual physical confrontation, the sheer volume and accumulation of these threats has the effect of intimidating women from using the Internet. And I think, you know, it's a really sad state where some people are saying, well, if you're not literally raped then everything is fine. I think we as a society should have a bit of a higher bar than that for, you know, taking action to make sure that women have equal opportunities in our society.[57]

At stake, then, is women's equality and participation in the increasingly significant public sphere that is the Internet, and gendertrolling attacks are, to a large extent, preventing women from full and unencumbered participation online.

Chapter 6

The Power of Naming

As we have seen, gendertrolling follows in a long-standing historical tradition of misogyny, in which women's voices and opinions have been barred from full participation in cultural, social, and political discourse, while women have simultaneously been shut out of professional opportunities. Gendertrolling is not only embedded in a historical tradition of misogyny; it is a new face to widespread misogynistic cultural patterns, values, and behaviors that underlie other more contemporary kinds of attacks on women.

WIDESPREAD, BUT UNSEEN

As we examine the phenomenon of gendertrolling more carefully in the context of other patterns of harassment, attacks, and abuses of women, we can see commonalities among them. These patterned misogynistic behaviors—domestic violence, rape, date rape, stalking, street harassment, sexual harassment in the workplace, and now, gendertrolling—are primarily aimed at and harm women, are pervasive rather than idiosyncratic or rare, and have a major impact and effect on women's lives. Nevertheless, before feminists campaigned to raise awareness about each of these types of patterned behaviors, they have been—at the same time they are ubiquitous—not widely recognized or acknowledged. As we examine each one of these behaviors, we can see that they, like gendertrolling, occurred on a fairly widespread basis even before they were widely recognized for the social harm they cause.

Domestic Violence

Domestic violence, which was brought to wider social consciousness after feminist activist campaigns in the 1970s and 1980s, has been a fairly common occurrence in women's lives over a long time period. Nevertheless, it took sustained and extensive activism to bring it into cultural awareness as something that is not just an aberration, but, in fact, a pattern. As Danielle Keats Citron reports in her book *Hate Crimes in Cyberspace*, before feminists campaigned around the issue of domestic violence, it was often viewed as a "lovers' quarrel." Citron explains that, in the 1960s and 1970s, when confronted with domestic violence, "The police officer's role was to 'soothe feelings' and 'pacify parties' involved in 'family matters.'"[1] Because domestic violence was not acknowledged, it was not seen as violence against women, but more as a problem of "fighting" between spouses. Although domestic violence affected large numbers of women even before it was so named, until feminist activism took place to raise awareness about it, it was rarely acknowledged or talked about.

Rape

Rape is another form of widespread assault on women that, while common—one out of six women in the United States experiences an attempted or completed rape during her lifetime[2]—is still seen as an exceptional or even rare experience for women. Even now, despite the known frequency of rape, when women report that they have been raped, there is a cloud of suspicion, and even sometimes accusations, of false rape claims that does not accompany the reporting of other crimes such as burglary or mugging. Ironically, although the rate of rape for women is considerably higher than the rate of rape for men in prison,[3] there is a high level of cultural awareness about the possibility of men getting raped in prison, as evinced by the widespread commentary and humor (e.g., "don't drop the soap") about men who go to prison. However, there is little, if any, public discourse about false rape allegations made by men in prison, although they surely must occur on occasion. So despite the pervasiveness of rape for women, it is much less recognized as a common occurrence than its prevalence would merit.

Date Rape

Although date rape or acquaintance rape has also been a common occurrence in women's lives for a long time, it was not named as such until the mid-1970s to 1980s. The term "date rape" first occurred in print in Susan Brownmiller's *Against Our Will: Men, Women, and Rape*, which was published in 1975, but it wasn't until a large-scale study on the topic in 1987 that the term began to be used more widely. Before the 1970s, women were undoubtedly raped by acquaintances or on dates, but they had no words or concepts to clearly understand what happened to them, so they tended to be silent about their experiences, often not even telling those closest to them. As one of the women who says Bill Cosby raped her explains, date rape "didn't exist" in 1969, when she says her rape occurred: "It never occurred to me to go to the police. It was a different time and 'date rape' was a concept that didn't exist. I just kept asking myself over and over in disbelief why this had happened to me. Other than my roommate, I did not discuss that night with anyone for 36 years."[4]

Stalking

Stalking is also an experience that took feminist activism to bring to awareness. Prior to 1990, stalking was not even illegal in the United States. A 2002 study found that 72 percent of female college students did not know that stalking was a crime, while 33 percent felt that police would not take it seriously, which resulted in 83 percent of stalking incidents not being reported to the police or campus law enforcement.[5] Although stalking was a phenomenon that occurred in women's (as well as many men's) experience, until it was given a name and a definition, it was not taken seriously.

Street Harassment

Harassment of women on public streets, while widespread throughout most parts of the world, is just starting to become recognized as a deterrent to women feeling comfortable walking in public. Although women have felt upset, disturbed, and even angered by the continual harassment and comments on their appearance as they pass through public venues, it is only recently that the concept of street harassment has begun to be named and acknowledged to as a harmful pattern of behavior that targets women. The harmful effects of street harassment are exacerbated by the awareness most women have of the possibility of being raped. College student Allie Myren, in a letter to the editor of the University of Wisconsin, Madison, school newspaper, explains that street harassment reminds women of the threat of rape and that it "creates vulnerability . . . by reminding me that I am not in control of my body. . . . [It] reminds me that I am safe and in possession of bodily autonomy only insofar as men decide not to violate it."[6] Street harassment is a form of misogynistic behavior that, although very widespread, is still in the process of being named and culturally recognized as destructive to women.

Sexual Harassment in the Workplace

There was little social consciousness about sexual harassment in the workplace in the minds of most people until feminists campaigned to call attention to it during the 1980s. This was the case even while sexual harassment was a not uncommon occurrence for working women, and it became increasingly more so as they began to enter into what had been previously all-male work arenas in the 1970s and 1980s. As Catharine MacKinnon, the legal theorist who did much to bring sexual harassment into social consciousness, phrases it, sexual harassment did not "socially exist," even while it existed in fact:

> The facts amounting to the harm did not socially "exist," had no shape, no cognitive coherence; far less did they state a legal claim. It just happened to you. To the women to whom it happened, it wasn't part of anything, much less something big or shared like gender. It fit no known pattern.[7]

Citron explains how sexual harassment in the workplace was viewed prior to activism to raise awareness about it: "Sexual harassment was a 'game played by male superiors' who 'won some' and 'lost some.'"[8] Sexual harassment in the workplace is another form of misogyny that was widespread yet simultaneously unacknowledged.

Gendertrolling

Gendertrolling follows this pattern of being increasingly widespread among women online and yet at the same time unacknowledged and invisible to most people. Feminist writer, media critic, and activist Soraya Chemaly highlights that hatred of women as a class, along with the attendant rampant online harassment and abuse against women, is so pervasive that it is ironically rendered invisible:

> The issue is there is no organization tracking [online harassment of women]. Women as a class is too big for anybody to think about. You might have the anti-defamation league looking at anti-Semitism or the NAACP looking at black hate.... The hatred that is focused on women as a class ... falls through

many cracks. When I talked to SPLC [Southern Poverty Law Center] about whether [online harassment of women] is on their radar, it really just isn't. I keep talking to various organizations. I hesitate to say it's an intersectional issue. Because it makes it almost sound like it's a variant of something and it really isn't a variant of something.[9]

Chemaly makes an important point—that hate crimes against women, along with gendertrolling, are not tracked. Generally, hate crime laws cover the categories of race, religion, national origin, ethnicity, disability, and sexual orientation—but not gender.[10] In fact, only 19 of 41 federal and state hate crimes statutes include gender as a category of hate crime.[11] Among the reasons given for not including gender as a category under hate crimes legislation is that "crimes against women are so prevalent that it would distort statistics for all other bases to cover them."[12] In other words, due to the sheer magnitude and frequency of the attacks, to count and record hate crimes against women would overwhelm the system. In fact, the FBI, which collects statistics on hate crimes pursuant to the 1990 Hate Crimes Statistics Act, does not include gender as one of the categories for hate crimes it documents.

It is a curiosity that these forms of harassment and abuse against women could be so prevalent, and yet, at the same time, be socially discounted and ignored to such an extent that they are effectively rendered unseen and unacknowledged by most people.

MATTER OF PRIVATE SHAME

Before domestic violence, date rape, street harassment, stalking, or sexual harassment in the workplace were named and therefore clearly defined and recognized, they tended to be matters of intense, private shame to those who were targeted, harassed, or attacked, or they were seen as idiosyncratic, individual, and rare occurrences.

For example, before feminist activists campaigned to make domestic violence a crime, battered women were shamed and stigmatized when they had been beaten or abused, as if they had done something to provoke the abuse. Without the knowledge that battering was something that happened to lots and lots of other women (in fact, one out of four women experiences violence in the context of an intimate relationship at some time during her life[13]), domestic violence victims tended to see their abuse as arising from some quality or deficiency in themselves.

Rape victims, in addition to the blame that the rest of society heaped on them, have tended to scrutinize their behavior, decisions, or way of dressing that they worry may have provoked their rape. Likewise, women who were date or acquaintance raped, especially before there was a name for it, tended to take the full shame of the attack on themselves. A woman might have blamed herself for, perhaps, not having suspected her date or friend would rape her, for having been in a place where the rapist could attack her, for having been flirtatious during the earlier part of the date, or for having dressed in an attractive or even sexy manner. Finally, women who were sexually harassed at work or on the street have likewise looked to themselves to find what they had done or worn that could have precipitated their harassment. The sense of self-blame and shame that women have felt after being harassed, attacked, or abused has isolated victims and contributed to their being silent about the abuse they were experiencing, which, in turn, further served to contribute to the sense that the problem was a purely individual one.

Although many women targeted by these kinds of abuse or harassment still tend to blame themselves, efforts to raise awareness work to counter this notion. The self-blaming tendencies are amplified to the extent that each woman believes herself to be individually targeted rather than seeing herself as part of a larger group that is being targeted as a class. Without a social reality to validate and make sense of these experiences as part of a pattern of harassment and abuse toward women, it has been difficult to see them other than as private, idiosyncratic, and relatively rare problems for which the targeted women were somehow individually culpable.

Conversely, seeing harassment and abuse as occurring due to being part of a targeted group can help overcome the sense that one is individually responsible for being attacked or abused. Through naming and recognizing harassing, abusive, and threatening behaviors as part of a larger pattern of misogynistic attacks, women can become empowered not only to quit blaming themselves but also to organize together to find ways to counter the assaults.

THE POWER OF NAMING

To name and create, as MacKinnon calls it, a "social existence" for a widespread activity is a vitally important step in challenging it, both culturally and legally. MacKinnon writes of the importance, for example, for sexually harassed women to "have been given a name for their suffering and an analysis that connects it with gender,"[14] rather than experiencing their abuse in shame and secrecy. She describes the effects of experiencing sexual abuse without social and, especially, legal recognition: "Sexual abuse mutes victims socially through the violation itself. . . . When the state also forecloses a validated space for denouncing and rectifying the victimization, it seals this secrecy and reinforces this silence."[15] Law professor Anita Hill concurs, explaining that at the time of the 1991 Senate hearings in which she testified about her sexual harassment by then-Supreme Court Justice nominee Clarence Thomas, "in a sense, we really hadn't developed the social consciousness of the problem, and we hadn't developed a vocabulary to tell people about why it was important for them to understand the issue of harassment in this setting."[16]

MacKinnon stresses the critical importance of creating social recognition of abuse, explaining that "if there is no right place to go to say, this hurt me, then a woman is simply the one who can be treated this way, and no harm, as they say, is done."[17] Even though MacKinnon would certainly agree that actual harm is in fact done to the woman, she is pointing out that there is no way to acknowledge that harm socially or legally, which adds considerably to the social isolation and stigma of women who are so harmed.

The effect of not acknowledging or recognizing widespread, common, and patterned abusive and harassing behaviors that women experience is that those behaviors are rendered effectively invisible, so their harm is not recognized, and the behaviors are therefore tolerated, albeit not explicitly, but rather by overlooking, ignoring, or dismissing their existence. Harassing and abusive behaviors that are ill-defined and nebulous are therefore cast under a cloud of confusion and ambiguity, which renders them nearly impossible to mobilize to fight against, either through collective action or through enacting laws that address the harms they cause.

Accurately describing and naming abuse, therefore, is an essential step in attempting to counter it. The power of naming lies in the recognition of a systematic pattern of abuse, maltreatment, or harassment, which, rather than seeing those acts as individual, idiosyncratic occurrences, enables people to see the behaviors as systemic, widespread, and embedded in cultural customs and values. Naming pervasive behaviors that target particular social groups, in this case, women, thus creates the possibility for people to mobilize collectively to advocate for changes in values, policies, and the law to recognize and address those harms.

ADVOCACY AFTER NAMING

Before feminist activists campaigned to raise awareness about these forms of harassment and abuse, they were unnamed, unacknowledged, and unrecognized. After feminists described, clearly named, and brought these widespread and systematic harmful practices into general social awareness, activists were better able to mobilize to create social, cultural, and legal changes to counter the harms. Citron observes that after "social movements successfully condemn and delegitimize a social practice, judges and politicians often jump on the bandwagon." She gives the example of how "the women's movement got the attention of lawmakers, courts, and law enforcement by discrediting the reasons behind society's protections of domestic violence and sexual harassment."[18]

Various abusive behaviors that now have widespread recognition for being harmful were not recognized as such until activists mounted extensive campaigns to raise awareness about them. For example, domestic violence was so named in order to draw attention to the fact that it was a social problem rather than a private family matter.[19] After domestic violence was named and described, feminist activists and lawyers were able to organize to create domestic violence shelters and to initiate legal reforms, including class-action lawsuits that claimed that it was a violation of equal protection when police failed to arrest batterers. Activists also campaigned to institute mandatory arrest policies, requirements to prosecute even if a battered woman decided to drop the charges, and tougher sentencing for batterers.[20] Likewise, after activists campaigned to make rape seen as an issue that happens to a significant number of women, they were then able to mobilize to create rape crisis shelters and to raise awareness that it is not women's fault when they are raped and that strategies to lessen rape should not only be ones that advise women how to change their behavior in order to avoid it.

Similarly, policies and laws against sexual harassment were enacted not long after it was described and named. Activists successfully lobbied for laws to be passed that made unemployment compensation cover cases where women left their jobs due to sexual harassment.[21] They also worked to get judges to see sexual harassment as interfering with equal opportunity to work.[22] Anita Hill reports that, although "in 1991, we had for so many women a disappointing outcome," subsequently, women "went forward in record numbers with their own complaints of sexual harassment and assault, and started filing complaints in record numbers. Just the idea that they knew now that the level of consciousness had been raised to that point allowed them to overcome their fears of bad treatment, and they decided that they must come forward."[23] Contributor to *Think Progress* Tara Culp-Ressler reports that after Hill's testimony, "other women finally had a name for what was happening to them in the workplace. The Equal Employment Opportunity Commission saw a sharp spike in the number of sexual harassment charges the following year."[24]

Stalking was also made illegal only after feminists described and named it: California was the first state to make it illegal, in 1990, with the rest of the states following suit within four years.[25]

In an interview, Citron describes, for the case of domestic violence, the tremendous power for social change that naming unleashed:

> And the women's movement in the 1960s and '70s said, look, [domestic violence] is not something women can prevent and cure, they can't walk away from it, they can't be blamed for it. This is something that's a public harm that we must take seriously. They named domestic violence for what it is, and explained its harms. Then [they] said, look, there are laws on the books we just enforce. They exist. Assault and battery. We, as a society, changed our mind and we changed ... the norm.[26]

Before these phenomena were named and brought into social consciousness, there were also few if any laws on the books that could redress the real and significant harms that they caused.

GENDERTROLLING: THE POWER OF A NAME

At this time, most people are not aware of the confluence of extreme, pervasive, prolonged, detailed, and graphic rape and death threats that constitute gendertrolling, and, indeed, they express surprise at the level of venom, threats, and attacks that are being unleashed on women online. This is partly because gendertrolling is a new phenomenon, but it is also because there has not heretofore been a word for the constellation of characteristics that comprise gendertrolling. This lack of awareness needs to change before the problem can be addressed—and an indispensable first step is accurately describing the phenomenon and giving it a name.

As it stands now, these online attacks on women tend to get lumped together with generic trolling, which covers up the unique characteristics of gendertrolling and obfuscates the fact that this is a pattern that happens to women. Chemaly points out the confusion that arises when the activities that characterize gendertrolling do not have a name and instead are classed with generic online harassment:

> When one hears "online harassment," he may, reasonably, think a woman's fear is exaggerated [because] "harassment" connotes name-calling or embarrassment. These epistemological differences have undoubtedly influenced the way that online systems are built and how companies assess user safety.[27]

Without a name for it, the cluster of characteristics that I am defining as gendertrolling is described clumsily, as people attempt to enumerate or list what is happening. Indeed, Arthur Chu, notable *Jeopardy!* champion and culture blogger, struggles to explain that there is a dramatic difference in the ways that men are harassed online compared to the harassment women receive, but without a word that accurately and clearly describes the phenomenon, he can only list generally a few of the distinctive aspects that happen to women.

> Guys claim to be harassed more often online than women do, but when guys are "harassed" it means being exposed to a generalized atmosphere of nasty comments and rude behavior. By contrast, women are the ones who get singled out, stalked, who become unwilling celebrities with a horde of people dedicated to "taking her down."[28]

Defining and naming a widespread harmful patterned behavior is essential before efforts toward raising awareness can take place and social, cultural, and legal remedies can be enacted. Yet, in describing and naming gendertrolling as a pattern that has distinct characteristics and unique features due to the particularities of the Internet, it must also be seen in the context of other more recognized patterned behaviors of misogyny: domestic violence, rape and date rape, stalking, street harassment, and sexual harassment in the workplace. Likewise, as detailed in the previous chapter, gendertrolling as a pattern is squarely situated within the broader, historical pattern of harassment and abuse of women for speaking publicly.

Chapter 7

Cultural Defense Mechanisms as Backlash

As discussed in Chapters 5 and 6, gendertrolling has much in common with other forms of harassment, abuse, and violence against women. They are all varied expressions of misogyny that have adapted to the culture and technological advances of the times. As feminists have mobilized to bring attention to misogynistic harassment, abuse, and attacks on women—domestic violence, rape, stalking, street harassment, and sexual harassment in the workplace—there has also been a substantial pushback against that mobilization, in what can be seen characterized as a massive cultural defense mechanism. This pushback helps ensure that even when women begin to develop a social awareness, a naming, of a patterned behavior that is targeting them, they face significant counterattacks. The cumulative effect of these defense mechanisms is to create a kind of smokescreen that obscures recognizing what is in fact a widespread pattern. The power of naming is in this manner subverted, and the phenomenon remains only quasi-visible, even to the people to whom it happens. These cultural defense mechanisms take characteristic forms that have much in common with each other.

Below, I lay out tactics that are typically deployed as cultural defense mechanisms. "Shooting the messenger" occurs when accusations are made against the integrity or trustworthiness of the people describing what happened to them, or, particularly in the case of women, they are shamed sexually as a way of creating a barrier to speaking out. A second tactic is denial that the patterned behaviors exist, which takes the form of discounting the seriousness of the phenomenon, accusing women of exaggerating or lying, or claiming oversensitivity on the part of the targets. A third tactic is to blur or even reverse the culpability of those doing abusive or harassing behavior. This can be done by claiming the attacks are the fault of the victim, asserting that the behavior of both parties is at fault, switching the focus to the perpetrator's intentions, or even reversing the culpability so that the perpetrator is seen as the victim. Finally (perhaps when all else fails), the offending or abusive behaviors, although they are perhaps acknowledged as unfortunate, are made out to be natural and therefore inevitable, implying that they are impossible to change.

SHOOTING THE MESSENGER

One way that systematic disadvantaging of women is maintained is through a pattern of attacking and vilifying women who speak out about their experiences. Shooting-the-messenger-type attacks effectively silence the victim by discrediting her from being seen as a reliable or trustworthy witness or by attacking the victim with such a level of animosity and threats that it makes the price of speaking out seem not worth it. When the cost of speaking out about abuse or harassment is made excessively high, it also induces others who observe the attacks to remain silent lest they experience the same ramped-up intensity of attacks.

"Shooting the messenger" happens when the reputation and character of women who accuse men of domestic violence, sexual harassment, rape, date rape, or street harassment are maligned. Domestic violence victims have had their reputations tarnished when their abuse comes to light. For example, Janay Palmer, whose then-boyfriend and prominent football player Ray Rice was shown in a video beating her in an elevator, was subsequently portrayed as a person of low character for being willing to put up with abuse in order to have access to her husband's money.[1]

It is also common for sexual harassment victims to have aspersions cast on their characters when they come forward. During the 1991 Senate hearings to appoint Clarence Thomas to the Supreme Court, Anita Hill accused Thomas of sexual harassment. As a result, she was cast as a "self-aggrandizing fame and fortune seeker, with a vindictive thirst for revenge";[2] as "a bitter old maid, a manhater, even perhaps, a lesbian, an erotomaniac (a category unknown to psychology), . . . and a cold, selfish, arrogant, ambitious person—an unwomanly woman";[3] and as having intentionally lied in her testimony before the Senate hearings on the matter.[4]

Rape victims who don't stay silent about their assault are also disparaged. In the 2012 Steubenville High School rape incident, where a high school girl who was barely—and sometimes not—conscious was videotaped being sexually assaulted, the Steubenville football coach initially dismissed the rape charges against the school's star football players by accusing the girl of using rape as an excuse for having been out partying.[5] Women who were date raped have been maligned as jilted lovers or as having morning-after regrets. "Shooting-the-messenger" behavior has even occurred when women seek to highlight their experiences of street harassment: Shoshana Roberts, a woman who was portrayed in a video demonstrating street harassment in New York City, received death threats after the video went viral.[6] The cost of attempting to raise awareness about street harassment was made very high for Roberts due to the fear and insecurity caused by the threats, which was a way of attacking the messenger in an attempt to silence her and others who might contemplate speaking on similar issues.

Sexual Shaming

One of the ways that women are particularly targeted is by maligning, insulting, and shaming them sexually. This intense sexual shaming often serves as a warning to others not to incur a similar risk by protesting their experiences of abuse or harassment. Dale Spender, feminist scholar and literary theorist, observes that sexual shaming has been used in the past as well: "From Aphra Behn through Mary Wollstonecraft to Germaine Greer we witness the technique of bringing a woman's character into disrepute by means of her sexuality, so that her ideas need not be addressed at all."[7] Spender goes on to assert that women's sexuality has been invoked as a means to refute their contributions to public discourse: "In the records which discuss women's contribution [to ideas]. . . we are also likely to encounter suggestions that the woman concerned was unbalanced in some way, abnormal, unrepresentative, and not to be trusted. So Harriet Martineau is portrayed as a crank, Christabel Pankhurst as a prude, Aphra Behn as a whore, Mary Wollstonecraft as promiscuous."[8]

Women who have brought charges of rape to law enforcement have been accused of being "sluts" or have had their sexual history brought up at trial, as a way of insinuating that their having been sexual in the past discredits their claim of having been raped. In another instance of sexual shaming, women who have been raped are sometimes pilloried for ostensibly bearing the sexual shame and stigma of being attacked. For example,

Rehtaeh Parsons, a 17-year-old girl who was gang raped at a party, killed herself after a photo of her rape was posted online, and she could not escape relentless online bullying that included shaming her for being a "slut," among other sexualized insults.[9]

Anita Hill testified during the Senate hearings on Thomas's nomination to the Supreme Court that Thomas harassed her with odd sexual comments ("Who has put pubic hair on my Coke?"[10]), as well as references to his penis size, to pornographic films he had seen, to an actor in one of the films, "Long Dong Silver," and to his interest in oral sex.[11] Because the comments were so graphic, Hill reported that she was embarrassed to recount them during the hearings. And because she was not believed, many of the senators as well as people attending or watching the hearings assigned the stigma and shame of having to repeat such graphic comments to Hill.

DENIAL

In addition to shooting the messenger, another way of countering claims when a targeted group calls attention to having been harassed, threatened, or assaulted is to use various forms of denial. Abuse and harassment are denied by downplaying it or not taking the problem seriously; by accusing women who talk about it of exaggerating or even lying; or by claiming women are just being overly sensitive.

Not Taking the Problem Seriously

Police and judges have a long history of not taking seriously such things as domestic violence, rape, stalking, voyeurs, and street harassment. Danielle Keats Citron, in discussing the "long history of dismissing gendered harms," explains that domestic violence was thought of

> as a man's right to discipline his wife. It wasn't a public problem, it was a matter of family government. [Police told] women to put their makeup on, and make their men dinner, and so they wouldn't be hit as much. The court called domestic violence a "trifle." And that view persisted until the 1970s when the women's movement, or battered women's movement, said enough is enough.[12]

Women have been denied restraining orders by judges who either thought the violence they reported was not significant enough to warrant protection or did not believe the woman's account of the violence perpetrated against her. Sadly, many women who sought, but were denied, restraining orders were subsequently killed by their abusers.[13]

Women who have expressed fear of rape or who have been raped have not had their concerns taken seriously: they have been advised that "if it's inevitable, just relax and enjoy it";[14] that "the female body has ways to shut that whole thing [pregnancy from rape] down";[15] that "if someone doesn't want to have intercourse, the body shuts down. . .[and] will not permit that to happen unless a lot of damage is inflicted";[16] and that "rape victims should make the best of a bad situation."[17] Maine's State Representative Lawrence Lockman exemplifies a stance of not taking rape seriously: "If a woman has [the right to an abortion], why shouldn't a man be free to use his superior strength to force himself on a woman? At least the rapist's pursuit of sexual freedom doesn't [in most cases] result in anyone's death."[18]

Stalking victims are also similarly discounted by law enforcement, with police telling victims to ignore their stalkers or that nothing can be done until the perpetrator actually harms them. Too often, women who are stalked have ultimately been attacked or even killed by their stalkers.[19] Indeed, stalking laws have only been enacted in the United States since the 1990s. Before that "stalking was treated as a 'summary harassment offense,' which is the legal equivalent of a traffic ticket," according to Christopher Mallios, an attorney with AEquitas, an organization focused on improving legal outcomes in cases of domestic and sexual violence and stalking.[20]

Voyeurism is another case of a crime that is perpetrated almost exclusively against women that is not taken seriously. "Peeping toms," or voyeurs, have been too-frequently viewed by police as harmless, and the police have often, therefore, advised women to ignore them and to simply close their curtains or blinds in response. However, studies have shown that a significant percentage of men who participate in voyeurism have admitted to having had sexual contact with a pre-pubescent child (52 percent) and to having raped an adult woman (37 percent).[21] It turns out that, although police tend to not take voyeurs seriously (and they have been the light-hearted subject of many cartoons and commentary), much of the time these men are engaging in "rape testing," that is, assessing the likelihood that they could get away with raping the woman they are observing. Certainly, many men who rape participated in voyeurism prior to raping.[22]

Street harassment is another pattern of misogynistic behavior that is not taken seriously in that women are often advised to ignore it or even to see it as a compliment. Recently, however, there have been many instances of street harassment culminating in violence: a 14-year-old girl in Florida who was walking along a road was accosted, choked till she lost consciousness, and run over several times by a man in an SUV after refusing his offer to have sex for money; a California woman who refused a ride from a man in a car was run over twice resulting in her being dragged behind the car; a Georgia woman was raped after she was accosted by three men who approached her on the street;[23] and a Detroit woman was killed after she rebuffed a man on the street who asked for her phone number.[24] In addition, a man who tried to defend several women from being harassed on the street was knocked unconscious by the harassers,[25] a woman's boyfriend was stabbed nine times—near fatally—by a man who catcalled the woman on the street as they were walking home,[26] and another man who tried to defend a woman from being harassed was beaten so badly by the harassers that he was hospitalized with a broken nose, a black eye, and a serious perforation in his intestine.[27] Indeed, a recent study found that 41 percent of women reported being the recipient of physically aggressive street harassment.[28]

Sexual harassment in the workplace has likewise been minimized and not taken seriously. Some men have tried to dismiss sexual harassment as merely letting a woman know that she is attractive, which they believe shouldn't constitute a hostile work environment. Women's experiences of sexual harassment in the workplace have been trivialized, especially so at the time feminists were first trying to raise awareness of it as a problem. Citron reports that "in a case involving a male supervisor who repeatedly tried to molest two female employees, the judge ruled that federal law could not interfere 'every time any employee made amorous or sexually oriented advances toward one another.'"[29] Women were also frequently advised that if they wanted to keep their jobs, then they had no standing to complain about sexual harassment, or they were told that, if a woman remained at a job where she was being sexually harassed, it indicated that she enjoyed the sexual harassment.[30]

Accusations of Exaggerating or Lying

Women who try to hold their attackers accountable are often accused of either exaggerating or lying outright as a way of denying the assault. Date rape victims have been accused of being a "girl who changed her mind afterwards," or having morning-after regrets after a "date gone wrong."[31] In a glaring example, Ken Buck, the district attorney for Weld County, Colorado, explained to a rape victim why he wouldn't prosecute her rape case saying, "A jury could very well conclude that this is a case of buyer's remorse. . . . It appears to me . . . that you invited him over to have sex with him."[32] Remarkably, this was a case in which the rapist had confessed to the police as well as to the victim in a recorded phone call. In another example of accusing women of lying or exaggerating claims of being raped, Lincoln University president Robert Jennings voiced his suspicions about women who reported that they had been raped on campus:

> We had on this campus last semester, three cases of young women, who after having done whatever they did with the young men, and then it didn't turn out the way they wanted it to turn out, guess what they did? They then went to Public Safety and said, "He raped me." ... Why am I saying all this, ladies? I'm saying this because, first and foremost, don't put yourself in a situation that would cause you to be trying to explain something that really needs no explanation had you not put yourself in that situation."[33]

Women are also accused of lying by making false rape accusations. However, it is estimated that less than 6 percent of rape accusations are false,[34] and false reports of rape are not any more common than false reports of other kinds of crimes including burglary, robbery, and mugging. In spite of the fact that there are similar rates of false reports of all kinds of crimes, when, for example, a robbery is reported, the suspicion of a false report is not commonly raised as a possibility unless specific circumstances warrant it.

In another illustration where women are seen to be exaggerating about violence perpetrated against them, Australian criminology scholar Adrian Howe points out that the actions of male perpetrators are diminished in criminology texts as well as in general discussions of violent acts through the "labeling of feminist speech about men's violence as 'extreme' or dismissing as hysteria women's allegations about violent men."[35]

The Trope of Being "Too Sensitive"

Another common accusation when women try to bring attention to behaviors they experience is being told they are overreacting or are too sensitive. Women who have brought domestic violence cases to court have been told by presiding judges that they should "kiss and make up and get out of my court," and that unless they sustained "permanent injury," abused women should work things out with their husbands.[36]

Women who respond to street harassers have been told by harassers, and by others, that they are overreacting, that the men are really paying them compliments, and that they should be flattered instead of upset. Regarding sexual harassment in the workplace, legal scholar Catharine MacKinnon points out that there was a frequent "charge [that] women who resented sexual harassment were oversensitive. Not that the acts did not occur, but rather that it was unreasonable to experience them as harmful."[37] Citron references a sexual harassment case in which a state unemployment board ruled against a woman who quit her job because her boss demanded that she sleep with him, saying "Today's modern world requires that females in business and industry have a little tougher attitude toward life in general."[38]

SHIFTING CULPABILITY

Another tactic that is employed to defuse and derail women's attempts to clearly name and define abusive and harassing behaviors is to shift the culpability for the behaviors in various ways. This blame-shifting takes various forms: the victim can be blamed for the abusive behavior, or, alternatively, both parties are seen as sharing in the blame. Or, without addressing who caused the abuse or harassment, the sympathy for the person who is wronged shifts from the person who was victimized to the perpetrator. Finally, in a clever and insidious move, cause and effect are reversed so that the targeted person is cast as the person who was really attacking the perpetrator.

Blaming the Victim

Rather than assigning full culpability for abusive and harassing behaviors to the perpetrators, a shift of focus occurs when targeted women are seen as bearing the responsibility for their harassment or abuse. Prior to feminist activism around domestic violence (and, unfortunately, even since) much of the attention on domestic violence was focused on the ways a battered woman was seen as provoking the attacks on her by not complying with the man's wants or by doing things that might upset him. Another common way of blaming domestic violence victims is to see women who defend themselves, even verbally, as having brought the violence on themselves; or the violence is seen as an understandable or even warranted response to "nagging" or "talking back." Paradoxically, women have also been blamed for allowing domestic violence by not leaving their abusers soon enough, despite the fact that there is a dramatically increased risk of victims being killed after they have left their abusers.[39] Partially as a result of widespread victim-blaming for domestic violence, many women internalize these messages and come to blame themselves for their own abuse. Citron summarizes victim-blaming attitudes toward women victims of domestic violence:

> Twentieth-century judges and caseworkers similarly treated battered women as the responsible parties rather than their abusers. If only they had cleaned

their homes and had dinner ready for their husbands, they would not have been beaten. Battered wives were advised to improve their appearance to prevent their husbands from beating them. Police training guides instructed officers that it would be unreasonable to remove abusive husbands from the home because they were simply responding to their wives' "nagging."[40] [citations omitted]

Victim-blaming is rampant among rape victims as well. One of the all-too-common things that women who have been raped often wonder is whether they had done something—been in the wrong place or with the wrong people, or worn something too provocative or revealing—that made them somehow culpable for their own rape. Date rape victims are also made to believe they must have done something to have led the rapist on. Women who were date raped have been accused of "wanting it" simply because they may have invited their date into their home, or gone with their date to his place. Paul Elam, founder of the popular men's rights activist's (MRA) site A Voice for Men, posted an inflammatory article online in which he asserted that women are to blame for being raped (although he has since taken the article down):

> And all the outraged PC demands to get huffy and point out how nothing justifies or excuses rape won't change the fact that there are a lot of women who get pummeled and pumped because they are stupid (and often arrogant) enough to walk th[r]ough life with the equivalent of a I'M A STUPID, CONNIVING BITCH—PLEASE RAPE ME neon sign glowing above their empty little narcissistic heads.[41]

Women who are harassed on the street or at their workplace have been admonished to dress or comport themselves differently, as if their dress or behavior had precipitated the harassment. Citron notes that before sexual harassment in the workplace was more widely accepted as the responsibility of the harasser, women were blamed for their own sexual harassment:

> Female employees were told that they "asked" supervisors to proposition them by dressing provocatively.... Courts legitimated this view by permitting employers to defeat sexual harassment claims with proof that female employees invited employers' sexual advances.... Society minimized the culpability of sexually harassing employers and maximized the responsibility of sexually harassed employees.[42]

In an extreme case that summarily debunks the idea that dressing provocatively is what causes women to be harassed, in Saudi Arabia, where women who venture out in public must cover themselves completely (using a niqab, which fully covers the body, the head, and the face and has only a narrow slit for the eyes), women are harassed on the street. Indeed, a study conducted by a Saudi researcher found that 78 percent of women respondents in Saudi Arabia said they had experienced sexual harassment, 15 percent were physically touched by the harasser,[43] and Saudi Arabia was ranked third in the rate of sexual harassment in a study of 24 mostly Western countries.[44] So even with the extremes of covering that women must comply with in Saudi Arabia, they are still sexually harassed while out in public. That this is so certainly belies the notion that sexual harassment is provoked by women wearing revealing clothing. Remarkably, one prominent Saudi cleric, Sheikh Muhammad al Habadan, proposed that street harassment of women in Saudi Arabia could be diminished if they were compelled to wear a niqab that allows only one eye—rather than both eyes—to be visible. This absurdity represents the lengths to which status quo defenders will go to hold women's actions to blame for the behavior of perpetrators.[45]

No-Fault Perpetration

Another way of shifting culpability is to claim that both people involved in an act of abuse or harassment were at fault. In this manner, events are blurred into a version where both parties participated and are therefore culpable, which belies the agency and intent of the perpetrator and renders the harm inflicted on the victim less visible. This is not to say that there are not many situations where both participants do share in the responsibility for a negative outcome; however, the trope of "it takes two to tango" is one that is conveniently used to deny and obscure the dynamics of situations where there is in fact a perpetrator and a target or victim, who, in fact, did nothing to cause or aggravate the harassment or assault.

An example of this is when police arrest both people during domestic violence assaults, based on the view that, since the battered woman may have defended herself against the abuse, she was equally to blame. The phenomenon of "mutual arrest" has been increasingly common as batterers have become aware of the mandatory arrest policies for domestic violence victims and therefore take advantage of the policy to accuse their victims of mutual assault when the police are called. Additionally, most states now have laws that require police to make an arrest for domestic violence calls, as a way of countering the previous police response where they would see a beaten woman but not arrest the batterer, perhaps out of misplaced sympathy. Unfortunately, this policy has often had the unintended consequence of both parties being arrested, out of a false equivalence that women who defend themselves from the abuse are equally culpable.

In an impassioned critique of the idea that "it takes two to tango," Patrick Stewart, the English film, television, and stage actor who most famously played Captain Jean-Luc Picard in the television series *Star Trek*, recounts what happened when his father beat his mother: "I heard police or ambulancemen, standing in our house, say, 'She must have provoked him,' or 'Mrs Stewart, it takes two to make a fight.'" In response, Stewart forcefully and unequivocally declares: "They had no idea. The truth is my mother did nothing to deserve the violence she endured."[46]

Shared culpability is also implied when, during a trial for the crime of rape, a victim's past sexual behavior is brought up, as if to suggest that a woman was partially to blame for her own rape simply because she may have had sex in the past.

In an example of attempting to make Anita Hill seem culpable for her own sexual harassment, David Brock, author of the book *The Real Anita Hill*, has admitted that he unethically endeavored to portray Hill as having a "perverse desire for male attention," a "'love-hate' complex with Thomas," and as being "a little bit nutty and a little bit slutty."[47] Brock, who has since expressed regret for his part in undermining Hill's credibility, was attempting to make her appear to be complicit in Thomas's alleged sexual harassment against her and even, perhaps, "asking for it."

Switch of Sympathies

Another effective tactic that contributes to obfuscating what women experience is to switch the focus from what actually happened to the targeted woman to the point of view of the person or people who caused the harm. When women have been raped, the focus has sometimes been switched to how the lives of the rapists will be ruined by the woman going forward with prosecution for the rape. Public sympathy often then switches from the woman who was raped to the rapist(s) because of the ways a rape conviction will affect his or their lives. For example, widespread sympathy was shown to British soccer player Ched Evans, who was convicted of rape in 2012, for being no longer able to play soccer due to his rape conviction. His defense counsel lamented, "Until now, [Evans] had a promising career to which he has devoted his whole life since his teens.... That career has now been lost."[48] (This is in stark contrast to the woman he was convicted of raping: she has had to live in hiding, moving five times in three years "after being hunted down by vile Internet trolls" who keep trying to locate her and then publicize her whereabouts.[49]) After the announcement of the guilty verdict in the Steubenville rape trial, CNN anchor Poppy Harlowe commiserated with the men who were found guilty of rape, commenting that they "had such promising futures, [were] star football players, very good students" and that they were "literally watch[ing] as they believed their life fell apart." She empathized with them, saying that she found it "incredibly difficult" to witness how upset they were at the guilty verdict.[50] Jennings, the college president who accused women of lying or exaggerating their rape claims, also showed concern for those who were accused of being rapists possibly facing jail time: "When you allege that somebody did something of that nature to you, you go to jail. I don't care how close they are to finishing the degree, their whole life changes overnight."[51]

When domestic violence victims testify in court against their abusers, the focus often becomes on whether the seemingly nice man who is appearing in front of the judge is capable of being physically abusive. Even in cases where a woman has been murdered by her partner, the public's sympathy can still be directed his way, to the point of overshadowing compassion for the victim. When Oscar Pistorius, the sprint runner whose legs were amputated below the knee at a young age, was convicted and sentenced for murdering his girlfriend Reeva Steenkamp, his psychologist lamented the conviction: "We are left with a broken man. . . [one] who has lost everything."[52] Less than one day after Pistorius was found guilty, sympathetic public sentiment for the Pistorius spurred Craig Spence, the International Paralympic Committee director of media and communications, to tell BBC Radio 5 Live, "Oscar's done a great deal for the Paralympic movement. He's been an inspiration to millions. . . . If he wishes to resume his athletics career then we wouldn't step in his way—we would allow him to compete again in the future."[53]

In these cases, the subjectivity of the woman who was abused, raped, or killed is subsumed by an outpouring of sympathy and concern toward the male perpetrators and how their promising lives were ruined by being convicted of the crimes they in fact committed. A consequence of the focus on the perpetrator is that it renders less visible the pain and harm experienced by the victims.

Another way to shift the subject is to focus on the motivations or intentions of the perpetrators rather than on the effects of the act on their target. So, for example, men who expose themselves in public to women are often seen as not having particularly malicious intentions and are sometimes even seen as humorously innocuous; however, for women who live in a world where one out of six women are raped, the effect of seeing a flasher is very likely to make them feel unsafe. In a similar way, street harassers are often seen—and see themselves—as not hurting the women they harass. In contrast, University of Wisconsin student Allie Myren eloquently describes the effects of street harassment on women who live in a context of the threat of being raped:

> It takes the next hour, day or week following the harassment to battle the self-consciousness reintroduced by my harassers, to fight the anger provoked by their belittling selfishness and to reconstruct the foundation of strong, independent, autonomous woman that makes me who I am. The vulnerability in being female that colors harassment lies in the fact that one unsolicited comment from a man is all it takes to remind me that he could own my body if he so chose.[54]

When Elliot Rodger shot and killed numerous people out of frustration that women would not go out with him, and women tweeted their outrage and frustration, the hashtag response was #NotAllMen, as if, since not all men act in the ways that women were complaining about, it diminished the experiences that women had. That "not all men" act in abusive or violent ways was in fact a non sequitur response to women speaking out about their experiences of some men becoming vengeful when rejected: it was a change of subject from women's experiences of abuse and harassment to the hurt feelings of those men who felt wrongfully implicated by women's comments. Ultimately, however, #NotAllMen was countered with the response #YesAllWomen, which proved to be prolifically popular on Twitter. Moreover, it was an effective switch-back to the point of view of women who are targeted by male violence. It took the discussion back from the digression of focusing on men and their feelings about women saying they are afraid of male violence and placed it squarely back on women's fears and experiences of male violence in their daily lives.

Switching the focus from the victims to the perpetrators is significant because whose reactions and perceptions are seen as relevant, accurate, and sympathetic influences whose reactions are privileged in public discourse. Public sentiment can indeed be swayed by sympathetic portrayals of perpetrators, which can then affect what social and legal consequences for abusive or harassing behavior are considered appropriate.

Perpetrators Feign Victimhood

In an especially brazen shift of culpability, perpetrators of abuse, harassment, and even violence to the point of murder can come to see themselves as victims. O.J. Simpson, who many people believe killed his former wife Nicole Brown Simpson in 1994, although he was not convicted of the crime, famously announced about his relationship with his wife, "I'm the real victim here—I was an abused husband."[55] Clarence Thomas, commenting about the Senate hearings in which testimony was heard from Anita Hill and others regarding his alleged sexual harassment of Hill, called the proceedings that considered Hill's testimony a "high-tech lynching."[56]

Men's rights activists focus on how men are innocent victims of domestic violence and rape accusations. In 2006, Darren Mack, a men's rights activist, admitted to killing his wife by stabbing her to death. He subsequently drove to a parking garage and shot the judge presiding over their divorce case through a courthouse window.[57] Although his wife had warned a friend that "he's out to get me and someday he will probably kill me,"[58] he was unrepentant at the trial and instead viewed himself as the "victim." His deceased wife's mother called him a "sociopath," whom she said "hypnotized himself into believing he's justified and he's the victim."[59] Men's rights groups were called on by others to distance themselves from defending Mack as an aggrieved victim. However, the few men's rights groups who were publicly critical of Mack's actions seemed to do so reluctantly.

MRAs also focus on the few wrongful convictions of men for rape and extrapolate from them that men are generally the victim when they are accused of rape. Elam, a prominent MRA, in an article explaining his view that most rape allegations by women against men are false, went so far as to announce "Should I be called to sit on a jury for a rape trial, I vow publicly to vote not guilty, even in the face of overwhelming evidence that the charges are true."[60]

Tamara N. Holder, a Chicago criminal defense attorney, explains how some abusive men have learned to game the system so that it looks like they are the victims:

> Unfortunately, many abusive men have learned to reshape domestic violence laws into another weapon of abuse. They are turning police and court protections upside down: The abusers themselves call 9–1–1; they have the women arrested for domestic violence; and then they do everything they can to try to have the women prosecuted and sentenced. In this way, the true victim is painted as the abuser.[61]

Indeed, turning the tables and feigning victimhood is one of the hallmark ploys of people who act abusively, so it is not surprising that this is a tactic that is commonly employed to distract from attempts to bring harassing, abusive, or threatening behavior to light.

CLAIMS OF INEVITABILITY

A fourth way that cultural defense mechanisms manifest is by making it seem that the abusive or harassing behaviors that women are critiquing are natural and, therefore, inevitable and immutable. The idea conveyed is that, because these kinds of harassing and abusive behaviors by men are part of men's "nature," they cannot be changed, and so to protest against them is akin to protesting against something as unavoidable and natural as, say, the rain. Women who would continue to complain or protest against something that is embedded in men's nature are seen as whiners who need to grow up and accept "reality." An additional implication of portraying these behaviors as natural is that it would be cruel and "emasculating" to ask the perpetrators to change since it is contrary to their nature and thus impossible. The conclusion to be drawn is that, just as "boys will be boys," so men will be men, and therefore, the only reasonable thing for women to do is to throw up their collective hands, perhaps give a resigned (and hopefully affectionately bemused) sigh, and accept that men cannot help behaving badly.

There are others, however, including many men, who do not buy this line of reasoning and instead see it as one that results in a society-wide tolerance of bad or abusive behavior. As Australian army chief Lt. Gen. David Morrison observed, in order to diminish sexual abuse in the military, certain behaviors must not be seen as normal. Morrison explained that "the standard you walk past is the standard you accept,"[62] urging people not to accept as normal things that are in fact unacceptable. Those who espouse the view that harassment and abuse of women is inevitable contribute to a climate where the behaviors are seen as, at a minimum, not unacceptable, and, worse, as something women should just put up with and accept.

A similar view is taken by some evolutionary psychologists and sociobiologists who view rape as an effective reproductive strategy that "may have increased the number of women with whom ancestral men copulated and, therefore, the reproductive success of rapist males."[63] These kinds of beliefs contribute to the notion that rape is a "natural" behavior for men, which reduces the sense of culpability for those who commit rape. In an elegant refutation of the supposed biological imperative for rape, Michael Kimmel, scholar and author on men and masculinity, explains,

> Evolutionary psychology cannot explain why most men do not rape. Rape rates also vary historically and cross-culturally, a fact that evolutionary psychology cannot explain. It also does not explain the variety of reasons why rape occurs or its relation to power and domination, such as rape used as a tool of warfare or gang rape. It ignores that rape is not always about sex and more often than not, not about reproduction as well.[64]

Sexual harassment has also been defended as behavior that men can't help due to their "natural urges." Citron explains, "Until the late 1970s, employers and judges defended male supervisors' 'amorous' activity as a normal and healthy development."[65] In 1975, the judge in a sexual harassment case in which a male supervisor harassed two female employees stated, "The only sure way an employer could avoid such charges would be to have employees who were asexual,"[66] with the implication that sexual harassment was simply the inevitable expression of human sexuality.

It is salient to note that claims of "natural" or supposedly biologically determined behaviors tend to be invoked in order to justify the inevitability of gender (as well as racial and other) hierarchies. Significantly, claims that certain behaviors are natural are rarely used to justify more egalitarian natural practices such as giving new mothers adequate time off from work to bond with their infants; or granting paid sick leave to all employees (as being sick is surely a natural condition); or even, perhaps, mandatory afternoon rest times at all jobs, since many people's bodies have a "natural" need for rest in the afternoon. Rather, claims that some behaviors are natural, and therefore immutable, are nearly always invoked to shore up existing hierarchies.

All of these cultural defense mechanisms—shooting the messenger, denial, shifting culpability, and claims of inevitability—have been employed to divert, confuse, deny, and distract from women speaking out about and clearly identifying harassment and attacks against them. In the next chapter, I will discuss how these cultural defense mechanisms have come into play as reactions against women trying to bring public attention to the harassment, threats, and abuse that are characteristic of gendertrolling.

Chapter 8

Gendertrolling: Cultural Defense Mechanisms at Work

As we saw in the last chapter, as women have fought to name and bring awareness to harassment and abuse, a pattern of cultural defense mechanisms emerges in response that impedes mobilizing to recognize the problem and to implement appropriate cultural and legal changes. Similarly, as the phenomenon of gendertrolling starts to reach the public's consciousness, even to a limited extent, the cultural defense mechanisms that have been employed to derail the public recognition of myriad other forms of harassment and abuse against women have come into play in full force. The pushback effect of these cultural defense mechanisms thwarts naming and defining gendertrolling as well as coming up with solutions that might address or ameliorate it.

SHOOTING THE MESSENGER

When women write about or otherwise expose the online abuse and threats they are subjected to, gendertrolls attempt to "shoot the messenger" by attacking or vilifying the women or otherwise maligning their character. When women speak or write about the attacks against them, gendertrolls often ramp up and greatly intensify their attacks on the women, as if in retribution for having spoken up or objected to the abuse. Not only are women attacked in coordinated campaigns, but those who speak up or call attention to the problem are doubly attacked for having spoken up. Melody Hensley, one of the atheist activists who has been gendertrolled, reported that after she posted online that she had PTSD from her online harassment, her harassment dramatically increased.[1]

> I had PTSD, and I decided that I was going to come out with that. I knew that I was going to get harassed by the usual suspects. What I didn't realize was that I was going to get harassed by veterans, that I was going to get harassed by the general public, that I was going to have tens of thousands of people start harassing me, all the time.... I came out with my PTSD, and people said that it was an insult to war veterans, that I was the worst human being in the world, that I should die.[2]

In a clear "shoot-the-messenger" ploy, her attempt to articulate the effects that online abuse had on her appeared to induce online harassers to redouble their efforts to attack her, thereby attempting to make the costs of having spoken up seem not worth it.

Sexual Shaming

As noted in Section 2 of Chapter 2, women who are gendertrolled are sent graphic and violent pornographic images with their faces superimposed on them, they are sent sexualized insults about their genitalia, and they are frequently called "whores," "sluts," "cunts," as well as other sexualized insults. Kathy Sierra, the technology guru who was driven offline in 2007, explains that gendertrolls attack women's sexuality, implying, among other sexualized insults, that they used sex to gain prominence in their profession:

> There is only one reliably useful weapon for the trolls to stop the danger you pose and/or to get max lulz: discredit you. The disinformation follows a pattern so predictable today it's almost dull: first, you obviously "fucked" your way into whatever role enabled your undeserved visibility. I mean ... duh. A woman. In tech....
> You are, they claim, CLEARLY "a whore".[3]

Sierra was told "Better watch your back on the streets whore.... Be a pity if you turned up in the gutter where you belong, with a machete shoved in that self-righteous little cunt of yours," and "The only thing Sierra is good for is her neck size," with a picture of a noose beside her head. In spite of the brutal nature of these messages and threats directed against her, she was "dismissed as a 'hysterical drama queen' who needed to 'toughen up.'"[4] Graphic and hypersexualized insults are another way of attempting to raise the costs of speaking out by shaming women sexually.

DENIAL

Not Taking the Problem Seriously

One way that the graphic, intensive, pervasive, and sustained threats and attacks on women that are characteristic of gendertrolling are not taken seriously is when people assume that they are similar to generic trolling and therefore do not acknowledge or recognize the drastically different character of the attacks and the levels of threat involved.

Online content providers such as Facebook have a track record of not taking such online abuse against women seriously. An Icelandic woman, Thorlaug Agustsdottir, found a Facebook group called "Men are better than women," with images such as "a young woman naked chained to pipes or an oven in what looked like a concrete basement, all bruised and bloody. She looked with a horrible broken look at whoever was taking the pic of her curled up naked."[5] After Agustsdottir complained about the group on her own Facebook page, someone on the group posted an image of Agustsdottir's face, Photoshopped to be bloodied and bruised, with the caption "Women are like grass, they need to be beaten/cut regularly."[6] Someone else in the group commented on the image, "You just need to be raped." Agustsdottir reported the page to Facebook, who determined that it did "not violate Facebook's Community Standards on hate speech, which includes posts or photos that attack a person based on their race, ethnicity, national origin, religion, sex, gender, sexual orientation, disability, or medical condition," and determined that the page qualified as "Controversial Humor."[7] In another instance of Facebook not taking abuse and threats against women seriously, feminist activist, author, and blogger Trista Hendren explained that Facebook did not consider threats that were posted to her and her family as credible or legitimate enough to remove, even though the FBI, whom Hendren had contacted regarding the threats, considered them credible enough to start an investigation.[8]

Independent video game developer and Gamergate target Zoe Quinn recounts her experiences of having the extensive and widely publicized harassment campaign against her not taken seriously in court:

> But then there's court, if you're lucky enough to get taken seriously.... Then there's the likelihood that you'll find yourself having to explain the Internet

to a judge who may or may not even want to know. Sometimes they understand, sometimes they tell you the Internet is not a big deal and maybe if you don't want to get harassed you shouldn't be online. Sometimes, when they tell you that, you tell them that your entire career is online and you'd have to give it up to effectively do that, and they tell you you're a smart young kid and should maybe just consider a new career.[9]

Accusations of Exaggerating or Lying

Women who are gendertrolled are also accused of exaggerating or making up the abuse and harassment or even of having been the perpetrator of their own abuse as a ploy to garner supporters or sympathy. A member of the 4chan online community, commenting about Quinn's harassment during the Gamergate episode, wrote "I don't doubt that people have given [Quinn] shit, but it's being played up to the nth degree to bring in sympathizers, and most of this 'abuse' actually takes the form of all the information we're making public on her. . . . She's at best hamming it up and at worst a liar."[10]

Incredibly, the women who were most targeted by threats in Gamergate, so much so that they felt they were in danger and needed to leave their homes for safety, were accused of participating in a "false flag" maneuver, that is, having been the ones who sent themselves the threats. False flag is a term derived from military use that describes creating actions that are perceived by others as if they were created by an opposing side. In this case, Gamergaters were accusing Quinn, Brianna Wu, and Anita Sarkeesian of having been the ones who propagated the threats made against them and having doxxed themselves under pseudonymous accounts that they themselves created.[11] Wu adamantly refuted the false flag allegations: "I'd like to think I'm a respected developer in this field. . . . At this point the FBI is involved. My local police department is involved, the Massachusetts cybercrime division is involved. If I made this up, I'll be going to jail. I can think of no quicker way to destroy my career than doing something stupid like that."[12]

After Sarkeesian appeared on the *Colbert Report*, an anonymous commenter who called himself "the Leader of Gamergate" concluded that, because she was willing to appear on a national television show, she must have been lying about the death threats she received: "I just realized, why would [Sarkeesian] go on national television in a studio with a well known location if she was in fear of her life. This is SOOOO GOOD FOR US."[13] Rather than taking Sarkeesian's appearance on the show (as well as her delivering three public speeches for which she had also received death threats) as a sign of her courage in the face of the threats made against her, this gendertroll concluded that she must be lying. Sarkeesian's show of bravery in the face of the ongoing and pervasive campaign against her, rather than being seen as evidence of her courage, was taken to mean that she must have been lying about receiving rape and death threats.

Sierra was also accused of lying about the extensive threats and harassment she experienced: as she explained, she was accused of being "a 'proven liar'. Or, as I was referred to yet again just yesterday by my favorite troll/hater/harasser: 'a charlatan.'"[14]

The Trope of Being "Too Sensitive"

In a similar vein, an all-too-common suggestion to women who bring their experiences of gendertrolling to light is that women are being oversensitive and need to grow a tougher skin. Women have been told that if they can't handle the insults, harassment, and rape and death threats they receive on the Internet, they should just log off. Astra Taylor, filmmaker and author of *The People's Platform: Taking Back Power and Culture in the Digital Age*, relates that women who are harassed online are frequently "told to 'lighten up' and that the harassment, however stressful and upsetting, isn't real because it's only happening online, that it's just 'harmless locker-room talk.'"[15] Amy Davis Roth, blogger at Free Thought Blogs, talks about the inadequacy of such advice:

> People say to "ignore it" or "grow a thicker skin" or to "just walk away" when online harassment is brought up. But that advice ignores the fact that women have every right to earn a living and to peacefully exist online without being threatened. This is not about mere critique as the harassers like to frame it, this is about bullying, intimidation and the stripping away of privacy. It is also about silencing and the idea that women are not allowed to have their own space, their own opinions or even the right to their own body *particularly* when online.[16]

Women have been accused of whining about similar kinds of abuse that men put up with without complaint. Mark Moulitsas, founder of the popular political blog the Daily Kos, commented about the harassment and threats Sierra received in 2007, implying that she needed to toughen up if she wanted to continue blogging,

> Look, if you blog, and blog about controversial shit, you'll get idiotic emails. Most of the time, said "death threats" don't even exist—evidenced by the fact that the crying bloggers and journalists always fail to produce said "death threats". . . . Email makes it easy for stupid people to send stupid emails to public figures. If they can't handle a little heat in their email inbox, then

really, they should try another line of work. Because no "blogger code of conduct" will scare away psycho losers with access to email.[17]

Brendan O'Neill, columnist and editor of the online magazine *Spiked*, wrote an opinion piece in the *Telegraph* making light of women complaining about online harassment and abuse, calling them the "21st-century equivalent of Victorian chaperones, determined to shield women's eyes and cover their ears lest they see or hear something upsetting." He concludes, "I would rather surf a web that caters for all, from the clever to the cranky, rather than put up with an Internet designed according to the needs of a tiny number of peculiarly sensitive female bloggers."[18]

Freelance writer and blogger Cath Elliot counters the idea of women being oversensitive:

> If I'd been trying to keep a tally I would have lost count by now of the number of abusive comments I've received since I first started writing online back in 2007. And by abusive I don't mean comments that disagree with whatever I've written—I came up through the trade union movement don't forget, and I've worked in a men's prison, so I'm not some delicate flower who can't handle a bit of banter or heated debate—no, I'm talking about personal, usually sexualised abuse, the sort that on more than one occasion now has made me stop and wonder if what I'm doing is actually worth it.[19]

The pervasiveness of the denial being used to negate women's experiences of gendertrolling online led Sarkeesian to declare, "One of the most radical things you can do is to actually believe women when they talk about their experiences."[20]

SHIFTING CULPABILITY

When women write or speak about online abuse, harassment, and threats, the facts and sometimes sequence of events are often twisted around by others in order to make it seem as though the woman was complicit or blameworthy in the acts committed against her. In another defense against clearly naming harassment and abuse, sympathy is sometimes extended for harassers, or harassers claim that they are the true victims.

Blaming the Victim

Women who have been harassed and threatened online are accused of being at fault for their own harassment. Women are told they would not have been targeted for the harassment campaigns against them if, for example, they hadn't spoken up about misogyny in videogames or campaigned for a women's face on a British banknote. An actor who works in television and commercials who was harassed with graphic and sexualized insults and threats explains that "I'm easily blamed for my choice of being on camera or told that it's my fault because I put myself out there in this fashion, but I refuse to accept that."[21]

Liz Ryerson, game critic and designer, postulated that Quinn was targeted because her Depression Quest video game was popular or because she herself was beginning to gain notoriety, which induced Gamergaters to somehow feel that she therefore deserved the abuse they heaped on her. Gamergaters then unleashed their "internalized misogyny and misdirected rage" at Quinn, accusing her of being "everything that is viewed as wrong with women—manipulativeness, sluttiness, being an 'attention-whore.'"[22]

On occasion, harassers have even created false online identities that accuse the woman of having made statements that would lead others to believe she deserves more harassment. Brianna Wu tweeted a link to a site that she found on which gendertrolls were engaged in a project they called "Operation Falseflag II," where they were planning on posing as feminists in fake Twitter accounts and then attacking Wu for objectifying women.[23]

No-Fault Perpetration

Some people have tried to split the difference of blame in online attacks, seeing both sides as having culpability. Kyle Wagner, staff writer at Deadspin and editor at *Gawker Media*, commented on a tendency in the media to attempt to see "both sides" of the Gamergate controversy, in spite of the fact that one "side" was issuing a torrent of rape and death threats, which caused many of the "other side" to flee their homes for safety:

> What's made [Gamergate] effective, though, is that it's exploited the same basic loophole in the system that generations of social reactionaries have: the press's genuine and deep-seated belief that you gotta hear both sides. Even when not presupposing that all truth lies at a fixed point exactly equidistant between two competing positions, the American press works under the assumption that anyone more respectable than, say, an avowed neo-Nazi is operating in something like good faith.[24]

Switch of Sympathies

The defensive tactic in which sympathies are shifted from the women being attacked to the attackers also occurs when women are gendertrolled. Sierra describes what she called one of the worst days of her life, when she realized that one of the people who was a prominent participant in the horrific gendertrolling campaign against her, Andrew "weev" Aurenheimer, dubbed the "web's most notorious troll,"[25] had managed to become a hero among technology professionals. Subsequent to his participation in the attacks on Sierra, Aurenheimer was prosecuted by the government for uncovering and exposing a flaw in the AT&T security system that allowed the email addresses of iPad users to be revealed. Because his prosecution was viewed as heavy handed on the part of the government, he was turned into a "hacktivist hero" online, which gained him newfound sympathy and support among people in the technology industry. Despite the fact that the gendertrolling attacks against Sierra, in which Aurenheimer was a key player, resulted in her abandoning her highly popular technology blog, dropping out of the technology field altogether and ending her career, and even moving to ensure the safety of her family, she describes how she, along with many others in the technology field, "had even begun to feel sorry for him." Commenting on how easy it was for her to switch the focus of her sympathy, even away from herself and onto her attacker, Sierra wrote, "Even I mistook the sociopath for a misunderstood outcast."[26]

Perpetrators Feign Victimhood

The defensive tactic of perpetrators being viewed by others as victims, or even the perpetrators coming to view themselves as victims, also occurs with gendertrolling, even in cases where gendertrolls have perpetrated graphic and vicious rape and death threats. In a stunning reversal of culpability, right-wing blogger Milo Yiannopoulos defended Gamergaters by arguing that they are the ones who are the real victims who are being attacked and terrorized. In Yiannopoulos's view, women are the ones wreaking terror online: "An army of sociopathic feminist programmers and campaigners, abetted by achingly politically correct American tech bloggers, are terrorising the entire community—lying, bullying and manipulating their way around the Internet for profit and attention."[27]

Arthur Chu, culture blogger and notable winner of game show *Jeopardy!*, sees the gendertrolling attacks of Gamergate as emanating from an "aggrieved underdog stance"[28] that derives from a "toxic swell of nerd entitlement."[29] Chu explains that "one of the most obnoxious but persistent beliefs that drives reactionary movements like Gamergate is the idea that the people screaming about having a 'feminist agenda' pushed on them are the true underdogs."[30]

T. C. Sottek, news editor at the *Verge*, also sees Gamergaters as being convinced that they are the ones who are experiencing some imagined harm:

What gives Gamergate power and momentum is its extremist conservative obstinacy; it is a reactionary movement against progressive voices that hoodwinks typically apolitical game players by convincing them of some harm that doesn't actually exist, like they are losing their right to free speech, or their hobby is being killed by an anti-gamer conspiracy.[31]

John Herrman, technology editor at *BuzzFeed* and editor at the *Awl*, explains that, in a strange twist, some men feel victimized and attacked by the fact that women feel threatened by them: "A great number of men, online and off, understand feminism as aggression—they feel as though the perception of their actions as threats *is itself a threat*."[32]

Kyle Wagner describes the "self-pity, self-martyrdom, an overwhelming sense of [their] own blamelessness"[33] that he sees part of Gamergaters' thinking, where they convince themselves that they are the aggrieved party, even while they are in positions of privilege:

Co-opting the language and posture of grievance is how members of a privileged class express their belief that the way they live shouldn't have to change, that their opponents are hypocrites and perhaps even the real oppressors. This is ... how you end up with an organized group of precisely the same video game enthusiasts to whom an entire industry is catering honestly believing that they're an oppressed minority.[34]

Sarkeesian concurs, saying that "the perpetrators do not see themselves as perpetrators at all."[35] Wu confirms this sense of the perpetrators feeling aggrieved, writing that "the people [sending threats and harassment] see themselves as noble warriors, not criminals."[36] Chu explains that these imagined victims see the women who are asking not to be sent horrific rape and death threats as "a powerful 'corrupt' force taking away the freedom of the vast mob of angry young male gamers and the billion-dollar industry that endlessly caters to them," so that, to them, bullying, harassing, and threatening the women in order "to shut them up and drive them out somehow constitutes justice."[37]

CLAIMS OF INEVITABILITY

The abusive online behavior of gendertrolls is taken as inevitable when, for example, people declare that online harassment and abuse are an unavoidable feature of the Internet. This sentiment is typically expressed with an air of futility, as if to say that the Internet will be the Internet, in much the same way that "boys will be boys" is used to rationalize other kinds of abusive behaviors. Tech guru and author Chris Locke concurs with the sentiment that online harassment, abuse, and threats are an inherent feature of the Internet. About the gendertrolling campaign that drove Sierra out of her career and off the Internet, he writes, "Evidently, there are some people who don't much like [Sierra]. . . . The same could be said of myself or indeed of anyone who blogs much. *It comes with the territory*" [italics added].[38]

Brendan O'Neill agrees with Locke's assessment that online harassment is integral to the Internet: "If I had a penny for every time I was crudely insulted on the Internet, labelled a prick, a toad, a shit, a moron, a wide-eyed member of a crazy communist cult, I'd be relatively well-off. For better or worse, *crudeness is part of the Internet experience. . .*" [italics added].[39] The message that is conveyed by statements such as these is that online abuse is inevitable and that therefore nothing can be done about it.

The claims that online abuse is an inherent and immutable feature of the Internet are also made by a segment of people, perhaps overrepresented on the Internet, who subscribe to a unique combination of ideas. These ideas include a belief that the Internet represents an imagined state of natural communications patterns that, if not tampered with, will reveal true human nature, so that absolute free speech with no restrictions must be preserved in order to maintain this envisioned techno-libertarian experiment. Another prevalent idea is that the Internet is separate and distinct from the rest of people's lives and that anonymity represents a chance to forgo the accountability of rules, laws, and civilities applied to other arenas of human expression. Finally, due to the iterative nature of the Internet, there is a common belief that it is a unique place for testing the marketplace of ideas, so that the ideas and memes that are most repeated are imbued with an inherent value, regardless of how abusive or threatening. Below, I lay out some of the ideas that comprise this ideology, which leads large numbers of people to conclude that the online harassment, abuse, and threats against women should not be regulated, or even discouraged, as doing so would do harm to what they conceive of as the inherent nature of the Internet.

The Internet as Natural

There is a particular and sizeable contingent of online denizens who subscribe to the idea that the Internet embodies a kind of state of nature or a free or natural expression of humanity, which they believe must be protected at all costs through wholly unencumbered Internet activities. They conceive of the Internet as having intrinsic qualities that arise organically out of some unspecified feature either of technology or of human nature. In viewing the Internet this way, they render the interactions that take place online as "natural," without a recognition that those interactions are, at least, to some—and probably to a great—extent, manifestations of the culture and values of the people who participate in those interactions. This "natural state" of the Internet is highly lauded and even revered among proponents of these beliefs—regardless of whether communication on the Internet is indeed evidence of a natural state and, even if so, whether such a "natural state" is worthwhile of preserving simply by virtue of its being natural.

The belief that the way people behave online is an inherent feature of the Internet and that it is therefore futile to attempt to change or curb online misogyny contributes to immunizing the perpetrators of threats and abuse from demands to change their behavior and makes it incumbent on women either to have to adapt to intolerable abuse or leave the Internet.

In this context, gendertrolling is defended as inevitable in that it is seen an unavoidable side effect of true free speech on the Internet. In this view, to create policies, laws, or even social norms to counter gendertrolling would necessarily destroy free speech. This stance is particularly ironic, given that gendertrolling has both the intent and the overwhelming effect of silencing women's speech on the Internet.

The Internet Should Be "Free"

Although the specific beliefs of those who subscribe to these ideas vary in some respects, their proponents can loosely be described as techno-libertarians. Deeply embedded in their view of the Internet is the idea that the Internet must remain totally "free," that is, free from any restrictions on speech whatsoever, regardless of how abusive and even threatening that speech may be. Many MRAs and Gamergaters, in particular those who frequent such sites as 4chan, 8chan, and Reddit, hold these beliefs. These sites tend to be havens where absolutist views on free speech reign and where even violent pornography or extreme threats of violence are acceptable, and even celebrated, as evidence of true freedom of speech.

The Internet Is a Separate World

Some of the people who subscribe to this ethos are very tech savvy and perhaps less skilled at interacting with people offline. Arthur Chu explains, based on his own past of having been extremely shy and "nerdy," the thinking of many people, frequently men, who see the Internet as imbued with special qualities that depart dramatically from offline life:

Being a nerd meant being good with computers, book knowledge, and data, and being bad with people. So the idea was that if you got really good at working with things and manipulating objects, you'd reach a point in life where you wouldn't need people to like you. You'd win purely by merit. There's nowhere on Earth where this is actually true, but there's people who believe that.

That's why so much of nerd culture involves these power fantasies full of magic. . . . It's also why a lot of the people in geeky subcultures gravitate towards libertarianism.[40]

There is a strong sense among many that the Internet is a world apart, a place where people can enter an alternate reality where the rules and limitations of offline life should not apply. As Jay Allen, contributor to the technology blog Boing Boing, describes it, anonymous imageboards such as 4chan "have their own idiosyncratic culture," where people who frequent these sites often feel are the "only place people can truly be themselves, without being burdened by their identity or consequences."[41] Astra Taylor observes that the Internet developed without regulation and without public input and was instead infused with a childishly idealistic sense of "how it was going to make everyone powerful and how everything would be free."[42]

The Value of Anonymity

Techno-libertarians also tend to be staunch supporters of anonymity, which adds to the mystique that the Internet is a special place distinct from offline life. Chu explains the significance of anonymity to those on 4chan:

> Look at 4chan culture, which is the ultimate version of shedding your IRL identity—you don't even keep a consistent screen name from thread to thread. That's very important to them, this belief in the possibility, that what I do online is completely separate from who I really am.[43]

Because forums such as Reddit, 4chan, and 8chan depend heavily on anonymity as a way of fostering freedom of expression without any consequences, doxxing, that is, to publicly reveal the identity of an anonymous poster on the boards, is the one unpardonable sin. Ironically, the proscription against doxxing is not applied to outsiders, especially women, with whom these techno-libertarians vehemently disagree on such topics as whether rape and death threats are acceptable, with the result that those outsiders are frequently doxxed.[44]

A Unique Marketplace of Ideas

Another tenet of techno-libertarian ethos is the belief that the Internet is the ultimate experiment in the "marketplace of ideas." Clyde Wayne Crews, who writes about technology, the Internet, and libertarianism, sees the Internet in that manner, saying that he "felt [the Internet] represented a demonstration project for spontaneous order, a chance to show that minimal regulation does work."[45]

Adherents to this ideology believe in a kind of evolutionary theory of ideas, where the best ideas, thoughts, images, or beliefs, referred to as "memes," are the ones that will be repeated and reposted most often and, in an analogy to evolution, they prove themselves to be more "fit" and therefore they "survive." Ideas that are not popular, on the other hand, will (naturally) fade away. In this view, any idea or meme that is popular, therefore, regardless of how offensive, cruel, or threatening, is seen as sacrosanct. In the minds of those who adhere to these ideas, the very fact that harassment, abuse, and threats are prevalent online indicates that they are inherently good and therefore should be defended.

Free-Speech Absolutism

These beliefs lead techno-libertarians to be Internet free-speech absolutists who take particular offense at anyone who would like to implement controls on Internet speech, even speech that goes so far as to constitute credible threats. Taylor confirms that "women who are increasingly speaking out against harassers are frequently accused of wanting to stifle free speech."[46]

Chris Kover, a writer for *Vice*, explains the nearly incomprehensible logic that emerges from this perspective: "What gets them really angry is when a feminist closes the comments on their YouTube videos or on their website. To them, that is an assault on free speech. So they harass her because she won't let them harass her on YouTube, basically."[47] Kathy Sierra believes she was targeted for gendertrolling for even suggesting comment moderation could be a solution to online abuse: "For the record, [as] far as most people have been able to determine, most of what happened to me long ago was triggered by a blog comment I made that said 'I'm not moderating my blog comments, but I support those who do and here's why.'"[48]

Legal scholar Danielle Keats Citron likewise lays out the reasoning of those who experience outrage when women try to protect themselves from online threats and harassment: "If victims seek legal help, they are accused of endangering the Internet as a forum of public discourse. The Internet is a free speech zone, a virtual Wild West, that cannot and should not bear the weight of regulation."[49] This convoluted logic holds that a woman who objects to harassment, no matter how dire, is violating the nearly sacred value of the completely unfettered free speech of those who are harassing her. In this manner, those who are being harassed are seen as attacking the harassers' free speech, and the harassed are therefore transformed, in that worldview, into being the attackers.

Ironically, when those who are among the strongest proponents of absolute Internet freedom have the tables turned on them, they sometimes realize how it feels to be on the receiving end of the kinds of harassment that they had been defending as essential to preserving the Internet. For example, the Federal Trade Commission recently issued an order that banned revenge porn site operator Craig Brittain from posting nude images of people without their consent and forced him to delete all such images and accompanying identity information that he had previously posted on his revenge porn site Is Anybody Down.[50] The terms of the order last for 20 years. But, in supreme irony, Brittain, who apparently objects to his online reputation being permanently besmirched by information about his nefarious online activities, has issued a takedown notice under the Digital Millennium Copyright Act. He is requesting that Google be made to erase unauthorized photos of him as well as articles about him on *Gawker*, *Huffington Post*, Reddit, *Forbes*, *Salon*, and *Vice* that discuss his history on the Internet. This is high irony from a person who made his living out of posting images of nude women without their consent, in which they were identified by name, that tarnished their reputations and limited their job prospects, and then charged them steep prices to remove their images through another site he allegedly ran. In a stunning display of hypocrisy, Brittain remains a techno-libertarian, saying that he still doesn't believe there should be any legal limitations on revenge porn,[51] although, apparently, he is willing to employ legal remedies when it comes to removing online information about himself.

In another instance of someone who didn't "get" what online harassment was about until he was attacked, Jan Rankowski, known as Jace Connors online, tried to make fun of Gamergaters by posing as an "over-the-top, super-hyper-macho armed" Gamergater.[52] He went so far as to post that he was targeting Brianna Wu and that he was, in fact, on his way to her house when his car crashed. Wu got wind of this and was understandably frightened, especially in view of the substantial number of rape and death threats she has received and her sense that Gamergaters are egging each other on in various online forums to attack her. When it came to light that Rankowski was actually trolling Gamergaters, they turned their attack apparatus on him. He told *BuzzFeed*, "People have been calling my old high school [and] calling my work and saying these nasty things about me. I was made to sign a contract at my job saying I wouldn't make any of these videos again."[53] He added that now that Gamergaters have targeted him so viciously, he has a better sense of what it has been like for women who have been targeted by Gamergate, explaining that previously he "didn't take this situation seriously, but I see what it means now to be in the other person's shoes. What her life must feel like. I have this newfound respect for the people who are having to deal with GamerGate, Brianna Wu and Anita [Sarkeesian]."[54]

Techno-libertarians want to maintain the Internet as a space that is exempt from the rules, laws, and civilities that apply to offline life. Fears abound that trying to limit or impose restrictions on threats, abuse, and harassment against women online would "break the Internet," that is, create a climate online where free speech is chilled, as if abuse, stalking, and rape and death threats are an indispensable component of free speech.

CRITICISMS OF ONLINE FREE SPEECH LIBERTARIANISM

Above, I have laid out some of the ideas that form the foundation of an online culture out of which rampant abuse has arisen. In the view of the proponents of these ideas, anything that arises out of this experiment is inherently worthwhile and evidence of true human nature. In this manner, whatever happens on the Internet is viewed as natural and inevitable. The conclusion drawn, therefore, is that online abuse and threats are inevitable and that no efforts should be made to create policies or enforce laws against them. There are, however, several important criticisms of the ideas that comprise techno-libertarian philosophies, which I detail below.

The Internet Is Not Natural

There is nothing natural or inevitable about the practices, discourse, and behaviors that have emerged on the Internet. To the contrary, the Internet is quintessentially unnatural; that is, it has certainly not arisen organically out of a state of nature. Astra Taylor highlights the irony of claiming a state of nature on the Internet:

> That's what the techno-optimists would have us believe, dismissing potential solutions as threats to Internet freedom and as forceful interference in a "natural" distribution pattern. The word "natural" is, of course, a mystification, given that technological and social systems are not found growing in a field, nurtured by dirt and sun. They are made by human beings and so can always be changed and improved.[55]

Neither are the interactions that take place online evidence of some imagined natural state of humanity. Rather, they are reflections of the social and cultural values of the people who participate in online conversations and activities. Similarly, the popularity or survival value of a meme is not useful as a singular measure of its value. (To wit, fast food is highly popular, but that fact alone is not a good indicator of its merits as natural or as food.) To see online interactions as evincing or uncovering true human nature ignores that they are merely expressions of the thoughts, priorities, and values of the people who are creating and shaping the interactions. The end result is a kind of tautological confirmation bias, where people who see the world a certain way go online and, because they cluster in havens where there are many others who see the world similarly, they are convinced that this is evidence that this is true human nature, emerging in its raw and unfettered form.

The Internet Is Real Life

A second criticism of techno-libertarians' slavish devotion to absolute free speech is that the Internet cannot be sharply divided in any real sense from offline life, as so many gendertrolled women have emphasized. The Internet is comprised of actual people who are communicating online; it is not some separate, magical, fantasy world where no harm can be done to living, breathing, flesh-and-blood people. Therefore, the Internet should not be exempt from laws, regulations, and policies that govern offline life. Although some of the most harassing and abusive online speech might well be popular due to its sensationalistic aspects and therefore is a "winning" meme, such speech nonetheless causes harm to those to whom it is directed. And threats, whether they are made off- or online, have real effects, in real life, to actual people.

Feminist writer, media critic, and activist Soraya Chemaly speaks of the impossibility of a sharply defined boundary between online and offline life:

> The culture at large creates a distinction, which is completely artificial and detrimental, between online and offline life. In fact, we live our lives seamlessly on both. We cannot work without the Internet. We connect with our families and friends on the Internet. We keep in touch with our children and parents online. That is just a completely false premise that somehow there is this abstracted virtual world that does not have consequence and meaning offline.[56]

Taylor echoes similar sentiments and focuses on the ways that offline marginalization is reinscribed online, in part due to the denial that online life is a reflection of real-world social problems:

The digital is not some realm distinct from "real" life, which means that the marginalization of women and minorities online cannot be separated from the obstacles they confront offline. Comparatively low rates of digital participation and the discrimination faced by women and minorities within the tech industry matter—and not just because they give the lie to the egalitarian claims of techno-utopians.[57]

Free Speech Rights Are Not Absolute

Freedom of speech is guaranteed by the First Amendment of the U.S. Constitution only insofar as the government cannot pass a law to abridge free speech; the doctrine of free speech does not mean that private companies, such as those who provide social media and other Internet platforms, have to tolerate or allow all kinds of speech. The guarantee of freedom of speech is a right that cannot be violated by the government and is applied only to attempts by the government to restrict speech. Private actors, such as online content providers or social media platforms, can regulate speech as much as they like without infringing on the First Amendment.

It is also important to bear in mind that in offline life, free speech is not absolute: for example, libelous or defamatory speech is not protected. Likewise, speech that constitutes copyright infringement, incites violence, or is an integral part of committing crimes, such as extortion or solicitation, is also not protected under the First Amendment. In addition, bribery, plagiarism, "fighting words," and speech that constitutes fraud are not protected.[58] Significantly, speech that constitutes a true threat, that is, "speech intended to convey a serious intent to hurt another person or that a reasonable person would interpret as expressing a serious intent to cause bodily harm," is also not protected speech.[59] Certainly, many of the posts or comments by gendertrolls can reasonably be considered to be true threats.

Free Speech Is Not the Most Important of All Values

Another criticism of techno-libertarians is that holding freedom of speech as a value above all others is simplistic and reductive. Arthur Chu speaks to this:

> I've already seen what happens when you get a culture that, rather than asking to what end we defend free speech, valorizes free speech for its own sake and thus perversely values speech more the more pointlessly offensive it is—because only then can you prove how devoted you are to freedom by defending it.[60]

Tim O'Reilly, founder of a company that publishes books on technology and computers, reiterates that "there's a strong undercurrent on the Internet that says that anything goes, and any restriction on speech is unacceptable." However, he believes that it is "ridiculous to accept on a blog or in a forum speech that would be seen as hooliganism or delinquency if practiced in a public space."[61] These commentators acknowledge that free speech is valued excessively on the Internet and believe that the value of free speech, while clearly important, should not trump all other values or considerations, such as, for example, the values of equality, justice, and equal opportunity to participate in public discourse, as well as the merits of engaging in discussions that are characterized by civility and logic in which ideas rather than insults and threats are exchanged.

Absolute Free Speech Tends toward Inequality

Finally, completely unrestricted free speech tends to augment inequality; in short, it enables bullying. Without any restraints on speech whatsoever, particularly those prohibiting true or credible threats, full rein is given to those who are willing to threaten and coerce others in order to intimidate them into withdrawing from full participation online. Astra Taylor cautions against "the tendency of open systems to amplify inequality—and new media thinkers' glib disregard for this fundamental characteristic."[62] Accordingly, a commitment to absolute and unrestricted free speech on the Internet has the ironic effect of stifling and silencing the speech of those who are bullied and harassed into silence or who withdraw entirely from Internet conversations due to harassment, abuse, and threats. Taylor explains that this "peculiar brand of libertarianism in vogue within technology circles means a minority of members—a couple of outspoken misogynists, for example—can disproportionately affect the behavior and mood of the group under the cover of free speech."[63] Ally Fogg, a British writer and journalist and columnist at the *Guardian*, eloquently sums up this idea, "the use of hate speech, threats and bullying to terrify and intimidate people into silence or away from certain topics is a far bigger threat to free speech than any legal sanction."[64] Chemaly summarizes how the value of unrestrained free speech privileges abusive dynamics:

> When we say to women, why don't you fight back, or just let it roll off your back, or it's not serious, we amplify that distinction because we're asking women to overcome decades of socialization in which their speech is supposed to be more quiet, less aggressive, more genteel, more polite, they're not supposed to interrupt, not supposed to disrupt. That's the dominant speech being expressed by harassers and abusers, and American interpretations of

freedom of speech and freedom of expression reward that abusive dominant male dynamic.[65]

Citron adds an important point about speech on the Internet: "Because the Internet serves as people's workspaces, professional networks, résumés, social clubs, and zones of public conversation, it deserves the same protection as offline speech. No more, no less."[66] Citron elaborates on how not having any restraints on destructive speech hampers the speech of those who are being attacked:

> Restraining a mob's most destructive assaults is essential to defending the expressive autonomy of its victims. Preventing mobs from driving vulnerable people offline would advance the reasons why we protect free speech in the first place, even though it would inevitably chill some speech of online mobs.[67]

Laurie Penny, British journalist and a contributing editor at the *New Statesman*, sums up,

> I believe the time for silence is over. If we want to build a truly fair and vibrant community of political debate and social exchange, online and offline, it's not enough to ignore harassment of women, LGBT people or people of colour who dare to have opinions. Free speech means being free to use technology and participate in public life without fear of abuse—and if the only people who can do so are white, straight men, the Internet is not as free as we'd like to believe.[68]

This is not to argue that there should be proscriptions against unpopular ideas, or even "hate speech," which is currently protected speech under the First Amendment. But laws that apply to speech that serves the sole purpose of threatening and frightening others through possible bodily harm—in other words, true threats—should be enforced online as well as offline.

The cultural defense mechanisms—shooting the messenger, denial, shifting culpability, and claims of inevitability—that have been employed in the past to stave off full recognition of myriad abuses against women have also been used to stymie women's attempts to name, define, and explore remedies for their unique experiences of harassment, abuse, and threats online. To the extent that these defense mechanisms are effective in creating confusion and doubt, patterned behaviors such as gendertrolling cannot be recognized, clearly defined, and accurately named. The lack of a clearly identifiable pattern in turn thwarts efforts to work toward enforcing existing laws, implementing new policies and laws, and raising awareness for cultural change. In order to have an effect on diminishing gendertrolling attacks on women, activists must therefore do the double work of clearly describing and naming the rampant harassment and abuse of women online, while also effectively countering the array of defenses brought to bear against their efforts.

Chapter 9

Recommendations for Change

In this chapter, I summarize some of the recommendations that a variety of people have made as to what changes might be useful to address the problem of gendertrolling. It is unclear which suggestions would be most effective, but I include a great many so that wiser minds than mine can sort through them and determine which have the most hopes of being successful. In the area of the law, legal scholars advocate increasing the enforcement of existing laws, especially laws against true threats, and training law enforcement to become more familiar with patterns of stalking and threats that take place online. Many also recommend amending or implementing new laws that specifically address the unique kinds of abuse and harassment that occur online.

Other advocates have recommended making changes to Internet policies and protocols, for example, eliminating or discouraging anonymity online or increasing comment moderation. Most of those who are attempting to bring attention to this topic recommend implementing technological fixes or policy changes for online content providers, especially social media. Many people have offered suggestions on how to ameliorate the damaging effects when women become victims of a gendertrolling campaign. Finally, because online life is a reflection of offline life, a preponderance of activists have come to the conclusion that widespread cultural change regarding attitudes toward women must take place before gendertrolling attacks will diminish.

INCREASE ENFORCEMENT OF EXISTING LAWS

Because gendertrolling campaigns induce terror and a fear of bodily harm in the targeted women to such an extent that they often alter their real-life routines, withdraw from the Internet, or even move in order to keep safe, a potentially powerful strategy to remedy this would be to extend enforcement of existing laws against offline threats to the credible threats that are made online. The Interstate Communications Act (18 U.S.C. § 875), which states "Whoever transmits in interstate or foreign commerce any communication containing . . . any threat to injure the person of another, shall be fined under this title or imprisoned not more than five years, or both,"[1] is widely interpreted to prohibit threatening people over the Internet. Danielle Keats Citron, a legal scholar whose work focuses on cyber law, affirms that "the First Amendment does not protect 'true threats' that communicate a serious intention to commit violence against particular individuals," and she argues that "threats of violence made via new technologies are not immunized from penalty on free speech grounds."[2]

Nevertheless, as it stands now, law enforcement by and large does not treat online threats with the same seriousness as offline threats. Video game developer Brianna Wu issued a statement calling on law enforcement generally, and the FBI specifically, to "to step it up. This will not stop until you show the public that there are consequences to these illegal acts."[3] British Member of Parliament Stella Creasy agrees, arguing that, legally, "there should be 'no distinction' between online and offline abuse."[4] Creasy compared the treatment of offline versus online threats: "If I received a bomb threat through the post, there is a protocol for dealing with that, but if I receive it online there is nothing in place. . . . We have to challenge this attitude that women just have to learn how to deal with these online threats, that they should be ignored."[5]

Increased enforcement of these laws would go a long way to rendering online activities safer for women, so that even if women still received horrific and graphic insults, they would have safeguards against the harassment escalating into potential physical harm. Enforcing the laws would also create a considerable chilling effect on those sending threats, once they observe that online threats are being taken seriously and that perpetrators fined or jailed, or both. In response to the online harassment of her constituent Brianna Wu, Congressperson Katherine Clark recently issued a public statement calling on the Department of Justice to enforce existing federal laws, such as the Interstate Communications Act, which makes it a crime to "to transmit threats of bodily injury in interstate commerce," or the Federal Cyberstalking Statute, which criminalizes using "electronic communication to place a person in reasonable fear of death or serious bodily injury."[6] Clark also sent a letter to other members of Congress as well as to the House Subcommittee on Commerce, Justice, Science, and Related Agencies asking them to specifically address online threats in the 2016 appropriations act.[7]

The recommendation to enforce laws against making true threats is separate from the issue as to whether hate speech laws should be adopted in the United States. Unlike hate speech, hate crimes, which are crimes whose motivation is interpreted as having arisen out of animus toward a particular group, are illegal. Although hate speech can help determine the presence of such animus, the hate speech itself is not the crime. Unlike many other countries around the world, the United States does not have laws against hate speech other than the legal prohibition against "fighting words."[8]

Citron describes what she sees as a fundamental difference between hate speech, which is "fully protected speech," and the kind of online harassment against women that is "targeted attacks on individuals," which "might constitute true threats or constitute intentional infliction of emotional harm or violate people's rights to privacy, sexual invasions of privacy, defamation."[9] Although some people do advocate implementing hate speech laws in the United States, actually enforcing laws against credible threats would go a long way toward addressing gendertrolling without having to create additional restrictions on speech.

The Supreme Court recently ruled on a case, *Elonis v. United States*, involving credible threats made on Facebook. Anthony Elonis posted on his Facebook page threats to kill his ex-wife, her father, coworkers, an FBI agent who was investigating his case, and some school children. He even referenced the Sandy Hook Elementary School shooting in one threat he posted, which he claimed were "song lyrics":

> Enough elementary schools in a ten mile radius to initiate the most heinous school shooting ever imagined And hell hath no fury like a crazy man in a kindergarten class.[10]

Elonis maintains that he did not intend his statements to be threatening and points to disclaimers he posted on his Facebook page saying that he was exercising his First Amendment rights to free speech. He also said that the statements he posted were rap lyrics and as such were artistic expression and therefore protected speech. He was convicted of making credible threats by a lower court and was sentenced to 44 months in prison, which he served.[11]

Garrett Epps, contributing editor to the *Atlantic*, argues that despite Elonis's assertion that he was just expressing himself by posting rap lyrics and that he didn't have the intention to threaten anyone, Elonis "knew he was terrifying his wife—a court had told him so and ordered him to stop. He posted that he intended to carry out 'the most heinous school shooting ever imagined'; when two federal agents visited him after the school threat, Tone Dougie [Elonis's assumed "rap name"] warned them that if they came again he would blow them up with a suicide vest."[12] After Elonis's ex-wife took out a restraining order against him, he posted "Fold up your [restraining order] and put it in your pocket / Is it thick enough to stop a bullet?"[13]

The case turned on whether a conviction for making credible threats "requires proof of the defendant's subjective intent to threaten . . . or whether it is enough to show that a 'reasonable person' would regard the statement as threatening."[14] The Supreme Court's decision avoided the First Amendment issues regarding protected speech and true threats, and ruled that criminal prosecutions, such as Elonis's, must take into account the intent of the perpetrator. The Court said that the prosecutors in Elonis's case had to establish that it was his purposeful intent to make threats in order to convict him of criminal behavior.

Justice Samuel Alito, who concurred in part and dissented in part with the decision, did grant that "whether or not the person making a threat intends to cause harm, the damage is the same."[15] Alito added that "statements on social media that are pointedly directed at their victims. . . are much more likely to be taken seriously [than actual song lyrics]. To hold otherwise would grant a license to anyone who is clever enough to dress up a real threat in the guise of rap lyrics, a parody, or something similar."[16] The Court's ruling does not mean that Elonis is not guilty of making credible threats; it is possible that his case will be retried with this higher standard for conviction in mind and that he could be found to have had the intent to threaten, in which case his previous conviction will stand.

A potential negative outcome of the Court's decision is that it establishes a more permissive environment with regard to those making online threats at a time when the opposite tack is needed. Rather than using a reasonable person standard in order to make a determination of credible threats, the Court held to the standard of a subjective intent to threaten, which raises an additional hurdle for women who are threatened online to get justice. This is an especially difficult hurdle because establishing intent can be more complicated and tricky than making an assessment as to how statements appear to a reasonable person. In addition, the person making the threats can simply make the claim that he did not intend his statements as threats. Criminal defendants can and do lie about their intentions. Feminist author and blogger Amanda Marcotte explains that "gaslighting is now being used as a legal tactic. . . . Gaslighting is why we can't locate the definition of a threat inside the brain of the person issuing it. Most abusers are fairly good about lying when called out and the odds that many will admit they are trying to scare and control people with threats are pretty damn low in most cases."[17] The standard of intent applied to the determination of credible threats adds a layer of difficulty at a time when it needs to be easier rather than harder to enforce the law against credible threats. Finally, the focus on the intentions of the perpetrators diverts attention from the social reality of those who are being victimized. Sandra J. Badin, coauthor of an amicus brief to the Elonis case by the National Network to End Domestic Violence, emphasizes that "the harms caused by threats of violence don't depend on the speaker's private intentions for communicating his threatening statements."[18] In an ironic note that lends credence to the assessment by Elonis's ex-wife for his propensity for violence, he was recently charged (*after* serving his prison sentence for threatening his ex-wife) with domestic-violence-related simple assault and harassment after hitting his girlfriend's mother in the head when she attempted to get him to leave her home.[19]

Although the ruling in this case was perhaps a step backward, nevertheless, implementing changes in laws and jurisprudence that would facilitate better and more streamlined enforcement of laws against credible threats would be a significant step toward undermining the climate of fear and uncertainty about personal safety that gives hate speech its additional power.

Increase Training for Law Enforcement

Increasing enforcement of the law against true threats will require special training of law enforcement, including the police and the FBI. As it stands now, law enforcement has been, for the most part, unresponsive and ill-equipped to respond adequately to gendertrolling attacks against women. Creasy emphasized the need for law enforcement to take online threats more seriously:

> Of course it's distressing to receive these threats. I was told my attacker would fuck my dead corpse—it's grim. . . . I want the police and other services to be able to understand the impact of these messages. I don't want them to tell me how to learn to cope—I want to hear they are doing something about it.[20]

Wu concurs and adds that law enforcement should be provided the tools it needs to enforce laws against online threats:

> [Wu's harasser is] still tweeting threats at me, and by doing nothing—law enforcement [is] enabling it. The long term solution is to make sure law enforcement has the tools it needs to prosecute online harassment. . . . This is going to require funding, it's going to require laws be [passed] that clearly outline whose responsibility it is to respond to these threats.[21]

Wu went on to detail that, despite the fact that the threats against her were detailed and credible, the police were mostly unresponsive:

> [The people who are threatening Wu online are] saying who, what, where, why, when. . . . They said I was going to be on the front page of your site when they murdered me.
>
> I had someone last week [who] made a video talking about how they're going to murder me. . . . This is not just, "I'm going to kill Brianna," this is like a multi-minute rant about why they want to murder me, how. Their face is visible in the video. I have their name and testimony from the people who know them and how unbalanced they are. This person lives 15 minutes from my house.
>
> This is what I want to emphasize for you—as much as you can have something going for you with death threats, I do. . . I have a very high profile case. There's so much media attention. I have the ear of the police. They have every reason to want to solve this crime, but at the same time nothing has happened, even giving them as much as information as I have.[22]

Journalist Anna Merlan, who also attempted to contact the police regarding her own online harassment, explained that "there are pretty good harassment and stalking laws on the books in most states that could be used to prosecute people who make clear threats online. But something about the online environment makes police lose interest."[23] She adds that "in practice, it's been hard for cops and courts to separate what constitutes a true threat online from what's protected as free speech."[24] Merlan also expresses frustration with the fact that many law enforcement personnel are not familiar enough with online environments in order to understand how online harassment and threats function: "We've heard from many women that local police are often well-intentioned and wanted to be helpful, but [they] may not even know what Twitter . . . is never mind the power it can have and the real effects it can have on someone's life and feelings of safety and ability make money."[25] According to Merlan, "Not a single violent threat made against Wu, Anita Sarkeesian or Zoe Quinn has result[ed] in an actual, prosecuted criminal case."[26]

Katherine Clark agrees that it is very difficult to get law enforcement to take online threats seriously and adds that the situation reminds her, as a former prosecutor, of "what we would see 20 years ago around domestic violence."[27]

Independent video game developer Zoe Quinn weighs in the frustrations of trying to get law enforcement to take online threats seriously:

> Think [Gamergate] is hard to explain to a friend? Try a legal system that doesn't really understand what the Internet is yet—it's like trying to push

cooked pasta through the eye of a needle. Try explaining shit like 4chan to an officer who types with henpeck hands and getting handed a police report that makes you feel like praying the abuse away may be more effective. Law enforcement is prepared for familiar things like "here is a death threat, here is someone violating a restraining order, here's where they openly discuss wanting to rape me", but trying to convey how things work online is frustrating.[28]

Merlan notes, however, that there have been several instances of law enforcement taking online threats very seriously—when the threats were aimed at the police. She notes that the FBI arrested Jeremiah Perez for a YouTube comment he posted that said, "WE VETERANS WILL KILL RETIRED HELPLESS COPS." Merlan reports that, within days of Perez making the threat, "the FBI contacted Perez's Internet service provider, started physically surveilling his house, ran his license plates, pulled his military records, executed a search warrant, and arrested him."[29] She also recounts a case of local police reacting quickly when they became aware of online threats against them. When Brooklyn resident Jose Maldonado posted "Might just go out and kill two cops myself!!!" on his Facebook page, he was tracked down and arrested by the New York police the same day.[30]

Increasing enforcement of the laws against credible online threats will require special training of law enforcement, including the police and the FBI as well as judges. It is important to educate law enforcement that advising women to leave the Internet is not useful, especially because of the Internet's centrality in performing many jobs and because social media is not only for "fun," but is also often used in professional activities. Training should also include information as to how social media sites work and the hazards incurred by doxxing and other "real-life" incursions of online activities, as well as how to track anonymous harassers by obtaining their IP addresses. Comprehensive training on these and other topics related to enforcing the law against true threats online will be essential if women are to be able to avail themselves of the full protection of current laws.

PROPOSED LEGAL REMEDIES

In addition to enforcing already-existing laws, scholars have recommended implementing various legal remedies to attempt to address gendertrolling and other abusive and harassing speech on the Internet. Existing state and federal laws have not fully kept up with changing technologies. For example, some harassment laws require that threats must be made directly from the harasser to the targeted person, as in an email; there is no provision in most laws for threats that are posted to third-party websites such as 4chan or 8chan. In addition, stalking laws are often outmoded in that they do not account for the ways that Internet harassment allows for wide dissemination of content, that harassers can be physically far removed from their targets and can remain anonymous, that harassers can impersonate a victim in order to create additional harm, and that harassers are often successful in egging others on to contribute substantially to harassment campaigns.[31]

What follow are some of the suggestions that legal scholars have made to amend the law in order to deal more effectively with online harassment, abuse, and threats.

Make Cyberharassment a Federal Crime

Telecommunications attorney Sarah Jameson argues that the federal government should and can legally recognize and define cyberharassment and that to do so would not violate privacy or free speech laws. She advocates defining cyberharassment as using "a computer network form of electronic communication to target a specific person for no defined purpose, and through the use of words or language, aim to harass, annoy, embarrass, abuse, threaten, induce fear of bodily harm, or a combination thereof, in a victim."[32] She advocates criminalizing cyberharassment, making it legal to trace IP addresses of anonymous parties who use the Internet to cyberharass, and making it a federal crime when a person goads another person to commit suicide as a direct result of cyberharassment.[33]

Amend the Communications Decency Act

An important law governing the Internet is the Communications Decency Act (CDA), which was passed in 1996. A key provision of this law, Section 230, states that "no providers or users of an interactive computer service shall be treated as the publisher or speaker of any information provided by another information content provider."[34] This section establishes that online content providers or those who operate websites or blogs cannot be held liable for user-generated content, such as comments or videos that are posted on the websites or blogs. Courts have ruled that this immunity holds for cases where an online content provider fails to remove content, even if the provider knows that the content is defamatory or invades the privacy of others.

Daniel J. Solove, a legal scholar on communication privacy law, suggests that, rather than providing for complete immunity for online content providers, Section 230 of the CDA should be modified in order to provide notice-and-takedown remedies, so that content that violates the law, such as content that is defamatory or invades privacy, must be taken down within a reasonable time period after notification to the online content provider.[35] In order to inhibit people from making false notice-and-takedown claims to extort money or otherwise harass people, Solove also recommends that penalties be imposed for those who abuse the notice-and-takedown provisions. He also advises that the damages awarded for defamation and invasion of privacy should be limited so as not to encourage abuse of this remedy.

Saul Levmore, a legal scholar who writes on Internet anonymity, however, does not see a notice-and-takedown policy as a good remedy because he says it is prohibitively expensive and does not help those who are not immediately aware that defamatory content about them has been posted.[36]

Amend the Federal Cyberstalking Statute

The Federal Cyberstalking Statute (18 U.S.C. § 2261A) makes it a felony to "use any 'interactive computer service or electronic communication service or electronic communication system' to engage in a 'course of conduct' with intent to harass or intimidate another person."[37] This statute includes penalties for placing "the other person in reasonable fear of serious bodily injury or death" or for causing "a reasonable person to 'suffer substantial emotional distress.'"[38] Citron points out that this statute is not useful for attacks that have the characteristics of gendertrolling because it does not take into account the cumulative actions of a cybermob on a targeted woman and is instead written with the acts of individual stalkers in mind.[39] Law professor Naomi Harlin Goodno also notes that this "statute does not squarely deal with situations where the cyberstalker pretends to be a victim and encourages third parties to innocently harass the victim."[40] Citron advocates that one way to strengthen this statute would be to include a takedown remedy so that if a court determines that content is constitutionally unprotected speech, such as a true threat, the court could order that the online content provider must remove the content.[41] Goodno recommends that existing doctrines, such as this statute, should be applied "liberally." She also advocates "recognizing new applications of firmly rooted doctrines" due to the unique characteristics of the Internet such as the permanence of online speech and its ability to reach an extremely wide audiences.[42]

Expand the Appropriation Tort

Solove also advocates expanding one of U.S. privacy torts, the appropriation tort, which already prohibits the use of someone else's name or likeness for financial gain.[43] The appropriation tort currently does not apply when a person's images appear on social networking sites, which means it cannot be used on issues related to the Internet. Solove concludes that the appropriation tort should be expanded to cover the Internet, but to apply only when a person's images or personal information are used in matters that are not of public concern.[44]

Use Civil Rights Law

Several commentators recommend adapting or expanding already-existing civil rights laws to provide legal protections against the new kinds of harassment and threats that are happening online. Citron sees the current state of online harassment and abuse as civil rights violations against women because "[s]o much of online harassment of women, without question, is because they are women"[45] and because such abuse and harassment "discourages [women] from writing and earning a living online. It interferes with their professional lives. It raises their vulnerability to offline sexual violence. It brands them as incompetent workers and inferior sexual objects. The harassment causes considerable emotional distress."[46] She recommends using a comprehensive legal approach that includes "traditional criminal prosecution, tort remedies, and civil rights actions," as well as specific remedies derived from civil rights law to address the problem.[47]

Citron suggests using the Civil Rights Act of 1968 (18 U.S.C. § 245), which states that "whoever... by force or threat of force willfully injures, intimidates or interferes with, or attempts to injure, intimidate or interfere with any person ... in order to intimidate such person ... from ... applying for or enjoying employment" shall be subject to a fine and imprisonment.[48] Citron also recommends using the Violence Against Women Act (VAWA), suggesting that "Congress could amend VAWA pursuant to its power to regulate an instrumentality of interstate commerce—the Internet—to punish anonymous cyber mobs that threaten individuals because of their gender or sexual orientation."[49] Other civil rights laws that Citron suggests could be useful in addressing the harms of online harassment and abuse of women or other targeted groups include Title VII of the Civil Rights Act of 1964 and the Ku Klux Klan Act of 1871.[50]

PROPOSED CHANGES TO ONLINE POLICIES

Anonymity

The Supreme Court has ruled that the First Amendment protects the right to speak anonymously, ruling that "anonymity is a shield from the tyranny of the majority."[51] However, some commentators are calling for restricting or eliminating entirely anonymity on the Internet. One legal scholar, Martha Nussbaum, sees anonymity as an inducement to online harassment:

> The anonymity of the AutoAdmit writers is a major source of their freedom to create for themselves a shame-free zone in which they can inflict shame on others: so my analysis suggests the importance of requiring identification as a condition of posting.[52]

It may well be the case that people are more willing to say or do socially unacceptable things if they have the cover of anonymity and are therefore less likely to be held to account for their actions. A recent study found that 44 percent of nonanonymous commenters versus only 15 percent of anonymous commenters posted civil comments on online news articles. The study reported that, of the 137 largest U.S. newspapers surveyed, nearly half no longer allow anonymous comments online.[53] The study's author concluded, "In short, when anonymity was removed, civility prevailed."[54] Levmore also notes that offline, hard-copy newspapers, except in special cases, do not publish articles or letters by anonymous authors.[55]

However, feminist writer, media critic, and activist Soraya Chemaly says she does not see anonymity as a primary contributor to online abuse and harassment:

> Anonymity is not the major driver of online harassment. The worst threats I've gotten have not been from anonymous people. They've been from people perfectly comfortable using their faces and names. Anonymity definitely frees some people to speak abusively. It's not really the cause of the abuse. I would argue that it is more the symptom of an overall abusive culture. Anonymity is vitally important for so many people who cannot speak freely.[56]

Most people agree that there are benefits to online anonymity that outweigh the costs of disallowing it. For example, domestic violence and sexual assault survivors may need anonymity in order to be able to freely participate in online life or to seek support. LGBT teenagers who are not able to be "out" to their parents or peers may need to be able to post anonymously in online support groups in order to participate. The same is true for people with medical conditions who may want to seek support from online forums without their colleagues or other people in their social or family circles being privy to their medical information or symptoms. Finally, political dissidents, especially those who live in countries where freedom of speech is sharply curtailed, need the cover of anonymity in order to express their political views online. Even Facebook, which has had a real-name policy in the past, is relenting on the policy, allowing users to have anonymous profiles on some new applications it is developing.[57]

Levmore sums up the benefit of anonymous communications: "The great promise of anonymity is that important information or viewpoints might be chilled if authors know they will be identified."[58] In addition, Levmore believes that not allowing anonymity is an unrealistic option for the Internet, if for no other reason than because it would be prohibitive in terms of the costs required to enforce such a policy.[59] He suggests instead that there may be an intermediate accommodation between prohibiting anonymity entirely and allowing complete anonymity, for example, requiring that the IP addresses of people who are accused of committing online harassment be made available to complainants in a legal action. Others have suggested that law enforcement should be empowered to have legal authority to access the IP addresses and identifying information of people against whom a claim of online harassment or abuse has been made. These measures are referred to as "traceable anonymity."

Levmore also recommends that, in order to discourage frivolous or harassing legal actions or actions filed merely to discover the identity of an anonymous poster, complainants be required to "overcome some modest hurdle."[60] Citron agrees that requirements for using real names is "too costly to self-expression,"[61] but also advocates that anonymity should be lifted for "speech that amounts to true threats, defamation, speech integral to criminal conduct, nonconsensual disclosure of sexually explicit images, and cruelty amounting to intentional inflection of emotional distress on purely private matters."[62]

Comment Moderation

Comment moderation is another contentious topic with regard to online forums. Many women who have been the targets of gendertrolling campaigns advocate moderating comments to online articles and posts. Chemaly says that she believes that online comments should be considered part of the content of a site.[63] Blogger Miri Mogilevsky advocates moderating comments and cites the example of the website of the magazine *Popular Science*, where comments were disabled on nearly all their articles.[64] The magazine found that there was bitter contention and trolling to such a degree that they felt it was detrimental to their readers' comprehension of the material they were posting. Their argument for shutting down comments was that "even a fractious minority wields enough power to skew a reader's perception of a story."[65]

Performer, editor, and contributor to Jezebel Lindy West (whose story is recounted in Chapter 2, Section 2) argues that moderating comments creates an elevated atmosphere of discussion and debate. She cites as an example a website she frequents that has moderated comments, saying "reading that website feels like a breath of fresh air because the comments are full of smart, happy, interesting people saying valuable things instead of garbage."[66] She explains, however, that when she suggests moderating the comments at other websites for which she writes, she is frequently told something to the effect of "you can't just start banning commenters because then no one will come to the website, and the website will die and you'll be fired."[67]

One drawback of comment moderation is the monetary cost to online content providers. As it stands now, online content hosts such as Tumblr, Facebook, Google, and Twitter already employ large numbers of people, most of whom are located overseas in countries where labor costs are low, to scrub their sites of offensive and illegal images.[68]

ONLINE CONTENT PROVIDERS

Among many people who are grappling with the problem of online abuse, the consensus seems to be that online content providers, especially social media platforms such as Twitter and Facebook, can do a lot to improve the policies that inform their platforms. Lindy West describes her frustration with social media providers: "It sucks to have to monitor my comments myself. It would be nice to have some institutional support.... There's no way that it's impossible for Facebook or Twitter to just have rules. I don't understand why that's so dangerous. I am not saying it would be easy to implement and figure out, but I don't think it's impossible."[69] Writer and contributor to the *Daily Beast* Samantha Allen also expresses a sense that online content providers need to make changes:

> If it seems like all we can do is hack at the branches of this problem rather than its roots, maybe it's because we're too focused on the people who use technologies rather than the technologies themselves. In other words, if we accept sexism as the more or less inevitable feature of our social world that it seems to be, efforts to combat Internet harassment would more properly be aimed at publishing platforms and social media services themselves rather than their users.[70]

Twitter

Twitter, for example, has been slow to make attempts to adapt to the abuse and harassment that takes place on its platform. Twitter has in the past defended its format as one that honors its strong commitment to free speech, and it cites the examples of the Arab Spring and the mass protests in Turkey in 2013, which were able to take advantage of Twitter's unique environment to advance political change in places where it might otherwise not have been possible.[71] However, culture blogger and notable *Jeopardy!* champion Arthur Chu points out that Twitter also has features that make it a unique haven for harassers, in particular Gamergaters:

> It's telling that [Gamergaters] were chased out of Reddit, chased out of 4chan, chased out of comments sections and forums—but they seized on Twitter as the perfect tool for getting out their message, because blasting Twitter with noise is very easy. Twitter is almost designed to facilitate large mobs of anonymous people harassing high-profile targets—the ability for you to talk smack directly to a celebrity you don't like is a huge part of Twitter's appeal that Twitter won't admit to.[72]

Many people have also complained of the lengthy process for registering a complaint of abuse or harassment. Caitlin Moran explained that it was unwieldy and cumbersome to use Twitter's multi-question forms when "on a big troll day, it can be 50 violent/rape messages an hour."[73] Another common criticism is that Twitter has not implemented restrictions on users who create multiple accounts. Those who use the social media platform for the sole purpose of harassing others often create multiple accounts as a way of continuing to harass a person who has blocked them on one account; it is much like a "never-ending game of whack-a-mole"[74] as the harasser keeps resurfacing in new Twitter accounts. Finally, Twitter had a long-standing policy of barring anyone who is not the actual target of abusive or harassing tweets, that is, users who only witness abuse and harassment, from reporting the tweets.

Twitter's advice to those who were dealing with harassing tweets has been either not to respond in the hopes that the harasser would lose interest, to unfollow or block the harassing person's account, and, if the abuse was extreme, to call the police. Twitter was only willing to ban offending users if they issued "direct, specific threats of violence against others."[75]

However, after Caroline Criado-Perez, along with many other women, were sent abusive tweets and bomb threats via Twitter in April 2013, an online petition was created to ask Twitter to create tools to deal with abusive tweets more efficiently.[76] In the fall of 2013, in response to the public outcry, Twitter responded by creating a "report abuse" button, which makes reporting abusive tweets more automatic.

Two incidents appear to have spurred Twitter to make additional changes to its platform. The first incident occurred when Zelda Williams, daughter of actor Robin Williams, who took his own life in August 2014, received such virulent and horrific harassment via Twitter shortly after her father's death that she abandoned the social media platform. Thereafter, Twitter partnered with Women, Action, and the Media, a nonprofit organization dedicated to gender justice in media, to investigate abuse and harassment of women on its platform. As a result, in early December 2014, Twitter improved its tools for reporting abuse, including adding the ability to report abusive and harassing tweets on behalf of others.[77]

The second incident occurred in late January 2015, when Lindy West relayed her story of being harassed online in a compelling episode of the popular podcast *This American Life*, which brought more mainstream attention to the topic of women being harassed online. On February 2, 2015, Twitter CEO Dick Costolo issued a statement saying he took "full responsibility for not being more aggressive" regarding harassment and abuse on Twitter and announced that Twitter would do more to improve how it deals with those who use the platform for the sole purpose of harassing others. Costolo announced, "We're going to start kicking these people off right and left and making sure that when they issue their ridiculous attacks, nobody hears them."[78] Shortly thereafter, Twitter also announced its decision to hire more staff for its moderation team.[79]

Despite its recent changes, many people feel that Twitter could still improve its platform. Some common recommendations from those who have been attacked on Twitter include placing restrictions on the creation of multiple accounts within a certain time frame and adding the ability to report multiple people at once, since harassers often mob a target so that reporting each one individually is time-consuming. *Slate* contributor and freelance writer Amanda Hess advocates prioritizing reports of threats over reports of spam and then following up with users about the outcome of their reports.[80] Developer and designer Danilo Campos recommends creating options that allow for blocking all users whose accounts are less than 30 days old, blocking new users whose "@" replies contain words specified by the blocker, and blocking anyone who has been blocked by more than a specified number of people whom the user is following.[81]

There is some danger of that these safeguards could be used against those who are being harassed. Certainly harassers can just as easily falsely report or flag Twitter accounts as abusive as an additional way to harass the account owner. In fact, Lindy West reports that gendertrolls have turned the system against her:

> Even if we did get better systems in place for Facebook, Twitter, and Youtube for reporting abuse, those systems could just as easily be used against people who are being victimized on those systems. When that rape joke thing was going on, trolls made a fake Facebook profile for me, and then my genuine

account ended up getting shut down because all of the trolls reported my genuine account as fake. It's unbelievably frustrating.[82]

This kind of thing may, however, be an inevitable side effect of providing remedies to people who are victimized, in the same way that domestic violence laws have been used by shrewd abusers who, claiming they are the victims, request protective orders against the people they are abusing. Most women who have been gendertrolled agree that better systems should be implemented even at the risk that they will, on occasion, be used against them.

Some people have been devising their own ways to deal with harassment on Twitter by creating applications that block groups of people who have been determined to send harassing or abusive tweets. Some of these blocking applications include BlockTogether, which hides messages from new or sparsely followed accounts; BlockBot, a three-tiered list of Twitter users that other Twitter users can choose to block; and Flaminga, which allows Twitter users to create secret lists that mute abusive and harassing users as well as to create filters that mute a specific user and all of their followers, which is especially useful in pile-on attacks.

One drawback with these blocking applications is that, on occasion, because abusiveness and harassment may be in the eye of the beholder, they have been used to block people who hold differing political opinions rather than for being abusive or harassing. For example, Caroline Criado-Perez, whose story of horrific gendertrolling is recounted in Section 3 of Chapter 2, and British journalist and deputy editor of the *New Statesman* Helen Lewis are now on one of BlockBot's proscribed lists.[83] It is ironic indeed that these two are now on Blockbot's list, as it was the publicity surrounding Criado-Perez's gendertrolling campaign that led to Twitter adopting its "report abuse" button, and Lewis is the author of the so-called Lewis's law, which originated in a tweet she sent that said, "The comments on any article about feminism justify feminism."

Facebook

Facebook is another social media platform that has had to grapple with online abuse and harassment. Although its terms of service have been lauded as exemplary because they include language about not allowing bullying, harassment, or hate speech, Chemaly says that the problem is with its enforcement decisions, describing the "applications of their terms of service [as] normatively male biased."[84] Chemaly describes Facebook as having had "implicit biases" in the way it has treated gender-based crimes such as rape, domestic violence, and stalking. As a result, according to Chemaly, Facebook pages that depicted, glorified, and promoted rape and domestic violence were frequently determined by Facebook moderators to be "controversial humor" and were therefore left up, although they were repeatedly reported as violating Facebook's terms of service. On the other hand, images of women breastfeeding or women who were engaged in public protests that used nudity as a tactic, for example, the Russian feminist group Femen, were often taken down by Facebook.[85]

In response to these problems, a Facebook Rape Campaign, #FBRape, was launched by Chemaly, Jaclyn Friedman, executive director of Women, Action, and the Media, and Laura Bates, founder of the Everyday Sexism Project, in early May 2013. The campaign, which generated more than 50,000 tweets, more than 4,500 emails, and a Change.org petition with over 222,000 signatures, urged Facebook to change many of its policies with regard to which content it deemed worthy of taking down and which content it decided was in accordance with its terms of service.[86] In May 2013, the campaign published an open letter to Facebook, signed by more than 50 organizations, demanding that it take action on "pages and images that explicitly condone or encourage rape or domestic violence or suggest that they are something to laugh or boast about."[87] The letter called on Facebook to recognize content that trivializes or glorifies violence against girls and women as falling into their category of prohibited hate speech; to train moderators to understand, especially given the context of offline violence against women, how online harassment affects women and men differently; and to recognize and remove such content.

The campaign also targeted companies that advertise with Facebook by showing them screenshots of their ads appearing on pages with highly offensive and abusive content. Nissan soon pulled its advertising from Facebook, and many other companies followed suit.[88] As a result, 15 advertisers pulled out of Facebook. On May 28, 2013, Facebook issued a public statement saying "it has become clear that our systems to identify and remove hate speech have failed to work as effectively as we would like. . . . We need to do better—and we will."[89] In the end, Chemaly reported that Facebook responded to their demands and implemented them, adding that "Facebook has done that very well."[90]

Although Facebook has shown dedication to making important changes, activists report that its performance could still be improved by notifying users regarding the outcome of their complaints and ensuring that reports of abuse such as harassment, nude images, and bullying are prioritized over reports of spam.[91] Citron also advocates that Facebook should make policy changes, including notifying and explaining to complainants the basis of their decisions and allowing an appeal process[92] and hiring more employees to deal with complaints, since its 1.3 billion users necessitate a sizeable number of staff to deal with these issues.

Diversify the Workforce at Internet/Technology Companies

A final recommendation for change is that online content providers would be more responsive to the diversity of people who frequent the sites by ensuring that their workforce is more representative of the larger population, especially in terms of race and gender diversity. Twitter's workforce is 70 percent male, its technology employees are 90 percent male,[93] and only 3 percent of Twitter's U.S. employees are Hispanic or Latino and 2 percent are black.[94] Facebook employees consist of about 31 percent women,[95] while only 15 percent of their technology employees are women and 1 percent are black.[96] Google's workforce is 30 percent women,[97] with women representing 17 percent and black people only 1 percent of its technology employees.[98] Only 6 percent of the chief executives of the top 100 technology companies are women,[99] and fewer than 1 percent of the founders of Silicon Valley companies are black.[100] Filmmaker and author Astra Taylor reports that Instagram didn't hire its first female engineer until 2013, although it was founded in 2010.[101] According to the *Boston Globe*, women are only 11 percent of game designers and 3 percent of programmers.[102]

Brianna Wu explains that "women make up half of all gamers, yet we make up only a fraction of this industry. . . . Women hold a shockingly disproportionate number of high level positions in game studios, game publishers and particularly in leadership roles."[103] She calls "upon the entire industry to examine its hiring practices at all levels."[104] Taylor believes that many women in technology are driven out by sexism, where women's contributions are routinely dismissed and undermined.

Chemaly explains the importance of incorporating diversity in technology companies:

> People really think that because these platforms are on the Internet, they are neutral and they are free. But they aren't. First of all, there's no such thing as a neutral platform. These platforms are created by people. Their architecture is designed by people, their moderation policies are written by people, and all of those people come to these processes with their own implicit biases and epistemologies. And because of the lack of diversity in tech engineering, and in the industry in general, the entire system only really reflects the life experiences and ways of knowing of an incredibly small special interest group who is like them.[105]

INDIVIDUAL RECOMMENDATIONS

Some recommendations involve suggestions as to what might be helpful to individual women who have been targeted by gendertrolling attacks as well as ways to support women who have been targeted. For those who have been targeted, Ashe Dryden, programming consultant, conference organizer, and writer, has a list of suggestions for women who are being attacked online including letting important people in the woman's life know that she is being gendertrolled, checking and adjusting her privacy settings on Facebook, blocking people on Twitter or using one of the blocking applications, asking her friends to screen her emails, and carefully documenting the abuse in case she needs to call on outside help such as law enforcement.[106]

Dryden also has advice for those who are seeking to support a woman who is being targeted with a harassment campaign. She advises, among other things, not offering suggestions as to how she could handle her harassment better, making sure it is all right with her before taking or posting her picture online, asking before posting private plans with her on social media, and asking before sharing her private contact information with anyone else such as telephone numbers, email addresses, or physical addresses.

Supportive Messages

Many people emphasize the critical importance of making efforts to show support to women who are attacked online. Atheist/skeptic blogger Amy Davis Roth endorses the power of sending positive messages, saying that "when someone sends in a [positive] email to Skepchick, it means the world to us. Say thank you, send a nice message."[107] Soraya Chemaly stays strong by focusing on the people who let her know that they are positively influenced by her writing. She says, "There are some mornings when I want to hide under my desk after I push that send message.... [But] I keep one [positive message] on my dashboard. When I get one of the terrible, obscene, slightly violent messages, I think of that person who I am talking to.[108] Ben Atherton-Zemon, spokesperson for the National Organization for Men Against Sexism, recommends writing supportive comments in the comments sections of articles and Facebook posts, sending supportive emails or tweets to the targeted woman, and reporting abusive comments and posts to the online content provider where possible.[109] Others recommend such simple acts as upvoting posts on Reddit or YouTube or "liking" Facebook content that is supportive of women who are being harassed. Lindy West proposes that "a good program would be 'Email a feminist and say hi.' [When] you see someone getting ripped to shreds online, send her an email and say I noticed what's going on with you."[110]

Support Networks

Many people advocate the importance for women who are being attacked by gendertrolls to create and reach out to support networks whenever possible. Women who have been the targets of long-standing harassment campaigns speak to how essential such a network can be to the mental health of those who are targeted. They attest that simply hearing from others who have been similarly targeted is a helpful reminder that the attacks are not personal, despite the fact that they feel intensely so. Activist Courtney Caldwell emphasizes that it is only because she has a strong support group that "the bullying tactics Open Carry Texas used to try to scare me into silence haven't worked."[111] She says her perseverance is not because of "some superhuman mental fortitude I possess. Again, it's only because of my support group. I worry about women who aren't fortunate enough to have the support that I do, and decide voicing their opinion isn't worth it."[112]

CULTURAL CHANGE

A preponderance of women who have been grappling with gendertrolling have concluded that making cultural change, that is, changing the values and ideas of those who commit the abuse and harassment, is what will ultimately be most effective. Creasy sees the cause of gendertrolling located not in some feature of social media or the Internet, but in the people who perpetrate it: "It's not Twitter, Facebook or Ask.fm that makes these people say these things: there's something in people that makes them say these sort of things."[113] British journalist Helen Lewis identifies the behavior as stemming from an underlying "deep-seated hatred towards women."[114] Actor and women's rights activist Ashley Judd concurs with Lewis in describing the motivation for the attacks she sustained for tweeting about a basketball game: "My tweet was simply the convenient delivery system for a rage toward women that lurks perpetually."[115] Nussbaum comes to a similar conclusion: "It is not enough to call the behavior . . . pathological, or the work of isolated nuts. It is rooted in American culture itself, and in one form or another, in most cultures of masculinity in the world."[116]

Although many people advocate changing values and norms, there are others who counter that advocating for such changes constitutes restrictions on free speech. In response to this claim, Chemaly says, "This isn't about censoring people, it's about changing norms for what is acceptable."[117] Lindy West eloquently articulates the importance of being mindful of words, even in an environment where free speech is permitted, by focusing on the power that words have to shape the social world: "What we say affects the world we live in. And we should make an effort to be more conscious about it because words have consequences. Words contribute to culture. Culture contributes to people's actions. These things are not separate. Words are both a reflection and a catalyst."[118]

The conclusion of many who are trying to tackle this problem is that, in order to truly effect change in gendertrolling behaviors, we need to reduce misogyny in general by changing the ideas, values, beliefs, and norms that determine how women are regarded and treated. Quinn writes about getting at the cultural systems that create the environment where online abuse toward women occurs. She concludes that the fact that these behaviors are systematic rather than unique and idiosyncratic offers hope for change:

> It's important to know that I am not special here—it's a fate I share with every other woman that is a high-profile target of online harassment. This is not a fluke or just a story of some shitty things happening to someone: this is how things work. This is a system so clearly defined it is predictive—the equation is essentially this. Feed into this machine an outspoken marginalized person with some degree of success or visibility, along with someone with a vendetta against that person, and what you get out is years of abuse and harassment directed at the marginalized individual along with galvanization & growth of communities who participate in that harassment and abuse. Some might see despair in this systematic abuse, but I see hope and opportunity. Systems are known quantities, systems can be disrupted, the variables can be tweaked and changed until they break down, if we have a decent map and try hard enough to understand how those mechanisms work.[119]

Quinn sees hope in naming and talking about the "system's existence" as key to dissecting it and to finding solutions:

> I post these updates and talk about the specific gears of this machine that I'm caught in, in the hope that it spreads. In the hope that we can talk about this and raise awareness of this system's existence, and finally do something about it. In the hopes that if the machinations of online abuse on this scale are laid bare, and actually TALKED ABOUT, the problem can get in front of enough eyes and brains to figure out what gears to stick monkey wrenches in, to finally cause it to grind to a halt instead of grinding down the people targeted by it.[120]

Although strategies for making cultural change are never clear-cut or easily identifiable, some suggestions have been proposed, including publicly speaking out about the problem and increasing social and legal sanctions against those who engage in gendertrolling campaigns.

Speak Out about the Problem

In line with Quinn's call to talk about the ways women are attacked online, many other people also advocate continually speaking out and writing about the problem as a method for effecting cultural change. Cath Elliot,

British feminist and trade union activist, says "it's imperative that women who write online continue to speak out about the abuse we're subjected to, and that we expose the Internet misogynists at every opportunity we get."[121] Brianna Wu also advocates speaking up as an effective strategy:

> First, major institutions in video games, which happen to be dominated by men, need to speak up immediately and denounce Gamergate. The dam started to break this week as Patrick Klepek of Giant Bomb broke the silence at their publication on Monday. Last week, the industry's top trade group, the Entertainment Software Association spoke out against Gamergate, saying "Threats of violence and harassment have to stop. There is no place in the video game community for personal attacks and threats."[122]

Atheist blogger Ophelia Benson concurs and asks specifically for the support of those who haven't been harassed: "I think it's really important for the people who are not affected by [online harassment], especially men, to be vocal about their objections to it."[123] Wu also stresses the importance of those who are not the direct victims of the attacks, but who are only witnesses to them, to speak out rather than remain silent:

> Some have [spoken out]. But many more have been silent. In the male-dominated video game media, many have chosen to sit by and do nothing as Gamergate picks us off, one by one. IGN [formerly Imagine Games Network, a website that focuses on video games, films, music, and other media] has not covered Gamergate. Game Informer has not covered Gamergate. Ironically, the people who most need to hear this message are not hearing it, because of an editorial choice to stay on the sidelines.[124]

Sarkeesian agrees that, in order to change norms of behavior, those who have remained on the sidelines, especially those who have prominence or power, need to be more forthright about their refusal to tolerate abuse of women:

> In terms of the immediacy of the harassment against women in gaming, I think developers and publishers and key figures in the gaming industry need to step up and say we do not accept this harassing behavior, we support women, and further outline steps that they are going to take to try to make the gaming community more inclusive and more diverse, both within their hiring practices and also with the games that they're making.[125]

Sanction Harassers

Another way to attempt changes in cultural values and norms is to increase social sanctions against those who wage gendertrolling campaigns and to institute policies of holding them accountable for their actions. Creasy is one who supports negatively sanctioning those who wage gendertrolling campaigns: "We need to be able to identify and engage with them and hold them to account for their behaviour. Because if we don't, the consequences could be quite severe."[126] Victoria McNally, writer and associate editor at the *Mary Sue*, a website for women who are interested in geek and pop culture, also urges that more effort be made toward implementing policies that sanction such behaviors:

> After all, it's very difficult to point out legitimate criticisms of Sarkeesian's analysis when so many assholes on the Internet are using those exact arguments as an excuse to call women sluts and threaten to rape them. Unless we are all committed to rooting out that kind of behavior when we see it, not just on an individual level but a systematic one, then it's going to continue to fester under the surface and irrevocably ruin the entire community.[127]

Kathy Sierra suggests creating and holding to norms of not allowing threatening or violent speech online, and especially, refraining from glorifying people who engage in harassing and threatening online behaviors and refusing to accept rationalizations or excuses for their behavior: "If you want to do something about it, do not tolerate the kind of abuse that includes threats or even suggestions of violence (especially sexual violence). Do not put these people on a pedestal. Do not let them get away with calling this 'social commentary', 'protected speech', or simply 'criticism.'"[128]

Chu also advocates distancing from and showing disapproval toward those who are targeting and harassing women. Referring to Gamergate, he says it's important to "make it clear that what they're about is unacceptable and that if they're going to continue to be about that they won't find friends or shelter in the industry."[129] Chu sees the potential end result of such a strategy as "once their reputation is shot enough, they stop winning regular victories and they start getting demoralized, people will peel off just from fatigue."[130] Citron cites an example of peer pressure working in the multiplayer online video game League of Legends, which solicits the help of its players to assist in monitoring abusive behavior, with some apparent success.[131]

Change Social Norms through Changing Laws

Many commentators see changing norms at least as important as or perhaps more important than changing laws. They also see changing laws as one way to induce cultural change and to signal to people that changes in norms and standards are taking place. Citron is among those who believe that legal change can result in changing cultural values and attitudes, writing that "education and law can help us combat destructive social attitudes."[132] Although Nussbaum believes changing laws is important, she sees cultural change as ultimately more effective: "The more general conclusion suggested by my analysis, however, is cultural rather than legal.... Changing [the culture]... requires changing pervasive cultural patterns of thinking and talking about masculinity."[133] Solove agrees that changing norms rather than just the law is essential to reducing online attacks on women: "The most effective solutions encourage norm change, and that occurs not just through the law but through increasing people's awareness of the consequences of their online speech."[134]

Feminist writer and blogger Amanda Marcotte sums up what she considers to be the long-term solution: "To fight for women's equality, and keep fighting until the idea that a woman is anything but equal to a man is a relic of the past."[135]

I have offered here but a few suggestions and recommendations for change that have been espoused by those who have been affected by or are attempting to remedy the problem of gendertrolling. There are undoubtedly many more suggestions that have been made and many more that will be made as more people become aware of and attempt to address this increasingly pervasive and virulent problem for women online. Immediate legal or technological fixes, while certainly helpful and practical, ultimately will not do much to change the motivations of gendertrolls to attack women. As we have seen, those who are bent on harassing, abusing, and threatening women seem to have endless capacities for adapting their tactics to new mediums and new technologies. Strategies that advocate for cultural change have the best hope of being effective at eradicating the motivations of those who attack women by tackling the root of the problem: misogyny.

Epilogue

they say goldfish have no memory
i guess their lives are much like mine
and the little plastic castle
is a surprise every time

—Ani DiFranco, "Little Plastic Castle"*

In this book, I have attempted to describe and name a new phenomenon, gendertrolling, which is happening to women online as misogyny has morphed to adapt to new technologies, in this case the Internet. I do not mean for this analysis of gendertrolling to be seen as a fixed phenomenon, or something that I have definitively nailed down. That is impossible, especially due to the ever-changing patterns that continually emerge on the Internet and to the demonstrated ability of misogyny to adapt to new technologies, structures, and conditions. However, I believe gendertrolling is a useful concept to identify something that is increasingly happening to women online that most people are not aware of, as well as to distinguish it from generic trolling. I look forward to many others weighing in and further refining, contributing to, and perhaps even correcting the analysis that I have presented in this book.

Perhaps more important than naming and describing gendertrolling, I am also attempting in this book to call attention to the fact that gendertrolling is not a new phenomenon that has arisen as an inevitable consequence of the Internet, but to demonstrate that it is simply a new form

---

*Song lyrics reprinted with permission from Ani DiFranco, from *Little Plastic Castle*.

of age-old misogyny. As feminists and women's rights activists continue to work to prevent the Internet from becoming a place that is hostile to women, it is important to bear in mind that this is by no means a new battle. Even the very methods suggested in the last chapter to make change are recognizably similar to those that have been employed, with varying degrees of success, to effect changes in attitudes and laws regarding other forms of misogyny, including domestic violence, rape, date rape, stalking, sexual harassment in the workplace, and street harassment.

It is doubtless the case that, even if we are able to implement laws and cultural changes that effectively diminish gendertrolling to the point that it is no longer as significant a problem, other new and creative forms of misogyny will emerge that future generations of women will have to contend with.

It's hard to say what will interrupt this tiresome and seemingly interminable process. One way I think that misogyny is able to succeed in continually morphing and adapting to new circumstances is that it surprises a new generation of women each time, who are caught off guard by not expecting it and who then have to spend their considerable time and energies describing, naming, and enacting changes for each new iteration of misogynistic behavior. Perhaps we are always, as the saying goes, fighting the last war, instead of anticipating the next new form that misogyny will take—or, at the very least, anticipating that it will, in all probability, morph to take a new form.

A place to start might be to come to expect these endlessly morphing iterations—to not be like the goldfish of Ani DiFranco's song that is continually surprised by the appearance of a little plastic castle. Perhaps if women and feminist activists were more prepared to anticipate the seemingly inevitable new iterations of misogyny, it would expedite the process of coming to recognize the commonalities each new form has with other earlier forms, which might enable women to identify and to fight them sooner, with less effort, and with more purpose. Certainly, not being aware of the history of the immense struggles that women have undertaken to secure even modest moves toward equality is something that contributes to the "little plastic castle" effect.

I am hopeful that this book makes a contribution by identifying not only gendertrolling, but the patterns that it shares in common with countless other modes of misogyny. I am therefore calling not only for increasing awareness of gendertrolling, but also for expecting, preparing, and even planning for a wide variety of new and creative forms of misogyny as it continues to adapt to the Internet, as well as to other as-of-yet unforeseen technologies that arise in the future.

Notes

CHAPTER 1

1. "I have every reason to believe that the majority of trolls on the English-speaking web are . . . white, male and somewhat privileged." From Whitney Phillips, "What an Academic Who Wrote Her Dissertation on Trolls Thinks of Violentacrez," *Atlantic*, October 15, 2012, http://www.theatlantic.com/technology/archive/2012/10/what-an-academic-who-wrote-her-dissertation-on-trolls-thinks-of-violentacrez/263631, accessed November 15, 2014.

2. "English Language & Usage Stack Exchange," October 11, 2011, English.stackexchange.com/questions/14149/trolling-billy-goats-gruff-or-fishing-reference, accessed March 21, 2015.

3. Alt.flame Google groups, July 8, 1992, https://groups.google.com/forum/#!msg/alt.flame/KuAxUGhfQDo/sSb0mRGmLUcJ, accessed March 21, 2015.

4. 4chan News, http://www.4chan.org/news, accessed March 22, 2015.

5. "How Popular Is 4chan.org?" Alexa, http://www.alexa.com/siteinfo/4chan.org, accessed March 22, 2015.

6. Jamie Dubs, "Rickroll: Part of a Series on Bait and Switch Videos," Know Your Meme, knowyourmeme.com/memes/rickroll, accessed March 21, 2015.

7. "Download More RAM," Know Your Meme, knowyourmeme.com/photos/367171-download-more-ram, accessed March 21, 2015; Download More Ram, Free, Fast, and Instant website, www.downloadmoreram.com, accessed March 21, 2015.

8. "Delete System32: Part of a Series on Trolling," Know Your Meme, knowyourmeme.com/memes/delete-system32, accessed March 21, 2015.

9. "10 Great Troll Moments in Internet History," *BuzzFeed*, September 4, 2013, http://www.buzzfeed.com/jacklinks/10-great-troll-moments-in-Internet-history#.tl3mP2NNw, accessed March 22, 2015.

10. "Let's Jam Up the NSA's Scanners," Operation Troll the NSA, trollthensa.com, accessed March 22, 2015.

11. Shell Harris, "Top 10 Internet Flame Wars," April 30, 2010, www.toptenz.net/top-10-Internet-flame-wars.php, accessed March 22, 2015.

12. Robin M. Kowalski, Susan P. Limber, and Patricia W. Agatston, *Cyberbullying: Bullying in the Digital Age*, second edition (Oxford: Wiley-Blackwell, 2012), 63.

13. Users are frequently sent to sites such as goatse.cx, which features sexually graphic imagery; lemonparty.org, which has an image of naked men engaging in sexual behavior; or bestgore.com, which has images and videos of murders, suicides, and violent accidents.

14. Steven Morris, "Internet Troll Jailed after Mocking Deaths of Teenagers," *Guardian*, September 13, 2011, http://www.theguardian.com/uk/2011/sep/13/Internet-troll-jailed-mocking-teenagers, accessed March 22, 2015; Whitney Phillips, "LOLing at Tragedy: Facebook Trolls, Memorial Pages, and Resistance to Grief Online," *First Monday* 16, no. 12 (December 5, 2011), http://firstMonday.org/ojs/index.php/fm/article/view/3168, accessed March 22, 2015.

15. Anna Merlan, "The Cops Don't Care about Violent Online Threats. What Do We Do Now?" Jezebel, January 29, 2015, http://jezebel.com/the-cops-dont-care-about-violent-online-threats-what-d-1682577343, accessed March 15, 2015.

16. Jeremy Stahl, "A Brief History of Swatting, the Criminal Hoax That Just Befell Lil Wayne," *Slate*, March 11, 2015, http://www.slate.com/blogs/the_slatest/2015/03/11/lil_wayne_swatted_a_brief_history_of_swatting_the_dangerous_Internet_hoax.html, accessed March 17, 2015.

17. Kevin Kolbye, quoted in "The Crime of 'Swatting': Fake 9–1–1 Calls Have Real Consequences," FBI website, September 3, 2013, http://www.fbi.gov/news/stories/2013/september/the-crime-of-swatting-fake-9–1–1-calls-have-real-consequences, accessed March 21, 2015.

18. Whitney Phillips, *This Is Why We Can't Have Nice Things: Mapping the Relationship between Online Trolling and Mainstream Culture* (Cambridge, MA, MIT Press, 2015), 24.

19. Claire Hardaker, quoted in Phillips, *This Is Why We Can't Have Nice Things*, 24.

20. Danielle Keats Citron, *Hate Crimes in Cyberspace* (Cambridge, MA: Harvard University Press, 2014), 52.

21. Phillips, "LOLing at Tragedy."

22. Hardaker, quoted in Phillips, *This Is Why We Can't Have Nice Things*, 25.

23. Laura Miller, "We're All Trolls Now, for Better and for Worse: How the Internet Lost Its Prankster Lulz and Found Its Outrage," *Salon*, May 9, 2015, http://www.salon.com/2015/05/09/were_all_trolls_now_how_the_Internet_lost_its_prankster_lulz_and_found_its_ideological_rage, accessed May 15, 2015.

24. Arthur Chu, quoted in John Biggs, "'The *Jeopardy!* Guy,' Talks about Gamergate and Web Harassment, *Tech Crunch*, December 1, 2014, http://techcrunch

.com/2014/12/01/arthur-chu-the-jeopardy-guy-talks-about-gamergate-and-web-harassment, accessed December 6, 2014.

25. Anonymous troll, quoted in Jamie Bartlett, "OG Internet Trolls Are Upset Their Hobby's Been Ruined," *Vice*, October 3, 2014, http://www.vice.com/read/trolls-jamie-bartlett-289, accessed March 21, 2015.

26. Maeve Duggan, "Online Harassment," Pew Research Center, October 22, 2014, http://www.pewInternet.org/2014/10/22/online-harassment, accessed December 28, 2014.

27. "WHOA Comparison Statistics, 2000–2013," Working to Halt Abuse Online, http://www.haltabuse.org/resources/stats/Cumulative2000–2013.pdf.

28. "Rape & Blackmailing MMS: Youth Booked," *Times of India*, February 27, 2015, http://timesofindia.indiatimes.com/city/indore/Rape-blackmailing-MMS-Youth-booked/articleshow/46391488.cms, accessed March 22, 2015; "Delhi Girl Allegedly Gang-Raped in Ghaziabad, Blackmailed with Video," New Delhi Television, June 6, 2013, http://www.ndtv.com/ghaziabad-news/delhi-girl-allegedly-gang-raped-in-ghaziabad-blackmailed-with-video-524573, accessed March 22, 2015; Uma Sudhir, "Girl Allegedly Raped by Boyfriend, His Friends; Accused Also Threaten to Circulate Her MMS," New Delhi Television, May 4, 2013, http://www.ndtv.com/south/girl-allegedly-raped-by-boyfriend-his-friends-accused-also-threaten-to-circulate-her-mms-521120, accessed March 22, 2015; "College Student Raped, Blackmailed," New Delhi Television, April 25, 2011, http://www.ndtv.com/jaipur-news/college-student-raped-blackmailed-453798, accessed March 22, 2015; "Young Girl Raped, Blackmailed with MMS," New Delhi Television, March 23, 2010, http://www.ndtv.com/cities/young-girl-raped-blackmailed-with-mms-413402, accessed March 22, 2015.

29. Rama Lakshmi, "Video Recordings of Gang Rapes on Rise in India in Effort to Shame, Silence the Victim," *Washington Post*, August 14, 2014, http://www.washingtonpost.com/world/video-recordings-of-gang-rapes-on-rise-in-india-in-effort-to-shame-silence-the-victim/2014/08/13/41d8be42–3360–4081–9ff0-dee2df54f629_story.html, accessed March 29, 2015.

30. Danielle Keats Citron, *Hate Crimes in Cyberspace* (Cambridge, MA: Harvard University Press, 2014), 11.

CHAPTER 2

1. Tiger Beatdown blog, November 10, 2011, tigerbeatdown.com/2011/11/10/but-how-do-you-know-its-sexist-the-mencallmethings-round-up, accessed August 10, 2014.

2. "Catch-Me-if-You-Can," anonymous troll, quoted in Greg Sandoval, "The End of Kindness: Weev and the Cult of the Angry Young Man," *Verge*, September 12, 2013, http://www.theverge.com/2013/9/12/4693710/the-end-of-kindness-weev-and-the-cult-of-the-angry-young-man, accessed August 15, 2014.

3. Tiger Beatdown blog.

4. Twitter user "Rapey1," quoted in Sandoval, "The End of Kindness."
5. "Feminista Jones," interview with author, January 11, 2015.
6. Ibid.
7. Ibid.
8. Ibid.
9. Ibid.
10. Ibid.
11. Ibid.
12. Ibid.
13. Ibid.
14. Ibid.
15. Ibid.
16. Ibid.
17. Ibid.
18. Ibid.
19. Ibid.
20. Ibid.
21. Ibid.
22. Laurie Penny, "A Woman's Opinion Is the Mini-Skirt of the Internet," *Independent*, November 4, 2011, http://www.independent.co.uk/voices/commentators/laurie-penny-a-womans-opinion-is-the-miniskirt-of-the-Internet-6256946.html, accessed August 21, 2014.
23. Dawn Foster, quoted in Helen Lewis, "'You Should Have Your Tongue Ripped Out': The Reality of Sexist Abuse Online," *New Statesman*, November 3, 2011, http://www.newstatesman.com/blogs/helen-lewis-hasteley/2011/11/comments-rape-abuse-women, accessed August 21, 2014.
24. Ben Dowell, "Website Hosting Abusive Mary Beard Comments Closes," *Guardian*, January 23, 2013, http://www.theguardian.com/media/2013/jan/23/mary-beard-website-abusive-closes, accessed January 2, 2015.
25. Janelle Asselin, "IT HAPPENED TO ME: I Received Rape Threats after Criticizing a Comic Book," XO Jane, April 24, 2014, http://www.xojane.com/it-happened-to-me/janelle-asselin-comic-book-rape-threats, accessed January 2, 2015.
26. Ashley Judd, "Forget Your Team: Your Online Violence toward Girls and Women Is What Can Kiss My Ass," *Mic*, March 19, 2015, http://mic.com/articles/113226/forget-your-team-your-online-violence-toward-girls-and-women-is-what-can-kiss-my-ass, accessed March 26, 2015.
27. Courtney Caldwell, interview with author, May 29, 2014.
28. Shauna James Ahern, "Warm Brown Rice and Grilled Vegetable Salad," Gluten Free Girl blog, August 30, 2011, http://glutenfreegirl.com/2011/08/warm-brown-rice-and-grilled-vegetable-salad, accessed December 31, 2014.
29. "Canada," quoted in Maria Streshinsky, editor, "This Is What the Harassment and Abuse of Women on the Internet Looks Like, Part II," *Pacific Standard*, January 14, 2014, http://www.psmag.com/navigation/nature-and-technology/

harassment-abuse-women-Internet-looks-like-part-ii-72768, accessed October 1, 2014.

30. Caroline Farrow, quoted in Lewis, "You Should Have Your Tongue Ripped Out."

31. Kathy Sierra, "Trouble at the Koolaid Point," Kathy Sierra's blog, October 7, 2014, http://seriouspony.com/trouble-at-the-koolaid-point, accessed October 10, 2014.

32. "Feminista Jones," interview with author, January 11, 2015.

33. Amanda Hess, quoted in "Internet Harassment Of Women: When Haters Do More Than Just Hate," *Tell Me More*, National Public Radio, January 8, 2014, http://www.npr.org/2014/01/08/260757625/Internet-harassment-of-women-when-haters-do-more-than-just-hate, accessed August 24, 2014.

34. Eleanor O'Hagan, quoted in Lewis, "You Should Have Your Tongue Ripped Out."

35. Ibid.

36. Melody Hensley, interview with author, August 15, 2014.

37. Amy Davis Roth, interview with author, May 26, 2014.

38. Danielle Keats Citron, "Civil Rights in Our Information Age," in ed. Saul Levmore and Martha C. Nussbaum, *The Offensive Internet: Privacy, Speech, and Reputation* (Cambridge, MA: Harvard University Press, 2010), 36.

39. Malorie Blackman, "Racist Abuse Will Not Stop Me Seeking More Diversity in Children's Literature," *Guardian*, August 27, 2014, http://www.theguardian.com/commentisfree/2014/aug/27/racist-abuse-diversity-in-childrens-literature?CMP=fb_gu, accessed October 10, 2014.

40. Zerlina Maxwell, quoted in Kelly Diels, "Women's Free Speech Is under Attack," *Salon*, August 13, 2013, http://www.salon.com/2013/08/13/womens_free_speech_is_under_attack, accessed November 15, 2014.

41. Zerlina Maxwell, quoted in Diels, "Women's Free Speech Is under Attack."

42. Imani Gandy, quoted in Catherine Buni and Soraya Chemaly, "The Unsafety Net: How Social Media Turned against Women," *Atlantic*, October, 9, 2014, http://www.theatlantic.com/technology/archive/2014/10/the-unsafety-net-how-social-media-turned-against-women/381261, accessed October 14, 2014.

43. Anita Sarkeesian, "Harassment, Misogyny and Silencing on YouTube," Feminist Frequency blog, June 7, 2012, www.feministfrequency.com/2012/06/harassment-misogyny-and-silencing-on-youtube, accessed October 4, 2014.

44. Mikki Kendall, quoted in "Internet Harassment of Women: When Haters Do More Than Just Hate," *Tell Me More*, National Public Radio, January 8, 2014, http://www.npr.org/2014/01/08/260757625/Internet-harassment-of-women-when-haters-do-more-than-just-hate, accessed August 24, 2014.

45. Mikki Kendall, quoted in Noah Berlatsky, "Online Harassment of Women Isn't Just a Gamer Problem," *PS Mag*, September 15, 2014, http://www.psmag.com/navigation/books-and-culture/online-harassment-women-isnt-just-gamer-problem-90518, accessed January 3, 2015, accessed November 15, 2014.

46. Robin Nelson, quoted in Barbara J. King, "A Toxic Stew: Risks to Women of Public Feminism," National Public Radio, February 26, 2015, http://www.npr.org/blogs/13.7/2015/02/26/389233371/a-toxic-stew-risks-to-women-of-public-feminism, accessed March 25, 2015.

47. Mark Melnychuk, "The Price Saskatchewan Women Pay for Speaking Up," *Leader Post*, March 23, 2015, http://www.leaderpost.com/touch/story.html?id=10909468, accessed March 25, 2015.

48. Penny, "A Woman's Opinion Is the Mini-Skirt of the Internet."

49. Mary Beard, "The Public Voice of Women," *London Review of Books*, 36, no. 6, March 20, 2014, 11–14, http://www.lrb.co.uk/v36/n06/mary-beard/the-public-voice-of-women, accessed October 10, 2014.

50. Chris Kover, "Do We Have to Worry about Someone Actually Killing or Raping a Feminist Activist?" *Vice*, September 8, 2014, http://www.vice.com/read/do-we-have-to-worry-about-someone-actually-killing-or-raping-a-feminist-activist-887, accessed October 10, 2014.

51. Dr. Nerdlove, "Ending Sexual Harassment in Geek Culture," April 18, 2014, http://www.doctornerdlove.com/2014/04/ending-sexual-harassment-geek-culture, accessed August 21, 2014.

52. Buni and Chemaly, "The Unsafety Net."

53. Tiger Beatdown blog.

54. Ibid.

55. Jenny Haniver, reporting on messages she received, on her Not in the Kitchen Anymore blog, http://www.notinthekitchenanymore.com, accessed August 10, 2014.

56. Cookies for Breakfast blog, www.breakfastcookie.tumblr.com/post/26879625651/so-a-girl-walks-into-a-comedy-club, accessed August 10, 2014.

57. Elissa Bassist, "Why Daniel Tosh's 'Rape Joke' at the Laugh Factory Wasn't Funny," *Daily Beast*, July 11, 2012, http://www.thedailybeast.com/articles/2012/07/11/why-daniel-tosh-s-rape-joke-at-the-laugh-factory-wasn-t-funny.html, accessed January 10, 2015.

58. Lindy West, interview with author, May 26, 2014.

59. Lindy West, "If Comedy Has No Lady Problem, Why Am I Getting So Many Rape Threats?" Jezebel, June 4, 2013, http://www.jezebel.com/if-comedy-has-no-lady-problem-why-am-i-getting-so-many-511214385, accessed May 30, 2014.

60. Lindy West, interview with author, May 26, 2014.

61. West, "If Comedy Has No Lady Problem, Why Am I Getting So Many Rape Threats?"

62. Lindy West, interview with author, May 26, 2014.

63. Ibid.

64. Ibid.

65. Lindy West, "A Feminist's Guide to Surviving the Internet," a talk delivered at the Women in Secularism III conference, Washington, DC, May 17, 2014.

66. Ibid.

67. Jim Norton, "I'm Disgusted by Suggestions Lindy West Should Be Raped," *XO Jane*, June 5, 2013, www.xojane.com/issues/jim-norton-lindy-west-rape-jokes, accessed May 26, 2014.

68. Lindy West, interview with author, May 26, 2014.

69. Ibid.

70. Ibid.

71. "Georgia," quoted in Streshinsky, editor, "This Is What the Harassment and Abuse of Women on the Internet Looks Like, Part IV."

72. "California," quoted in Streshinsky, editor, "This Is What the Harassment and Abuse of Women on the Internet Looks Like, Part II."

73. Ibid.

74. Jennifer Pozner, quoted in Ben Atherton-Zeman, "How Some Men Harass Women Online and What Other Men Can Do to Stop It," *Ms. Magazine* blog, January 23, 2013, http://msmagazine.com/blog/2013/01/23/how-some-men-harass-women-online-and-what-other-men-can-do-to-stop-it, accessed July 14, 2014.

75. Kate Smurthwaite, quoted in Lewis, "You Should Have Your Tongue Ripped Out."

76. Natalie Dzerins, quoted in Lewis, "You Should Have Your Tongue Ripped Out."

77. Dawn Foster, quoted in Lewis, "You Should Have Your Tongue Ripped Out."

78. Melody Hensley, interview with author, August 15, 2014.

79. Caroline Farrow, quoted in Lewis, "You Should Have Your Tongue Ripped Out."

80. Penny, "A Woman's Opinion Is the Mini-Skirt of the Internet."

81. Judd, "Forget Your Team."

82. Courtney Caldwell, interview with author, May 29, 2014.

83. Rebecca Mead, "The Troll Slayer," *New Yorker*, September 1, 2014, http://www.newyorker.com/magazine/2014/09/01/troll-slayer, accessed January 10, 2015.

84. Elizabeth Day, "Mary Beard: I Almost Didn't Feel Such Generic, Violent Misogyny Was about Me," *Guardian*, January 26, 2013, http://www.theguardian.com/books/2013/jan/26/mary-beard-question-time-internet-trolls, accessed August 21, 2014.

85. Mary Beard, "Internet Fury: Or Having Your Anatomy Dissected Online," January 27, 2013, http://www.timesonline.typepad.com/dons_life/2013/01/Internet-fury.html, accessed October 14, 2014.

86. Ophelia Benson, interview with the author, May 26, 2104.

87. "Indiana," quoted in Streshinsky, editor, "This Is What the Harassment and Abuse of Women on the Internet Looks Like, Part III."

88. "New York," quoted in Streshinsky, editor, "This Is What the Harassment and Abuse of Women on the Internet Looks Like, Part II."

89. Miri Mogilevsky, interview with author, May 27, 2014.

90. Tiger Beatdown blog.

91. Cheryl Lindsey Seelhoff, on her Womensspace blog, August 4, 2008, https://womensspace.wordpress.com/2007/08/04/blogging-while-female-warning-may-trigger/#comments, accessed March 31, 2015.

92. Adrienne Vogt, "Not Gonna Take It: Taming the Twitter Rape Trolls," *Daily Beast*, August 3, 2013, http://www.thedailybeast.com/witw/articles/2013/08/02/preventing-rape-threats-on-twitter.html.

93. Alice Philipson, "Woman Who Campaigned for Jane Austen Bank Note Received Twitter Death Threats," *Telegraph*, July 28, 2013, http://www.telegraph.co.uk/technology/10207231/Woman-who-campaigned-for-Jane-Austen-bank-note-receives-Twitter-death-threats.html, accessed October 10, 2014.

94. Ibid.

95. Elizabeth Day, "Caroline Criado-Perez: 'I Don't Know if I Had a Kind of Breakdown,'" *Guardian*, December 7, 2013, http://www.theguardian.com/society/2013/dec/08/caroline-criado-perez-jane-austen-review-2013, accessed November 4, 2014.

96. Caroline Criado-Perez, video, "Twitter Row Victim Caroline Criado-Perez: 'I Feel under Siege,'" July 30, 2013, http://www.bbc.com/news/uk-23498146, accessed December 12, 2014.

97. Caroline Criado-Perez, quoted in Helen Lewis, "John Nimmo and Isabella Sorley: A Tale of Two 'Trolls,'" *New Statesman*, January 8, 2014, http://www.newstatesman.com/media/2014/01/john-nimmo-and-isabella-sorley-tale-two-trolls, accessed December 13, 2014.

98. Diels, "Women's Free Speech Is under Attack."

99. Caroline Criado-Perez, "After the Jane Austen Announcement I Suffered Rape Threats for 48 Hours, but I'm Still Confident the Trolls Won't Win," *New Statesman*, July 27, 2013, http://www.newstatesman.com/media/2013/07/after-jane-austen-announcement-i-suffered-rape-threats-48-hours-im-still-confident-tro, accessed December 12, 2014.

100. Jennifer Cockerell, "Twitter 'Trolls' Isabella Sorley and John Nimmo Jailed for Abusing Feminist Campaigner Caroline Criado-Perez," *Independent*, January 24, 2014, http://www.independent.co.uk/news/uk/crime/twitter-trolls-isabella-sorley-and-john-nimmo-jailed-for-abusing-feminist-campaigner-caroline-criadoperez-9083829.html, accessed December 13, 2014.

101. Emily Greenhouse, "Twitter's Free-Speech Problem," *New Yorker*, August 1, 2013, http://www.newyorker.com/tech/elements/twitters-free-speech-problem, accessed September 29, 2014.

102. Paul Bracchi, "The Women-Hating Twitter Trolls Unmasked," *Daily Mail*, August 2, 2013, http://www.dailymail.co.uk/news/article-2383808/The-women-hating-Twitter-trolls-unmasked-From-respected-military-man-public-schoolboy-men-anonymously-spew-vile-abuse-online.html, accessed September 14, 2014.

103. Laura Smith-Spark, "Calls for Action as Female Journalists Get Bomb Threats on Twitter," CNN, August 2, 2013, http://edition.cnn.com/2013/08/01/world/europe/uk-twitter-threats/index.html, accessed September 14, 2014.

104. Ibid.

105. Kharunya Paramaguru, "British Female Journalists React to Bomb Threats Received Via Twitter," *Time* magazine, August 1, 2013, http://world.time.com/2013/08/01/british-female-journalists-receive-bomb-threats-via-twitter, accessed September 14, 2014.

106. Day, "Caroline Criado-Perez."

107. Jill Stark, "Twitter Criticised for Failing to Respond to Caroline Criado-Perez Rape Threats," *Sunday Age*, July 29, 2013, http://www.theage.com.au/digital-life/digital-life-news/twitter-criticised-for-failing-to-respond-to-caroline-criadoperez-rape-threats-20130729–2qu8d.html, accessed October 10, 2014.

108. Greenhouse, "Twitter's Free-Speech Problem."

109. Paul Bracchi, "The Women-Hating Twitter Trolls Unmasked," *Daily Mail*, August 2, 2013, http://www.dailymail.co.uk/news/article-2383808/The-women-hating-Twitter-trolls-unmasked-From-respected-military-man-public-schoolboy-men-anonymously-spew-vile-abuse-online.html, accessed October 19, 2014.

110. Ibid.

111. Cockerell, "Twitter 'Trolls' Isabella Sorley and John Nimmo Jailed for Abusing Feminist Campaigner Caroline Criado-Perez."

112. Criado-Perez, "After the Jane Austen Announcement I Suffered Rape Threats for 48 Hours, but I'm Still Confident the Trolls Won't Win."

113. Penny, "A Woman's Opinion Is the Mini-Skirt of the Internet."

114. Soraya Chemaly, "The Digital Safety Gap and the Online Harassment of Women," *Huffington Post*, January 28, 2013, http://www.huffingtonpost.com/soraya-chemaly/women-online-harassment_b_2567898.html, accessed January 10, 2015.

115. "New Jersey," quoted in Streshinsky, editor, "This Is What the Harassment and Abuse of Women on the Internet Looks Like, Part IV."

116. "Michigan," quoted in Streshinsky, editor, "This Is What the Harassment and Abuse of Women on the Internet Looks Like, Part II."

117. Judd, "Forget Your Team."

118. Rebecca Watson, interview by author, May 6, 2014.

119. Miri Mogilevsky, interview with author, May 27, 2014.

120. Rebecca Watson, "Facebook Says a Page about Murdering a Feminist Isn't Harassment," Skepchick blog, October 5, 2013, http://skepchick.org/2013/10/facebook-says-a-page-about-murdering-a-feminist-isnt-harassment, accessed November 17, 2014.

121. Courtney Caldwell, "The Perils of Being a Woman Online," Cult of Courtney blog, October 5, 2013, http://cultofcourtney.com/2013/10/05/the-perils-of-being-a-woman-online, accessed August 15, 2014.

122. "California," quoted in Streshinsky, editor, "This Is What the Harassment and Abuse of Women on the Internet Looks Like, Part V."

123. Kover, "Do We Have to Worry about Someone Actually Killing or Raping a Feminist Activist?"

124. Stella Creasy, quoted in Greenhouse, "Twitter's Free-Speech Problem."

125. "Virginia," quoted in Streshinsky, editor, "This Is What the Harassment and Abuse of Women on the Internet Looks Like, Part II."

126. "North Carolina," quoted in Streshinsky, editor, "This Is What the Harassment and Abuse of Women on the Internet Looks Like, Part IV."

127. "Texas," quoted in Streshinsky, editor, "This Is What the Harassment and Abuse of Women on the Internet Looks Like, Part V."

128. Amanda Hess, quoted in "Internet Harassment of Women."

129. Anita Sarkeesian, "Harassment, Misogyny and Silencing on YouTube," Feminist Frequency blog, June 7, 2012, www.feministfrequency.com/2012/06/harassment-misogyny-and-silencing-on-youtube, accessed July 12, 2014.

130. Helen Lewis, "Dear the Internet, This Is Why You Can't Have Anything Nice," *New Statesman*, June 12, 2012, www.newstatesman.com/blogs/Internet/2012/06/dear-internet-why-you-cant-have-anything-nice, accessed February 3, 2015.

131. Ken Clarke, "Internet Trolls Targeted in New Bill to Tackle Defamation Online," *Guardian*, June 12, 2013, http://www.theguardian.com/law/2012/jun/12/Internet-trolls-bill-defamation-online, accessed March 26, 2015; "Arrest Warrant Issued for Louise Mensch's Troll," *Telegraph*, June 8, 2012, http://www.telegraph.co.uk/technology/Internet/9319014/Man-convicted-of-sending-abusive-messages-to-Louise-Mensch-tells-court-his-computer-was-hacked.html, accessed March 26, 2015.

132. Anonymous troll, quoted in Jaclyn Friedman, "From the Archive: Wack Attack," *Bitch Magazine*, Spring 2008, no. 39, http://bitchmagazine.org/article/from-the-archive-wack-attack, accessed July 7, 2014.

133. Kim B., interviewed by Cheryl Lindsey Seelhoff, "Threatened into Silence," *off our backs*, 37, no. 1 (2007), 28.

134. Ibid.

135. Jezebel staff, "We Have a Rape Gif Problem and Gawker Media Won't Do Anything about It," Jezebel, August 11, 2014, http://www.jezebel.com/we-have-a-rape-gif-problem-and-gawker-media-wont-do-any-1619384265, accessed November 22, 2014.

136. Laura Hudson, "How Indifferent Corporations Help Sexist Internet Trolls Thrive," *Wired Magazine*, August 11, 2014, http://www.wired.com/2014/08/jezebel-gawker-rape-gifs, accessed September 29, 2014.

137. Cath Elliot, quoted in Lewis, "You Should Have Your Tongue Ripped Out."

138. Citron, "Civil Rights in Our Information Age," 34.

139. Kover, "Do We Have to Worry about Someone Actually Killing or Raping a Feminist Activist?"

140. Caitlin Dewey, "Rape Threats, Then No Response: What It Was Like to Be a Woman on Twitter in 2014," *Washington Post*, December 17, 2014, http://www

.washingtonpost.com/news/the-intersect/wp/2014/12/17/rape-threats-then-no-response-what-it-was-like-to-be-a-woman-on-twitter-in-2014, accessed February 11, 2015.

141. National Center for Injury Prevention and Control, Centers for Disease Control and Prevention, Atlanta, Georgia, "Executive Summary: Key Findings, Sexual Violence by Any Perpetrator," in *The National Intimate Partner and Sexual Violence Survey: 2010 Summary Report*, November 2011, based on The National Intimate Partner and Sexual Violence Survey, http://www.cdc.gov/violenceprevention/pdf/nisvs_executive_summary-a.pdf, 1, accessed March 1, 2015.

142. Kathy Sierra, "Trouble at the Koolaid Point," Kathy Sierra's blog, October 7, 2014, http://seriouspony.com/trouble-at-the-koolaid-point, accessed October 10, 2014.

143. Marcela Kunova, "Netizens Come Together against Online Harassment of Women," June 29, 2013, *Huffington Post*, http://www.huffingtonpost.co.uk/marcela-kunova/netizens-come-together-against-online-harassment-of-women_b_3666712.html, accessed October 10, 2014.

144. Amy Davis Roth, "Online Activism" panel presented at the Women in Secularism III conference, Alexandria, VA, May 16, 2014.

145. Kate Smurthwaite, quoted in Lewis, "You Should Have Your Tongue Ripped Out."

146. Dawn Foster, quote in Lewis, "You Should Have Your Tongue Ripped Out."

147. Diels, "Women's Free Speech Is under Attack."

148. Ibid.

149. "Ohio," quoted in Streshinsky, editor, "This Is What the Harassment and Abuse of Women on the Internet Looks Like, Part V."

150. Ibid.

151. Jill Filipovic, "I've Received More Rape Threats Than I Can Count. This Is a Call for Kinder Online Debate," *Guardian*, January 9, 2014, http://www.theguardian.com/commentisfree/2014/jan/09/twitter-call-for-kinder-more-humble-online-debate, accessed March 26, 2015.

152. Jill Filipovic, "Let's Be Real: Online Harassment Isn't 'Virtual' for Women," *Talking Points Memo*, January 10, 2014, http://talkingpointsmemo.com/cafe/let-s-be-real-online-harassment-isn-t-virtual-for-women, accessed May 22, 2014.

153. Jennifer Pozner, quoted in Atherton-Zeman, "How Some Men Harass Women Online and What Other Men Can Do to Stop It."

154. Lindy West, interview with author, May 26, 2014.

155. Amanda Hess, "The Pick-Up Artist Community's Predictable, Horrible Response to a Mass Murder," *Slate*, May 24, 2014, http://www.slate.com/blogs/xx_factor/2014/05/24/elliot_rodger_the_pick_up_artist_community_s_predictable_horrible_response.html, accessed December 4, 2014.

156. Kat Stoeffel, "Q&A: A Reformed Pickup Artist on Elliot Rodger's Anger," *New York Magazine*, May 30, 2014, http://nymag.com/thecut/2014/05/reformed-pickup-artist-on-rodgers-anger.html, accessed June 24, 2014.

157. Katie J. M. Baker, "The Angry Underground World of Failed Pickup Artists," Jezebel, May 2, 2012, http://jezebel.com/5906648/the-angry-underground-world-of-failed-pickup-artists, accessed January 11, 2015.

158. Allegheny County Police Superintendent Charles Moffatt, quoted in "Police: Gym Shooter 'Had a Lot of Hatred' for Women, Society," CNN, August 5, 2009, http://www.cnn.com/2009/CRIME/08/05/pennsylvania.gym.shooting/index.html?eref=onion, accessed January 12, 2015.

159. Ibid.

160. Julie Bindel, "The Montreal Massacre: Canada's Feminists Remember," Guardian, October 3, 2012, http://www.theguardian.com/world/2012/dec/03/montreal-massacre-canadas-feminists-remember, accessed January 12, 2015.

161. Ibid.

162. Tiger Beatdown blog.

163. Ibid.

164. Kevin Dobson, tweeted to Anita Sarkeesian, August 27, 2014.

165. Cheryl Lindsey Seelhoff, interview with author, May 4, 2014.

166. Ibid.

167. Ibid.

168. Ibid.

169. Ibid.

170. Ibid.

171. Ibid.

172. Ibid.

173. Ibid.

174. "2013 Online Harassment/Cyberstalking Statistics," report by Working to Halt Online Abuse, whoa.org, http://www.haltabuse.org/resources/stats/2013Statistics.pdf, accessed January 12, 2015.

175. "Washington, DC," quoted in Streshinsky, editor, "This Is What the Harassment and Abuse of Women on the Internet Looks Like, Part I."

176. Shanley Kane, "My Statement," Pastebin.com, January 20, 2015, http://pastebin.com/3jAQARCy, accessed January 21, 2015.

177. James Ahern, "Warm Brown Rice and Grilled Vegetable Salad."

178. Rebecca Watson, quoted in Kris Holt, "Misogynist Trolls Have Turned Storify into a Harassment Tool," Daily Dot, August 16, 2013, http:dailydot.com/lifestyle/elevtorgate-storify-feminist-harassment, accessed December 15, 2014.

179. Ana Mardoll, quoted in Holt, "Misogynist Trolls Have Turned Storify into a Harassment Tool."

180. Ibid.

181. Melody Hensley, quoted in Holt, "Misogynist Trolls Have Turned Storify into a Harassment Tool."

182. Rebecca Watson, quoted in Holt, "Misogynist Trolls Have Turned Storify into a Harassment Tool."

183. User @CarolineIsDead sent a tweet to Caroline Criado-Perez, quoted in Adrienne Vogt, "Not Gonna Take It: Taming the Twitter Rape Trolls," *Daily Beast*, August 3, 2013, http://www.thedailybeast.com/witw/articles/2013/08/02/preventing-rape-threats-on-twitter.html, accessed September 12, 2014.

184. Sarkeesian, "Harassment, Misogyny and Silencing on YouTube."

185. Tweeted to Anita Sarkeesian, quoted in Emily Greenhouse, "Twitter's Free-Speech Problem," *New Yorker*, August 1, 2013, http://www.newyorker.com/tech/elements/twitters-free-speech-problem, accessed November 3, 2014.

186. Anita Sarkeesian, "Harassment Via Wikipedia Vandalism," Feminist Frequency blog, June 10, 2012, http://www.feministfrequency.com/2012/06/harassment-and-misogyny-via-wikipedia, accessed July 17, 2014.

187. Lewis, "Dear the Internet, This Is Why You Can't Have Anything Nice."

188. Sarkeesian, "Harassment Via Wikipedia Vandalism."

189. Greenhouse, "Twitter's Free-Speech Problem."

190. Lewis, "Dear the Internet, This Is Why You Can't Have Anything Nice."

191. Lewis, "This Is What Online Harassment Looks Like."

192. Sarkeesian, quoted in Lewis, "This Is What Online Harassment Looks Like."

193. Helen Lewis, "Game Theory: Making Room for the Women," *New York Times*, December 25, 2012, http://artsbeat.blogs.nytimes.com/2012/12/25/game-theory-making-room-for-the-women, accessed August 23, 2014.

194. Lewis, "This Is What Online Harassment Looks Like."

195. Sarkeesian, "Harassment Via Wikipedia Vandalism."

196. Ian Miles Cheong, "Ben Spurr Makes Game Advocating Physical Violence against Anita Sarkeesian," Gameranx, July 6, 2012, http://www.gameranx.com/features/id/7810/article/ben-spurr-makes-game-advocating-physical-violence-against-anita-sarkeesian, accessed July 28, 2014.

197. Lewis, "This Is What Online Harassment Looks Like."

198. Katherine Fernandez-Blance, "Gamer Campaign against Anita Sarkeesian Catches Toronto Feminist in Crossfire," *The Star*, July 10, 2012, http://www.thestar.com/news/gta/2012/07/10/gamer_campaign_against_anita_sarkeesain_catches_toronto_feminist_in_crossfire.html, accessed August 28, 2014.

199. Colin Campbell, "Sarkeesian Driven Out of Home by Online Abuse and Death Threats," *Polygon*, August 27, 2014, www.polygon.com/2014/8/27/6075679/sarkeesian-driven-out-of-hoome-by-online-abuse-and-death-threats, accessed November 1, 2014.

200. Soraya Nadia McDonald, "Gaming Vlogger Anita Sarkeesian Is Forced from Home after Receiving Harrowing Death Threats," *Washington Post*, August 29, 2014, http://www.washingtonpost.com/news/morning-mix/wp/2014/08/29/gaming-vlogger-anita-sarkeesian-is-forced-from-home-after-receiving-harrowing-death-threats, accessed March 14, 2014.

201. Kyle Wagner, "The Future of the Culture Wars Is Here, And It's Gamergate," *Deadspin*, October 14, 2014, deadspin.com/the-future-of-the-culture-wars-is-here-and-its-gamerga-1646145844, accessed November 1, 2014.

202. Anita Sarkeesian, quoted in Brian Crecente, "FBI Working with Game Developer Association to Combat Online Harassment," *Polygon*, September 4, 2014, www.polygon.com/2014/9/6105185/fbi-game-developer-harassment, accessed November 1, 2014.

203. Anita Sarkeesian, quoted in Sean T. Collins, "Anita Sarkeesian on GamerGate: 'We Have a Problem and We're Going to Fix This,'" *Rolling Stone*, October 17, 2014, http://www.rollingstone.com/culture/features/anita-sarkeesian-gamergate-interview-20141017, accessed October 25, 2014.

204. Crecente, "FBI Working with Game Developer Association to Combat Online Harassment."

205. Matt Thorson, quoted in Keith Stuart, "Anita Sarkeesian Gets Cameo Role in TowerFall Game," *Guardian*, February 10, 2015, http://www.theguardian.com/technology/2015/feb/10/anita-sarkeesian-cameo-role-towerfall-game, accessed March 27, 2015.

206. Philipson, "Woman Who Campaigned for Jane Austen Bank Note Received Twitter Death Threats."

207. Miri Mogilevsky, interview with author, May 27, 2014.

208. Kane, "My Statement."

209. Kim B., interviewed by Cheryl Lindsey Seelhoff, "Threatened into Silence," 29.

210. Amy Davis Roth, quoted in Atherton-Zeman, "How Some Men Harass Women Online and What Other Men Can Do to Stop It."

211. S. E. Smith, "On Blogging, Threats, and Silence," Tiger Beatdown blog, October 11, 2011, http://tigerbeatdown.com/2011/10/11/on-blogging-threats-and-silence, accessed January 3, 2015.

212. Rebecca Watson, interview with author, May 6, 2014.

213. Kate Smurthwaite, quoted in Lewis, "You Should Have Your Tongue Ripped Out."

214. Kate Smurthwaite, "Sometimes It's Hard to Be a Woman...," New Internationalist blog, March 24, 2015, http://newint.org/blog/2015/03/24/social-media-hate-comments, accessed March 25, 2015.

215. Catherine Buni and Soraya Chemaly, "The Unsafety Net: How Social Media Turned against Women," *Atlantic*, October, 9, 2014, http://www.theatlantic.com/technology/archive/2014/10/the-unsafety-net-how-social-media-turned-against-women/381261, accessed February 26, 2015.

216. Melody Hensley, interview with author, August 15, 2014.

217. Tiger Beatdown blog.

218. Quoted in Katie J.M. Baker, "Woman Writes about Sexism in the Skeptic Community; Men Get Violently Upset about Their Own Feelings," Jezebel, October 25, 2012, http://jezebel.com/whats-amazing-to-me-is-that-rebecca-watson-has-claimed-459719443, accessed March 14, 2015.

219. Rebecca Watson, "Why I Don't Just Go to the Cops," Skepchick blog, October 10, 2013, http://skepchick.org/2013/10/why-i-dont-just-go-to-the-cops, accessed November 16, 2014.

220. Rebecca Watson, "It Stands to Reason, Skeptics Can Be Sexist Too," *Slate*, October 24, 2012, http://www.slate.com/articles/double_x/doublex/2012/10/sexism_in_the_skeptic_community_i_spoke_out_then_came_the_rape_threats.html, accessed November 4, 2014.

221. Rebecca Watson, "About Mythbusters, Robot Eyes, Feminism, and Jokes," YouTube video, http://www.youtube.com/watch?v=uKHwduG1Frk, accessed November 10, 2014.

222. Watson, "It Stands to Reason, Skeptics Can Be Sexist Too."

223. Watson, "Why I Don't Just Go to the Cops."

224. Rebecca Watson, interview with author, May 6, 2014.

225. Watson, "It Stands to Reason, Skeptics Can Be Sexist Too."

226. Rebecca Watson, interview with author, May 6, 2014.

227. Watson, "Why I Don't Just Go to the Cops."

228. Ibid.

229. Ibid.

230. Rebecca Watson, interview with author, May 6, 2014.

231. Ibid.

232. Ibid.

233. Ibid.

234. Kane, "My Statement."

235. "Canada," quoted in Streshinsky, editor, "This Is What the Harassment and Abuse of Women on the Internet Looks Like, Part I."

236. "Massachusetts," quoted in Streshinsky, editor, "This Is What the Harassment and Abuse of Women on the Internet Looks Like, Part III."

237. Jenny Haniver, reporting on messages she received, on her Not in the Kitchen Anymore blog, http://www.notinthekitchenanymore.com, accessed on December 28, 2014.

238. Anonymous harasser, quoted in Dr. Nerdlove, "Ending Sexual Harassment in Geek Culture," April 18, 2014, http://www.doctornerdlove.com/2014/04/ending-sexual-harassment-geek-culture, accessed on December 15, 2014.

239. Message to Kathy Sierra, quoted in "Just Say No to Death Threats, *Wired* magazine, March, 27, 2007, http://www.wired.com/2007/03/just_say_no_to_, accessed on December 7, 2014.

240. Stephen Totilo, "Another Woman in Gaming Flees Home Following Death Threats," Kotaku.com, October 11, 2014, http://kotaku.com/another-woman-in-gaming-flees-home-following-death-thre-1645280338, accessed October 21, 2014; Christopher Zumski Finke, "Why You Need to Know about a Gross Thing Called #GamerGate—And the Women Who Fight It," *Yes Magazine*, October 22, 2014, http://www.yesmagazine.org/people-power/why-you-need-to-know-about-a-gross-thing-called-gamergate, accessed October 28, 2014.

241. Christopher Zumski Finke, "Why You Need to Know about a Gross Thing Called #GamerGate—And the Women Who Fight It," *Yes Magazine*, October 22, 2014, http://www.yesmagazine.org/people-power/why-you-need-to-know-about-a-gross-thing-called-gamergate, accessed October 28, 2014; Amy Goodman

interviewing Anita Sarkeesian, "'Women Are Being Driven Offline': Feminist Anita Sarkeesian Terrorized for Critique of Video Games," Democracy Now, October 20, 2014, https://www.youtube.com/watch?v=WRinZyeugfY&feature=youtu.be, accessed October 21, 2014.

242. Greg Tito, "Exclusive: 4Chan and Quinn Respond to Gamergate Chat Logs," *Escapist*, September 7, 2014, http://www.escapistmagazine.com/news/view/137293-Exclusive-Zoe-Quinn-Posts-Chat-Logs-Debunking-GamerGate-4Chan-and-Quinn-Respond, accessed October 19, 2014.

243. Mike Pearl, "Zoe Quinn Told Us What Being Targeted by Every Troll in the World Feels Like," *Vice*, September 12, 2014, http://www.vice.com/read/we-talked-to-zoe-quinn-about-whats-next-for-the-gaming-world-999, accessed October 14, 2014.

244. T. C. Sottek, "Stop Supporting Gamergate," *Verge*, October 8, 2014, http://www.theverge.com/2014/10/8/6919179/stop-supporting-gamergate, accessed October 12, 2014.

245. Ibid.

246. Ibid.

247. Wagner, "The Future of the Culture Wars Is Here, And It's Gamergate."

248. Sottek, "Stop Supporting Gamergate."

249. Ibid.

250. Jay Hathaway, "What Is Gamergate, and Why? An Explainer for Non-Geeks," Gawker, October 10, 2014, http://gawker.com/what-is-gamergate-and-why-an-explainer-for-non-geeks-1642909080, accessed October 20, 2014.

251. Anna Merlan, "Anita Sarkeesian on Colbert: Gamergate Is 'Terrorizing Women,'" Jezebel, October 29, 2014, http://jezebel.com/anita-sarkeesian-on-colbert-gamergate-is-terrorizing-w-1652705621, accessed October 30, 2014.

252. Zoe Quinn, quoted in Victoria McNally, "A Disheartening Account of the Harassment Going On in Gaming Right Now (and How Adam Baldwin Is Involved)," Mary Sue, August 28, 2014, www.themarysue.com/video-game-harassment-zoe-quinn-anita-sarkeesian, accessed November 1, 2014.

253. Sarah Kaplan, "With #GamerGate, the Video-Game Industry's Growing Pains Go Viral," *Washington Post*, September 12, 2014, www.washingtonpost.com/news/morning-mix/wp/2014/09/12/with-gamergate-the-video-game-industrys-growing-pains-go-viral, accessed October 12, 2014.

254. Simon Parkin, "Zoe Quinn's Depression Quest," *New Yorker*, September 9, 2014, www.newyorker.com/tech/elements/zoe-quinns-depression-quest, accessed on October 30, 2014.

255. Jesse Singal, "Gaming's Summer of Rage," *Boston Globe*, September 20, 2014, www.bostonglobe.com/arts/2014/09/20/gaming-summer-rage/VNMeHYTc5ZKoBixYhz1JL/story.html, accessed October 12, 2014.

256. "GamerGate," Know Your Meme, www,knowyourmeme.com/memes/events/gamergate, accessed November 1, 2014; Ophelia Benson, "Remember, #gamergate Isn't about Attacking Women," Butterflies and Wheels blog, October 11, 2014, http://freethoughtblogs.com/butterfliesandwheels/2014/10/remember-gamergate-isnt-about-attacking-women, accessed October 14, 2014.

257. Keith Stuart, "Brianna Wu and the Human Cost of Gamergate: 'Every Woman I Know in the Industry Is Scared,'" *Guardian*, October 17, 2014, http://www.rawstory.com/rs/2014/10/brianna-wu-and-the-human-cost-of-gamergate-every-woman-i-know-in-the-industry-is-scared, accessed October 21, 2014.

258. Brianna Wu, quoted in Stephen Totilo, "Another Woman in Gaming Flees Home Following Death Threats," *Kotaku*, October 11, 2014, http://kotaku.com/another-woman-in-gaming-flees-home-following-death-thre-1645280338, accessed October 21, 2014.

259. Brianna Wu, "Rape and Death Threats Are Terrorizing Female Gamers. Why Haven't Men in Tech Spoken Out?" *Washington Post*, October 20, 2014, http://www.washingtonpost.com/posteverything/wp/2014/10/20/rape-and-death-threats-are-terrorizing-female-gamers-why-havent-men-in-tech-spoken-out, accessed October 21, 2014.

260. Stuart, "Brianna Wu and the Human Cost of Gamergate."

261. Ibid.; Totilo, "Another Woman in Gaming Flees Home Following Death Threats."

262. Totilo, "Another Woman in Gaming Flees Home Following Death Threats."

263. Wu, "Rape and Death Threats Are Terrorizing Female Gamers."

264. Zoe Quinn, quoted in Mike Pearl, "Zoe Quinn Told Us What Being Targeted by Every Troll in the World Feels Like," *Vice*, September 12, 2014, http://www.vice.com/read/we-talked-to-zoe-quinn-about-whats-next-for-the-gaming-world-999, accessed October 14, 2014.

265. Wagner, "The Future of the Culture Wars Is Here, And It's Gamergate."

266. Zoe Quinn, in Pearl, "Zoe Quinn Told Us What Being Targeted by Every Troll in the World Feels Like."

267. Ibid.

268. Wagner, "The Future of the Culture Wars Is Here, And It's Gamergate."

269. "8chan," Know Your Meme, www.knowyourmeme.com/memes/sites/8chan, accessed November 1, 2014.

270. Pearl, "Zoe Quinn Told Us What Being Targeted by Every Troll in the World Feels Like."

271. Totilo, "Another Woman in Gaming Flees Home Following Death Threats."

272. Arthur Chu, quoted in John Biggs, "'The *Jeopardy*! Guy,' Talks about Gamergate and Web Harassment, *Tech Crunch*, December 1, 2014, http://techcrunch.com/2014/12/01/arthur-chu-the-jeopardy-guy-talks-about-gamergate-and-web-harassment, accessed December 6, 2014.

273. "BioWare Writer Received Death Threats to Family," *Metro*, August 16, 2013, http://metro.co.uk/2013/08/16/bioware-writer-quits-after-death-threats-to-family-3925970, accessed November 1, 2014.

274. Sarkeesian, quoted in Collins, "Anita Sarkeesian on GamerGate."

275. Brianna Wu, "It Happened to Me: I've Been Forced Out of My Home and Am Living in Constant Fear because of Relentless Death Threats from Gamergate," *XO Jane*, October 16, 2014, http://www.xojane.com/it-happened-to-me/brianna-wu-gamergate, accessed November 8, 2014.

276. Ibid.

277. Stuart, "Brianna Wu and the Human Cost of Gamergate."
278. Wu, "Rape and Death Threats Are Terrorizing Female Gamers."
279. Lindy West, interview with author, May 26, 2014.
280. Melody Hensley, interview with author, August 15, 2014.
281. Arthur Chu, "Of Gamers, Gates, and Disco Demolition: The Roots of Reactionary Rage," *Daily Beast*, October 16, 2014, http://www.thedailybeast.com/articles/2014/10/16/of-gamers-gates-and-disco-demolition-the-roots-of-reactionary-rage.html, accessed December 6, 2014.
282. Eleanor O'Hagan, quoted in Lewis, "You Should Have Your Tongue Ripped Out."
283. Rebecca Solnit, "How Male Trolls, Harassment, Sexism, and Racism Can Dominate Women's Web Experience," *Alternet*, April 10, 2014, http://www.alternet.org/gender/disappearing-woman-and-life-Internet, accessed September 11, 2014.
284. Adria Richards, quoted in Diels, "Women's Free Speech Is under Attack."
285. "Infographic: Battle of the Sexes—How Men and Women Use the Social Web," http://www.infographicsarchive.com/social-media/infographic-battle-of-the-sexes-hoe-men-and-women-use-the-social-web, accessed September 15, 2014.
286. "Misogyny: The Sites," in *Intelligence Report*, no. 145 (Spring 2012), Southern Poverty Law Center, www.splcenter.org/get-informed/intelligence-report/browse-all-issues/2012/spring-misogyny-the-sites.
287. Rob Price, "The Web's Most Infamous Misogynist Regrets Nothing," *Daily Dot*, February 13, 2014, www.dailydot.com/lifestyle/roosh-v-mens-rights-sexism-misogyny.
288. Lindy West, interview with author, May 26, 2014.
289. Amy Davis Roth, interview with author, May 26, 2014.
290. Amy Davis Roth, "Online Activism" panel at the Women in Secularism III conference, held in Alexandria, VA, May 16, 2014.
291. Cheryl Lindsey Seelhoff, interview with author, May 4, 2014.
292. Citron, "Civil Rights in Our Information Age," 35.
293. Ibid.
294. Cheryl Lindsey Seelhoff, interview with author, May 4, 2014.
295. Citron, *Hate Crimes in Cyberspace*, 54.
296. Arthur Chu, quoted in Biggs, "'The *Jeopardy!* Guy,' Talks about Gamergate and Web Harassment."
297. "California," quoted in Streshinsky, editor, "This Is What the Harassment and Abuse of Women on the Internet Looks Like, Part II."
298. Lindy West, interview with author, May 26, 2014.
299. David Futrelle, interviewed by Chris Kover, "Do We Have to Worry about Someone Actually Killing or Raping a Feminist Activist?" *Vice*, September 8, 2014, http://www.vice.com/read/do-we-have-to-worry-about-someone-actually-killing-or-raping-a-feminist-activist-887, accessed November 27, 2014.
300. Arthur Chu, "I'm Not 'That Creepy Guy from the Internet': How Gamergate Gave the Geek Community a Bad Name," October 30, 2014, *Salon*, www

.salon.com/2014/10/30/that_creepy_guy_from_the_Internet_how_gamergate_shattered_faith_in_the_geek_community, accessed December 6, 2014.

301. Ibid.

302. Chu, quoted in Biggs, "'The *Jeopardy!* Guy,' Talks about Gamergate and Web Harassment."

303. David Futrelle, interviewed by Chris Kover, "Do We Have to Worry about Someone Actually Killing or Raping a Feminist Activist?"

304. Lindy West, interview with author, May 26, 2014.

305. Soraya Chemaly, "Online Activism" panel presented at the Women in Secularism III conference, Alexandria, VA, May 16, 2014.

CHAPTER 3

1. Lindy West, interview with author, May 26, 2014.
2. Rebecca Watson, interview with author, May 6, 2014.
3. Ibid.
4. Filipovic, "Let's Be Real."
5. Ibid.
6. Amy Davis Roth, "A Woman's Room Online," Skepchick blog, September 4, 2014, http://skepchick.org/2014/09/a-womans-room-online, accessed November 14, 2014.
7. "California," quoted in Streshinsky, editor, "This Is What the Harassment and Abuse of Women on the Internet Looks Like, Part V."
8. Citron, "Civil Rights in Our Information Age," 36.
9. Catherine Mayer, "I Got a Bomb Threat on Twitter. Was I Right to Report It?" *Time* magazine, August 2, 2013, http://world.time.com/2013/08/02/i-got-a-bomb-threat-on-twitter-was-i-right-to-report-it, accessed January 2, 2015.
10. Mikki Kendall, quoted in "Internet Harassment Of Women: When Haters Do More Than Just Hate," *Tell Me More*, National Public Radio, January 8, 2014, http://www.npr.org/2014/01/08/260757625/Internet-harassment-of-women-when-haters-do-more-than-just-hate, accessed August 24, 2014.
11. Smurthwaite, "Sometimes It's Hard to Be a Woman. . . ."
12. Filipovic, "Let's Be Real."
13. Ibid.
14. Day, "Caroline Criado-Perez."
15. Caroline Farrow, quoted in Lewis, "You Should Have Your Tongue Ripped Out."
16. Rosamund Urwin, quoted in Lewis, "You Should Have Your Tongue Ripped Out."
17. Kathy Sierra, quoted in Dan Fost, "The Attack on Kathy Sierra," SF Gate Blog, March 27, 2007, http://blog.sfgate.com/techchron/2007/03/27/the-attack-on-kathy-sierra, accessed October 15, 2014.
18. Citron, "Civil Rights in Our Information Age," 31.
19. Penny, "A Woman's Opinion Is the Mini-Skirt of the Internet."

20. Ashe Dryden, "Harassment," Ashe Dryden's blog, December 3, 2014, http://www.ashedryden.com/tags/harassment, accessed January 2, 2015.

21. Emily May, quoted in Atherton-Zeman, "How Some Men Harass Women Online and What Other Men Can Do to Stop It."

22. Kane, "My Statement."

23. Sarah Kendzior, "On Being a Thing," Sarah Kendzior's blog, June 7, 2014, http://sarahkendzior.com/2014/06/07/on-being-a-thing, accessed October 8, 2014.

24. "Washington," quoted in Streshinsky, editor, "This Is What the Harassment and Abuse of Women on the Internet Looks Like, Part IV."

25. "California," quoted in Streshinsky, editor, "This Is What the Harassment and Abuse of Women on the Internet Looks Like, Part II."

26. "Unknown," quoted in Streshinsky, editor, "This Is What the Harassment and Abuse of Women on the Internet Looks Like, Part V."

27. "Massachusetts," quoted in Streshinsky, editor, "This Is What the Harassment and Abuse of Women on the Internet Looks Like, Part III."

28. Jennifer McCreight, quoted in Watson, "It Stands to Reason, Skeptics Can Be Sexist Too."

29. Diels, "Women's Free Speech Is under Attack."

30. Kunova, "Netizens Come Together against Online Harassment of Women."

31. Wu, "Rape and Death Threats Are Terrorizing Female Gamers."

32. Brianna Wu, "I'm Brianna Wu, and I'm Risking My Life Standing Up to Gamergate," *Bustle*, February 11, 2015, http://www.bustle.com/articles/63466-im-brianna-wu-and-im-risking-my-life-standing-up-to-gamergate, accessed February 11, 2015.

33. Kathy Sierra, quoted in Theresa Cook, "Female Bloggers Face Threats: What Can Be Done?" *ABC News*, May 1, 2007, http://abcnews.go.com/TheLaw/story?id=3107139&page=1, accessed March 14, 2015.

34. Kathy Sierra, "Trouble at the Koolaid Point," Kathy Sierra's blog, October 7, 2014, http://seriouspony.com/trouble-at-the-koolaid-point, accessed October 10, 2014.

35. Amy Goodman interviewing Anita Sarkeesian, "'Women Are Being Driven Offline': Feminist Anita Sarkeesian Terrorized for Critique of Video Games," *Democracy Now*, October 20, 2014, https://www.youtube.com/watch?v=WRinZyeugfY&feature=youtu.be, accessed October 21, 2014.

36. Liz Ryerson, "On Right-Wing Videogame Extremism," Ellagura blog, August 22, 2014, ellaguro.blogspot.com/2014/08/on-right-wing-videogame-extremism.html, accessed November 23, 2014.

37. Lana Polansky, quoted in Ryerson, "On Right-Wing Videogame Extremism."

38. Soraya Chemaly, quoted in Diels, "Women's Free Speech Is under Attack."

39. Eleanor O'Hagan, quoted in Lewis, "You Should Have Your Tongue Ripped Out."

40. "California," quoted in Streshinsky, editor, "This Is What the Harassment and Abuse of Women on the Internet Looks Like, Part III."

41. "United States," quoted in Streshinsky, editor, "This Is What the Harassment and Abuse of Women on the Internet Looks Like, Part III."

42. "Europe," quoted in Streshinsky, editor, "This Is What the Harassment and Abuse of Women on the Internet Looks Like, Part II."

43. Dawn Foster, quoted in Lewis, "You Should Have Your Tongue Ripped Out."

44. Kate Smurthwaite, quoted in Lewis, "You Should Have Your Tongue Ripped Out."

45. Dr. Nerdlove, "Ending Sexual Harassment in Geek Culture," April 18, 2014, http://www.doctornerdlove.com/2014/04/ending-sexual-harassment-geek-culture, accessed October 8, 2014. (Italics in original.)

46. Filipovic, "Let's Be Real."

47. Dryden, "Harassment."

48. Kane, "My Statement."

49. Wu, "Rape and Death Threats Are Terrorizing Female Gamers."

50. Adi Robertson, "Trolls Drive Anita Sarkeesian Out of Her House to Prove Misogyny Doesn't Exist," *Verge*, August, 27, 2014, http://www.theverge.com/2014/8/27/6075179/anita-sarkeesian-says-she-was-driven-out-of-house-by-threats, accessed February 8, 2015.

51. Smith, "On Blogging, Threats, and Silence."

52. Diels, "Women's Free Speech Is under Attack."

53. Watson, "It Stands to Reason, Skeptics Can Be Sexist Too."

54. Kendall, quoted in "Internet Harassment of Women: When Haters Do More Than Just Hate."

CHAPTER 4

1. "Canada," quoted in Streshinsky, editor, "This Is What the Harassment and Abuse of Women on the Internet Looks Like, Part I."

2. "New York," quoted in Streshinsky, editor, "This Is What the Harassment and Abuse of Women on the Internet Looks Like, Part I."

3. "Texas," quoted in Streshinsky, editor, "This Is What the Harassment and Abuse of Women on the Internet Looks Like, Part I."

4. Anna Merlan, "The Cops Don't Care about Violent Online Threats. What Do We Do Now?" Jezebel, January 29, 2015, http://jezebel.com/the-cops-dont-care-about-violent-online-threats-what-d-1682577343, accessed March 15, 2015.

5. Amy Davis Roth, interview with author, May 26, 2014.

6. Watson, "Why I Don't Just Go to the Cops."

7. Ibid.

8. Ibid.

9. Ibid.

10. Ibid.

11. Amy Davis Roth, interview with author, May 26, 2014.

12. Ibid.

13. "Washington," quoted in Streshinsky, editor, "This Is What the Harassment and Abuse of Women on the Internet Looks Like, Part I."

14. Catherine Mayer, "I Got a Bomb Threat on Twitter. Was I Right to Report It?" *Time* magazine, August 2, 2013, http://world.time.com/2013/08/02/i-got-a-bomb-threat-on-twitter-was-i-right-to-report-it, accessed January 2, 2015.

15. Amanda Hess, quoted in "Internet Harassment of Women: When Haters Do More Than Just Hate."

16. Sierra, "Trouble at the Koolaid Point."

17. Ahern, "Warm Brown Rice and Grilled Vegetable Salad."

18. Lindy West, quoted in Adrienne Vogt, "Not Gonna Take It: Taming the Twitter Rape Trolls," *Daily Beast*, August 3, 2013, http://www.thedailybeast.com/witw/articles/2013/08/02/preventing-rape-threats-on-twitter.html, accessed October 22, 2014.

19. Iram Ramzan, "Muslim Women Must Not Be Driven Off the Net by Trolls," *Left Foot Forward*, December 28, 2013, www.leftfootforward.org/2013/12/muslim-women-Internet-trolls, accessed October 10, 2014.

20. Wu, "It Happened to Me."

21. Kane, "My Statement."

22. "California," quoted in Streshinsky, editor, "This Is What the Harassment and Abuse of Women on the Internet Looks Like, Part IV."

23. Chemaly, "The Digital Safety Gap and the Online Harassment of Women."

24. Citron, *Hate Crimes in Cyberspace*, 108.

25. Jill Filipovic, "Feministe's Next Top Troll," Feministe blog, www.feministe.us./blog/archives/tag/feministes-next-top-troll, accessed October 16, 2014.

26. Miri Mogilevsky, "Online Activism" panel presented at the Women in Secularism III conference, Alexandria, VA, May 16, 2014.

27. Rebecca Watson, "Page O' Hate," Skepchick blog, www.skepchick.org/page-o-hate, accessed November 12, 2014.

28. Anita Sarkeesian, "One Week of Harassment on Twitter," Feminist Frequency Tumblr page, January 20, 2015, http://femfreq.tumblr.com/post/109319269825/one-week-of-harassment-on-twitter, accessed January 31, 2015.

29. Lindy West, interview with author, May 26, 2014.

30. "If You Don't Have Anything Nice to Say, SAY IT IN ALL CAPS," *This American Life*, January 23, 2015, http://www.thisamericanlife.org/radio-archives/episode/545/if-you-dont-have-anything-nice-to-say-say-it-in-all-caps, accessed January 30, 2015.

31. Alanna Vagianos, "Young Men Read Mean Tweets Sent to Women," *Huffington Post*, March 26, 2015, http://www.huffingtonpost.com/2015/03/26/young-men-read-mean-tweets-chelsea-woolley_n_6946786.html?ncid=tweetlnkushpmg00000067, accessed March 31, 2015.

32. Amy Davis Roth, "A Woman's Room Online," Skepchick blog, September 4, 2014, http://skepchick.org/2014/09/a-womans-room-online, accessed October 15, 2014.

33. Ibid.

34. Amy Davis Roth, interview with author, May 26, 2014.

35. Davis Roth, "A Woman's Room Online." (Italics in original.)

CHAPTER 5

1. Amanda Marcotte, "Harassment of Women Is Nothing New—The Internet Just Makes It Easier," *Daily Beast*, January 17, 2014, http://www.thedailybeast.com/articles/2014/01/17/harassment-of-women-is-nothing-new-the-Internet-just-makes-it-easier.html, accessed January 2, 2015. (Italics in original.)

2. Ibid.

3. Dale Spender, *Women of Ideas and What Men Have Done to Them* (London: Pandora, 1992), 42.

4. Mary Astell, quoted in Spender, *Women of Ideas and What Men Have Done to Them*, 86.

5. Spender, *Women of Ideas*, 86.

6. "Sophia, a Person of Quality," quoted in Spender, *Women of Ideas and What Men Have Done to Them*, 78.

7. Penny, "A Woman's Opinion Is the Mini-Skirt of the Internet."

8. Spender, *Women of Ideas and What Men Have Done to Them*, 95. (Italics in original.)

9. "Maryland," quoted in Streshinsky, editor, "This Is What the Harassment and Abuse of Women on the Internet Looks Like, Part IV."

10. Kover, "Do We Have to Worry about Someone Actually Killing or Raping a Feminist Activist?"

11. Wu, "It Happened to Me."

12. Wu, "Rape and Death Threats Are Terrorizing Female Gamers."

13. Sierra, "Trouble at the Koolaid Point."

14. David Futrelle, interviewed by Kover, "Do We Have to Worry about Someone Actually Killing or Raping a Feminist Activist?"

15. Mary Beard, "The Public Voice of Women," *London Review of Books*, 36, no. 6 (March 20, 2014), http://www.lrb.co.uk/v36/n06/mary-beard/the-public-voice-of-women.

16. Ibid.

17. King James Bible 1 Corinthians 14:34.

18. Priscilla Mason, quoted in Barbara Miller Solomon, *In the Company of Educated Women: A History of Women and Higher Education in America* (New Haven, CT: Yale University Press, 1985), 28.

19. Solomon, *In the Company of Educated Women*, 28.

20. Jone Johnson Lewis, "Seneca Falls: Seneca Falls 1848 Women's Rights Convention," http://womenshistory.about.com/od/suffrage1848/a/seneca_falls.htm, accessed November 13, 2014.

21. Ibid.

22. Solomon, *In the Company of Educated Women*, 29.

23. Susan Douglas Franzosa, "Schooling Women in Citizenship," *Theory into Practice*, 27, no. 4 (September 1988): 278.

24. Spender, *Women of Ideas and What Men Have Done to Them*, 51.

25. Ibid., 33.

26. Cindy Tekobbe, interviewed by Ben Kieffer, "Engaging in #GamerGate: 'There Is That Fear Going into It, as a Woman,'" Iowa Public Radio, September 30, 2014, www.iowapublicradio.org/post/engaging-gamergate-there-fear-going-it-woman, accessed November 1, 2014.

27. Kane, "My Statement."

28. Eleanor O'Hagan, quoted in Lewis, "You Should Have Your Tongue Ripped Out."

29. Marcotte, "Harassment of Women Is Nothing New."

30. Anonymous blogger, quoted in Lewis, "You Should Have Your Tongue Ripped Out."

31. Kunova, "Netizens Come Together against Online Harassment of Women."

32. Melody Hensley, interview with author, August 15, 2014.

33. Lindy West, "Comedy Doesn't Belong to the A**holes Anymore," *Daily Dot*, November 10, 2014, http://www.dailydot.com/opinion/artie-lange-twitter-rant-comedy-lindy-west, accessed November 30, 2014.

34. Beard, "The Public Voice of Women."

35. Spender, *Women of Ideas and What Men Have Done to Them*, 42. (Italics in original.)

36. Eleanor O'Hagan, quoted in Lewis, "You Should Have Your Tongue Ripped Out."

37. Dawn Foster, quoted in Lewis, "You Should Have Your Tongue Ripped Out."

38. Mary Beard, quoted in Day, "Mary Beard: I Almost Didn't Feel Such Generic, Violent Misogyny Was about Me."

39. Natalie Dzerins, quoted in Lewis, "You Should Have Your Tongue Ripped Out."

40. Dawn Foster, quoted in Lewis, "You Should Have Your Tongue Ripped Out."

41. Ramzan, "Muslim Women Must Not Be Driven Off the Net by Trolls."

42. Robert Scoble, quoted in "Blog Death Threats Spark Debate," *BBC News*, March 27, 2007, news.bbc.co.uk/2/hi/technology/6499095.stm, accessed October 15, 2014.

43. David Allen Green, quoted in Lewis, "You Should Have Your Tongue Ripped Out."

44. Atherton-Zeman, "How Some Men Harass Women Online and What Other Men Can Do to Stop It."

45. John Scalzi, "The Sort of Crap I Don't Get," John Scalzi blog, August 31, 2011, http://whatever.scalzi.com/2011/08/31/the-sort-of-crap-i-dont-get, accessed December 31, 2014.

46. Ibid.

47. Miri Mogilevsky, interview with author, May 27, 2014.

48. "Feminista Jones," interview with author, January 11, 2015.

49. Astra Taylor, "How Male Trolls, Harassment, Sexism, and Racism Can Dominate Women's Web Experience," *AlterNet*, April 10, 2014, http://www.alternet.org/gender/disappearing-woman-and-life-Internet, accessed September 11, 2014.

50. Terrell Jermaine Starr, "The Unbelievable Harassment Black Women Face Daily on Twitter," *Alternet*, September 16, 2104, http://www.alternet.org/unbelievable-harassment-black-women-face-daily-twitter, accessed October 14, 2014.

51. Sydette Harry, quoted in Starr, "The Unbelievable Harassment Black Women Face Daily on Twitter."

52. Jane Fae, quoted in Lewis, "You Should Have Your Tongue Ripped Out." (Italics in original.)

53. McNally, "A Disheartening Account of the Harassment Going On in Gaming Right Now (and How Adam Baldwin Is Involved)."

54. Ibid.

55. Atherton-Zeman, "How Some Men Harass Women Online and What Other Men Can Do to Stop It."

56. Wu, "It Happened to Me."

57. Amanda Hess, quoted in "Internet Harassment of Women: When Haters Do More Than Just Hate," *Tell Me More*, NPR show, January 8, 2014, http://www.npr.org/2014/01/08/260757625/internet-harassment-of-women-when-haters-do-more-than-just-hate, accessed August 24, 2014.

CHAPTER 6

1. Citron, *Hate Crimes in Cyberspace*, 80–81.

2. Patricia Tjaden and Nancy Thoennes, "Prevalence, Incidence, and Consequences of Violence against Women: Findings from the National Violence against Women Survey," National Institute of Justice/Centers for Disease Control and Prevention, November 1998, https://www.ncjrs.gov/pdffiles/172837.pdf, accessed December 30, 2014.

3. Allen J. Beck and Paige M. Harrison, Sexual Victimization in State and Federal Prisons Reported by Inmates, 2007, Bureau of Justice Statistics Special Report, December 2007, http://www.bjs.gov/content/pub/pdf/svsfpri07.pdf, accessed December 30, 2014.

4. Cindra Ladd, "Cosby: 'Trust Me,'" *Huffington Post*, January 26, 2015, http://www.huffingtonpost.com/cindra-ladd/bill-cosby-trust-me_b_6526064.html, accessed January 30, 2015.

5. Citron, *Hate Crimes in Cyberspace*, 84.

6. Allie Myren, "Letter to the Editor: Sexual Harassment Perpetuates a System of Vulnerability," *The Badger Herald*, February 6, 2015, http://badgerherald.com/opinion/2015/02/06/letter-the-editor-sexual-harassment-perpetuates-a-system-of-vulnerability/#.VNtw4fnF9V0, accessed February 11, 2015.

7. Catharine A. MacKinnon, "Sexual Harassment: Its First Decade in Court," *Feminism Unmodified: Discourses on Life and Law* (Cambridge, MA: Harvard University Press), 106.

8. Citron, *Hate Crimes in Cyberspace*, 90.

9. Soraya Chemaly, "Online Activism" panel presented at the Women in Secularism III conference, Alexandria, VA, May 16, 2014.

10. Kathy Ewing, "Make Violence against Women a Hate Crime," Cleveland.com, August, 15, 2013, www.cleveland.com/opinion/indix.ssf/2013/08/make_violence_against_women_a.html, accessed September 4, 2014.

11. "Hate Crime Laws: The ADL Approach," Report by the Anti-Defamation League, 2012, http://adl.org/assets/pdr/combating-hate/Hate-Crimes-Law.pdf.

12. Ann Noel, "Rethinking Violence against Women as Hate Crimes," California Association of Human Relations Organizations, www.cahro.org/2011/08/rethinking-violence-against-women-as-hate-crimes, accessed September 28, 2014.

13. Tjaden and Thoennes, "Extent, Nature, and Consequences of Intimate Partner Violence: Findings from the National Violence against Women Survey."

14. MacKinnon, "Sexual Harassment: Its First Decade in Court," 104.

15. Ibid.

16. Anita Hill, quoted in David Palumbo-Liu, "Anita Hill on Clarence Thomas' Delusions: 'What You Are Calling "High-tech Lynching" Is Not How Lynching Worked Historically,'" *Salon*, February 9, 2015, http://www.salon.com/2015/02/09/a_frightening_experience_anita_hill_on_the_clarence_thomas_hearings_and_why_she_feels_more_optimistic_today/, accessed May 30, 2015.

17. MacKinnon, "Sexual Harassment: Its First Decade in Court," 104.

18. Citron, *Hate Crimes in Cyberspace*, 99.

19. Ibid., 98–99.

20. Ibid.

21. Ibid., 98.

22. Citron, quoted in Soraya Chemaly, "'Hate Crimes in Cyberspace' Author: 'Everyone Is at Risk, from Powerful Celebrities to Ordinary People,'" *Salon*, September 9, 2014, http://www.salon.com/2014/09/02/hate_crimes_in_cyberspace_author_everyone_is_at_risk_from_the_most_powerful_celebrity_to_the_ordinary_person, accessed January 1, 2015.

23. Anita Hill, quoted in David Palumbo-Liu, "Anita Hill on Clarence Thomas' Delusions."

24. Tara Culp-Ressler, "23 Years Later, Senator Who Interrogated Anita Hill Still Doesn't Understand Sexual Harassment," *Think Progress*, May 7, 2014, http://thinkprogress.org/health/2014/05/07/3435242/anita-hill-alan-simpson, accessed May 30, 2015.

25. Citron, *Hate Crimes in Cyberspace*, 102–103.

26. Citron, quoted in Chemaly, "'Hate Crimes in Cyberspace' Author."

27. Soraya Chemaly, "Why Women Get Attacked by Trolls: A New Study Unpacks the Digital Gender Safety Gap," *Salon*, October 23, 2014, http://www.salon.com/2014/10/23/why_women_get_attacked_by_trolls_a_new_study_unpacks_the_digital_gender_safety_gap, accessed October 30, 2014.

28. Arthur Chu, "The Plight of the Bitter Nerd: Why So Many Awkward, Shy Guys End up Hating Feminism," *Salon*, January 9, 2015, http://www.salon.com/2015/01/10/the_plight_of_the_bitter_nerd_why_so_many_awkward_shy_guys_end_up_hating_feminism, accessed January 10, 2015.

CHAPTER 7

1. AkaEnragedGoddess, "Revictimizing Janay Rice: She's a Gold Digger because You Don't Like Her Choices," *Daily Kos*, September 9, 2014, http://www.dailykos.com/story/2014/09/09/1328435/-Revictimizing-Janay-Rice-She-s-a-gold-digger-because-you-don-t-like-her-choices#, accessed February 8, 2015.

2. Ed Rampell, "Anita Hill Finally Tells All in Oscar-Winner's New Film," *The Progressive*, February 12, 2014, http://www.progressive.org/news/2014/02/186985/anita-hill-finally-tells-all-oscar-winners-new-film, accessed January 4, 2015.

3. Caryl Rivers, *Slick Spins and Fractured Facts: How Cultural Myths Distort the News* (New York: Columbia University Press, 1996), 107.

4. David Brock, excerpt from *Blinded by the Right: The Conscience of an Ex Conservative*, www.randomhouse.com/boldtype/0203/brock/excerpt.html, accessed November 4, 2014.

5. Jen Roesch, "How a Victim-Blaming System Excuses Rape," *Socialist Worker*, January 7, 2013, www.socialistworker.org/2013/01/07/victim-blaming-system-excuses-rape, accessed November 8, 2014.

6. "Woman in Street Harassment Video: 'I Do Not Feel Safe Right Now,'" National Public Radio, November 1, 2014, http://www.npr.org/2014/11/01/360494480/woman-in-street-harassment-video-i-do-not-feel-safe-right-now, accessed January 4, 2015.

7. Spender, *Women of Ideas and What Men Have Done to Them*, 31.

8. Ibid.

9. Christine Salek, "Rehtaeh Parsons: Nova Scotia Girl Raped, Bullied, and Commits Suicide," April 11, 2013, http://mic.com/articles/33989/

rehtaeh-parsons-nova-scotia-girl-raped-bullied-and-commits-suicide, accessed February 8, 2015.

10. "Hearings before the Senate Committee on the Judiciary on the Nomination of Clarence Thomas to Be Associate Justice of the Supreme Court of the United States, Hill, Anita F. Testimony and prepared statement," US Government Printing Office, October 11–13, 1991, 38, www.gpoaccess.gov/congress/senate/judiciary/sh102–1084pt4/41–124.pdf, accessed November 4, 2014.

11. Culp-Ressler, "23 Years Later, Senator Who Interrogated Anita Hill Still Doesn't Understand Sexual Harassment."

12. Citron, quoted in Chemaly, "'Hate Crimes in Cyberspace' Author."

13. Mathew Walberg, Liam Ford, and Clifford Ward, "Weeks before Slaying, Protection Order Denied," *Chicago Tribune*, November 20, 2012, articles.chicagotribune.com/2012–11–20/news/ct-met-darien-stabbing-1120–20121120_1_protection-order-emergency-order-domestic-violence, accessed November 23, 2014; Rheana Murray, "Mom Killed by Husband in Murder-Suicide Asked for Restraining Order 6 Days before Death," *New York Daily News*, April 29, 2012, www.nydailynews.com/news/national/mom-killed-husband-murder-suicide-asked-restraining-order-6-days-death-report-article-1.1065156, accessed November 23, 2014; "High Point Teacher Dies from Shooting Injuries," *Fox8News*, September 7, 2013, myfox8.com/2013/09/07/high-point-teacher-dies-from-shooting-injuries, accessed November 23, 2014; "Tacoma Woman Denied Protection Order Found Murdered," King5.com, January 24, 2011, www.king5.com/story/news/local/2014/07/30/12935918, accessed November 23, 2014.

14. Clayton Williams, quoted in Katie Halper, "Clayton 'Rape Victims Should Relax and Enjoy It,' Williams Is Funding TX Gov GOP Nominee Greg Abbott," *Raw Story*, October 8, 2014, www.rawstory.com/rs/2014/10/clayton-rape-victims-should-relax-and-enjoy-it-williams-is-funding-tx-gov-gop-nominee-greg-abbott, accessed November 2, 2014.

15. Todd Akin, quoted in David Weigel, "The Female Body Has Ways to Shut That Whole Thing Down," *Slate*, August 20, 2012, www.slate.com/blogs/weigel/2012/08/20/todd_akin_rape_comments.html, accessed November 2, 2014.

16. Judge Derek Johnson, quoted in Amanda Marcotte, "California Judge Claims Rape Victim 'Didn't Put Up a Fight,'" *Slate*, December 14, 2012, www.slate.com/blogs/xx_factor/2012/12/14/judge_derek_johnson_admonished_claimed_rape_victim_didn_t_put_up_a_fight.html, accessed November 2, 2014.

17. Rick Santorum, quoted in Tanya Somanader, "Santorum to Rape Victims: 'Make the Best Out of a Bad Situation,'" *Think Progress*, January 23, 2012, www.thinkprogress.org/health/2012/01/23/409242/santorum-to-rape-victims-make-the-best-out-of-a-bad-situation, accessed November 2, 2014.

18. Lawrence Lockman, quoted in Nina Liss-Schultz, "Maine Republican Has Not Apologized for Comparing Abortion to Rape," RH Reality Check, October 17, 2014, ww.rhrealitycheck.org/article/2014.10.17/maine-republican-apologized-comparing-abortion-rape, accessed November 2, 2014.

19. Vikram Dodd and Alan Travis, "Stalking Victims Claim Crime Not Taken Seriously Enough," *Guardian*, November 13, 2011, www.theguardian.com/law/2011/nov/13/stalking-not-taken-seriously, accessed October 3, 2014; Paisley Gilmour, "Stalking Victim Begged Cops for Help 120 Times before Maniac Stabbed Her Eight Times," *Mirror*, May 3, 2014, www.mirror.co.uk/news/uk-news-helen-pearson-stalking-victim-begged-3493512, accessed October 4, 2014.

20. Marjorie Korn, "Why You Should Worry about Online Stalking," *Self Magazine*, January 18, 2013, http://www.self.com/life/health/2013/01/worry-about-online-stalking, accessed December 31, 2014.

21. Gene G. Abel, Judith V. Becker, Jerry Cunningham-Rathner, Mary Mittelman, and Joanne L. Rouleau, "Multiple Paraphilic Diagnoses among Sex Offenders," *Bulletin of the American Academy of Psychiatry and the Law*, 16, no. 2 (1988): 164.

22. Rachel Gray, "Man Back in Jail on Rape Charges after Previous Peeping Tom Arrest," *Marietta Daily Journal*, April 23, 2014, http://mdjonline.com/bookmark/24978123-Man-back-in-jail-on-rape-charges-after-previous-peeping-tom-arrest, accessed March 2, 2015; Frank Heinz and Randy McIlwain, "Rape Suspect Was Linked to Peeping Tom Cases: Police," *Dallas Ft. Worth NBC*, April 10, 2013, http://www.nbcdfw.com/news/local/Rape-Suspect-May-be-Linked-to-Peeping-Tom-Cases-Police-202331951.html, accessed March 2, 2015; "Peeping Tom in Montgomery County Convicted of Rape and Sodomy," WDBJ, May 22, 2012, http://articles.wdbj7.com/2012-05-22/dna-samples_31817159, accessed March 2, 2015; Cassie Foss, "Peeping Tom Suspect Had History of Offenses Involving Children, Records Show," *Island Packet*, July 23, 2011, http://www.islandpacket.com/2011/07/23/1735506/peeping-tom-suspect-had-history.html, accessed March 2, 2015; Christine Dempsey, "Serial Rapist Linked to New Haven Case," *Hartford Courant*, December 17, 2009, http://articles.courant.com/2009-12-17/news/09121712525421_1_serial-rapist-police-briefs-raped, accessed March 2, 2015; Jamie Satterfield, "Knox Jury Finds Peeping Tom Guilty of Rape," *Knoxville News-Sentinel*, March 27, 2009, http://www.timesfreepress.com/news/local/story/2009/mar/27/knox-jury-finds-peeping-tom-guilty-rape/213394, accessed March 2, 2015.

23. Holly Kearl, "When Street Harassment Is More Deadly Than Catcalls," *Ms. Magazine* blog, October 21, 2013, http://www.msmagazine.com/blog/2013/10/21/when-street-harassment-is-more-deadly-than-catcalls, accessed November 3, 2014.

24. "Mass Shooting Kills Mother of Three, Wounds Five Others," My Fox Detroit, October 6, 2014, http://www.myfoxdetroit.com/story/26719319/mass-shooting-kills-mother-of-three-wounds-five-others, accessed October 30, 2014.

25. Tara Culp-Ressler, "Man Knocked Unconscious for Trying to Stick Up for Women Being Catcalled," *Think Progress*, August 13, 2014, http://thinkprogress.org/health/2014/08/13/3470631/philadelphia-street-harassment, accessed November 15, 2014.

26. Jenny Kutner, "Man Stabbed 9 Times after Asking Catcaller to Stop Harassing His Girlfriend, *Salon*, November 21, 2014, www.salon.com/2014/11/21/man_stabbed_9_times_after_asking_catcaller_to_stop_harassing_his_girlfriend, accessed November 22, 2014.

27. Emily Woodbury, Ben Kieffer, and Lindsey Moon, "ISU Student Severely Injured after Intervening in Street Harassment," Iowa Public Radio, February 20, 2015, http://iowapublicradio.org/post/isu-student-severely-injured-after-intervening-street-harassment, accessed February 22, 2015.

28. Holly Kearl, "Unsafe and Harassed in Public Spaces: A National Street Harassment Report," Stop Street Harassment, Spring 2014, http://www.stopstreetharassment.org/our-work/nationalstudy, accessed November 20, 2014.

29. Citron, *Hate Crimes in Cyberspace*, 80.

30. Ibid., 81–82.

31. Michael Kimmel, "Rape and Women's Voice," *Huffington Post*, August 23, 2012, http://www.huffingtonpost.com/michael-kimmel/rape-and-womens-voice_b_1820021.html, accessed February 21, 2015.

32. Ken Buck, quoted Scot Kersgaard, "Buck's Refusal to Prosecute 2005 Rape Case Reverberates in U.S. Senate Race," *The Colorado Independent*, October 11, 2010, www.coloradoindependent.com/63491/bucks-refusal-to-prosecute-2005-rape-case-reverberates-in-u-s-senate-race, accessed November 2, 2014; Nick Baumann, "The Ken Buck Rape Case," *Mother Jones*, October 26, 2010, www.motherjones.com/politics/2010/10/ken-buck-rape-case, accessed November 2, 2014.

33. David Edwards, "College Pres. Warns Women Not to Report Rapes: Girls Lie if Sex Doesn't 'Turn Out the Way They Want,'" *Raw Story*, November 10, 2014, http://www.rawstory.com/rs/2014/11/college-pres-warns-women-not-to-report-rapes-girls-lie-if-sex-doesnt-turn-out-the-way-they-want, accessed December 27, 2014.

34. David Lisak, Lori Gardinier, Sarah C. Nicksa, and Ashley M. Cote, "False Allegations of Sexual Assault: An Analysis of Ten Years of Reported Cases," *Violence against Women* 16, no. 12 (December 2010): 1318–1334.

35. Adrian Howe, *Sex, Violence and Crime: Foucault and the "Man" Question* (New York: Routledge-Cavendish, 2008), 55.

36. Citron, *Hate Crimes in Cyberspace*, 80–81.

37. MacKinnon, "Sexual Harassment: Its First Decade in Court," 108.

38. Citron, *Hate Crimes in Cyberspace*, 90.

39. "Predictors of Domestic Violence Homicide," National Center on Domestic and Sexual Violence, www.ncdsv.org/images/FWV_PredictorsDVHomicide_2004.pdf, accessed November 10, 2014.

40. Citron, *Hate Crimes in Cyberspace*, 82.

41. Paul Elam, "Challenging the Etiology of Rape a Voice for Men," originally published on A Voice for Men blog, November 14, 2010, http://www.scribd.com/doc/234696235/Challenging-the-Etiology-of-Rape-a-Voice-for-Men, accessed February 8, 2015.

42. Citron, *Hate Crimes in Cyberspace*, 81–82.

43. Noura bint Afeich, "Saudi Women Turn to Social Media to Combat Harassment," *Al-Monitor*, February 14, 2014, www.al-monitor.com/pulse/culture/2014/02/sexual-harassment-rise-saudi-arabia.html, accessed November 10, 2014.

44. Ibid.

45. "Saudi Cleric Favours One-Eye Veil," *BBC News*, October 3, 2008, www.news.bbc.co.uk/2/hi/middle_east/7651231.stm, accessed November 10, 2014.

46. Patrick Stewart, "Patrick Stewart: The Legacy of Domestic Violence," *Guardian*, November 26, 2009, http://www.theguardian.com/society/2009/nov/27/patrick-stewart-domestic-violence, accessed November 4, 2014.

47. David Brock, excerpt from *Blinded by the Right: The Conscience of an Ex Conservative*, www.randomhouse.com/boldtype/0203/brock/excerpt.html, accessed November 4, 2014.

48. Frances Ryan, "The 'Ruined Lives' of Oscar Pistorius and Ched Evans: Why Do Men Matter More Than Women?" *New Statesman*, October 14, 2014, http://www.newstatesman.com/politics/2014/10/ruined-lives-oscar-pistorius-and-ched-evans-why-do-men-matter-more-women, accessed October 22, 2014.

49. Amanda Perthen, "Ched Evans's Rape Victim Is Forced to Move for FIFTH Time to Flee Trolls as Attorney General Comes under Fire from Her Father," *Daily Mail*, December 27, 2014, http://www.dailymail.co.uk/news/article-2888732/Ched-Evans-s-rape-victim-forced-FIFTH-time-flee-trolls-Attorney-General-comes-fire-father.html, accessed June 4, 2015.

50. Winston Ross, "CNN Feels Sorry for Steubenville Rapists; World Can't Believe Its Ears," *Daily Beast*, March 18, 2013, www.thedailybeast.com/articles/2013/03/18/cnn-feels-sorry-for-steubenville-rapists-world-can-t-believe-its-ears.html, accessed November 4, 2014; "CNN Grieves That Guilty Verdict Ruined 'Promising' Lives of Steubenville Rapists," March 17, 2013, www.youtube.com/watch?&v=MvUdyNko8LQ, accessed November 4, 2014.

51. Edwards, "College Pres. Warns Women Not to Report Rapes."

52. Ryan, "The 'Ruined Lives' of Oscar Pistorius and Ched Evans."

53. Ibid.

54. Myren, "Letter to the Editor."

55. Ansar Haroun and David Naimark, *Poker Face in Mental Health Practice; A Primer on Deception Analysis and Detection* (New York: W.W. Norton & Company, 2011), 74.

56. "Anita Hill vs. Clarence Thomas: The Backstory," *CBS News*, October 20, 2010, http://www.cbsnews.com/news/anita-hill-vs-clarence-thomas-the-backstory, accessed February 8, 2015.

57. Arthur Goldwag, "Leader's Suicide Brings Attention to Men's Rights Movement," *Intelligence Report*, Spring 2012, Issue Number 145, Southern Poverty Law Center, http://www.splcenter.org/get-informed/intelligence-report/browse-all-issues/2012/spring/a-war-on-women, accessed February 15, 2015.

58. Martha Bellisle, "Charla Mack Foresaw Violent Acts," *Reno Gazette-Journal*, June 16, 2006, http://archive.rgj.com/article/20060616/NEWS10/606160401/Charla-Mack-foresaw-violent-acts, accessed November 29, 2014.

59. Mark Sayre, "Darren Mack Enters Guilty Plea for Murder," 8 News Now, KLAS-TV, Las Vegas, November 5, 2007, http://www.8newsnow.com/story/7313458/darren-mack-enters-guilty-plea-for-murder, accessed February 17, 2015.

60. Paul Elam, "Jury Duty at a Rape Trial? Acquit!" A Voice for Men blog, July 20, 2010, http://www.avoiceformen.com/mens-rights/jury-duty-at-a-rape-trial-acquit, accessed February 11, 2015.

61. Tamara N. Holder, Foreword to Janie McQueen, *Hanging On by My Fingernails: Surviving the New Divorce Gamesmanship, and How a Scratch Can Land You in Jail* (Atlanta, GA: Burning Sage, 2012), x.

62. Lt. Gen. David Morrison, quoted in Mary Elizabeth Williams, "Can Fark's Anti-Misogyny Policy Work?" *Salon*, August 21, 2014, http://www.salon.com/2014/08/21/can_farks_anti_misogyny_policy_work, accessed October 4, 2014.

63. William F. McKibbin, Todd K. Shackelford, Aaron T. Goetz, and Valerie G. Starratt, "Why Do Men Rape? An Evolutionary Psychological Perspective," *Review of General Psychology* 12, no. 1 (March 2008): 88.

64. Michael Kimmel, "An Unnatural History of Rape," in *The Gender of Desire: Essays on Male Sexuality* (Albany: State University of New York Press, 2005), 220.

65. Citron, *Hate Crimes in Cyberspace*, 90.

66. Ibid., 80.

CHAPTER 8

1. Melody Hensley, interview with author, August 15, 2014.
2. Ibid.
3. Sierra, "Trouble at the Koolaid Point."
4. Citron, *Hate Crimes in Cyberspace*, 75.
5. Buni and Chemaly, "The Unsafety Net."
6. Ibid.
7. Ibid.
8. Ibid.
9. Zoe Quinn, "Dispatches from the Quinnspiracy," Zoe Quinn's Blog, January 11, 2015, http://ohdeargodbees.tumblr.com/post/107838639074/august-never-ends, accessed March 15, 2015.
10. Anonymous commenter, quoted in Wagner, "The Future of the Culture Wars Is Here, And It's Gamergate."
11. Stuart, "Brianna Wu and the Human Cost of Gamergate."
12. Brianna Wu, quoted in Stuart, "Brianna Wu and the Human Cost of Gamergate."

13. Screen cap image, dated October 29, 2014, in David Futrelle, "The Top 22 Most Ridiculous Things Said by 8channers about Anita Sarkeesian's Appearance on the Colbert Report," We Hunted the Mammoth blog, October 30, 2014, http://wehuntedthemammoth.com/2014/10/30/the-top-22-most-ridiculous-things-said-by-8channers-about-anita-sarkeesians-appearance-on-the-colbert-report, accessed October 30, 2014.

14. Sierra, "Trouble at the Koolaid Point."

15. Astra Taylor, "How Male Trolls, Harassment, Sexism, and Racism Can Dominate Women's Web Experience," *Alternet*, April 10, 2014, http://www.alternet.org/gender/disappearing-woman-and-life-Internet?paging=off&current_page=1#bookmark, accessed September 11, 2014.

16. Amy Davis Roth, "A Woman's Room Online," Skepchick blog, September 4, 2014, http://skepchick.org/2014/09/a-womans-room-online, accessed October 15, 2014. (Italics in original.)

17. Markos Moulitsas, "Death Threats and Blogging," Daily Kos, April 11, 2007, http://www.dailykos.com/story/2007/04/12/322169/-Death-threats-and-blogging, accessed December 31, 2014.

18. Brendan O'Neill, "The Campaign to 'Stamp Out Misogyny Online' Echoes Victorian Efforts to Protect Women from Coarse Language," *Telegraph*, November 7, 2011, http://blogs.telegraph.co.uk/news/brendanoneill2/100115868/the-campaign-to-stamp-out-misogyny-online-echoes-victorian-efforts-to-protect-women-from-coarse-language, accessed December 31, 2014.

19. Cath Elliot, quoted in Lewis, "You Should Have Your Tongue Ripped Out."

20. Casey Newman, "Anita Sarkeesian Shares the Most Radical Thing You Can Do to Support Women Online," *Verge*, September 13, 2014, www.theverge.com/2014/9/13/6145169/anita-sarkeesian-shares-the-most-radical-thing-you-can-do-to-support, accessed September 28, 2014.

21. "California," quoted in Streshinsky, editor, "This Is What the Harassment and Abuse of Women on the Internet Looks Like, Part V."

22. Liz Ryerson, "On Right-Wing Videogame Extremism," Ellaguro blog, August 22, 2014, ellaguro.blogspot.com/2014/08/on-right-wing-videogame-extremism.html, accessed November 23, 2014.

23. Stuart, "Brianna Wu and the Human Cost of Gamergate."

24. Wagner, "The Future of the Culture Wars Is Here, And It's Gamergate."

25. Fernando Alfonso III, "What Happens When the Web's Most Notorious Troll Forum Pranks Itself?" *Daily Dot*, April 1, 2013, http://www.dailydot.com/society/4chan-pranks-itself-sht-4chan-says, accessed June 2, 2015.

26. Sierra, "Trouble at the Koolaid Point."

27. Milo Yiannopoulos, quoted in Zaid Jilani, "Gamergate's Fickle Hero: The Dark Opportunism of Breitbart's Milo Yiannopoulos," *Salon*, October 28, 2014, http://www.salon.com/2014/10/28/gamergates_fickle_hero_the_dark_opportunism_of_breitbarts_milo_yiannopoulos, accessed 10/31/14.

28. Arthur Chu, "Of Gamers, Gates, and Disco Demolition: The Roots of Reactionary Rage," *Daily Beast*, October 16, 2014, http://www.thedailybeast

.com/articles/2014/10/16/of-gamers-gates-and-disco-demolition-the-roots-of-reactionary-rage.html, accessed December 6, 2014.

29. Chu, "I'm Not 'That Creepy Guy from the Internet.'"

30. Ibid.

31. T. C. Sottek, "Don't Be Fooled by 'Gamers' Who Want to Enlist You for Abuse," *Verge*, October 8, 2014, http://www.theverge.com/2014/10/8/6919179/stop-supporting-gamergate, accessed October 21, 2014.

32. John Herrman, "Two Minutes of Walking on the Internet as a Woman," *The Awl*, October 28, 2014, http://www.theawl.com/2014/10/two-minutes-of-walking-on-the-Internet-as-a-woman, February 15, 2015. (Italics in original.)

33. Wagner, "The Future of the Culture Wars Is Here, And It's Gamergate."

34. Ibid.

35. Sarkeesian, quoted in Casey Newton, "Anita Sarkeesian Shares the Most Radical Thing You Can Do to Support Women Online."

36. Wu, "I'm Brianna Wu, And I'm Risking My Life Standing Up to Gamergate."

37. Chu, "Of Gamers, Gates, and Disco Demolition."

38. Chris Locke, quoted in Liz Tay, "Blogger Spat Rages Over Sierra 'Death Threats,'" *Computerworld*, March 28, 2007, http://www.computerworld.com.au/article/180214/blogger_spat_rages_over_sierra_death_threats_, accessed January 3, 2015.

39. O'Neill, "The Campaign to 'Stamp Out Misogyny Online' Echoes Victorian Efforts to Protect Women from Coarse Language."

40. Arthur Chu, "This 'Jeopardy!' Champ and Proud Geek Gives Swirlies to Gamergaters in His Spare Time," *Mother Jones*, November 11, 2014, www.motherjones.com/media/2014/11/arthur-chu-jeopardy-gamergate, accessed December 6, 2014.

41. Jay Allen, "How Imageboard Culture Shaped Gamergate," Boing Boing, December 31, 2014, http://boingboing.net/2014/12/31/how-imageboard-culture-shaped.html, accessed February 2, 2015.

42. Taylor, "How Male Trolls, Harassment, Sexism, and Racism Can Dominate Women's Web Experience."

43. Chu, "This 'Jeopardy!'"

44. Allen, "How Imageboard Culture Shaped Gamergate."

45. Clyde Wayne Crews Jr., "Techno-Libertarianism: Building the Case for Separation of Technology and State," *Forbes*, July 17, 2014, http://www.forbes.com/sites/waynecrews/2014/07/17/techno-libertarianism-building-the-case-for-separation-of-technology-and-state, accessed February 26, 2015.

46. Taylor, "How Male Trolls, Harassment, Sexism, and Racism Can Dominate Women's Web Experience."

47. Kover, "Do We Have to Worry about Someone Actually Killing or Raping a Feminist Activist?"

48. Sierra, "Trouble at the Koolaid Point."

49. Citron, *Hate Crimes in Cyberspace*, 19.

50. Thomas Fox-Brewster, "Craig Brittain: Confessions of an 'Accidental' Revenge Porn Pusher," *Forbes*, February 6, 2015, http://www.forbes.com/sites/thomasbrewster/2015/02/06/revenge-porn-apology-craig-brittain, accessed February 26, 2015.

51. Ibid.

52. Joseph Bernstein, "GamerGate's Archvillain Is Really a Trolling Sketch Comedian," *BuzzFeed*, February 23, 2015, http://www.buzzfeed.com/josephbernstein/gamergates-archvillain-is-really-a-trolling-sketch-comedian#.jep63xqYr9, accessed February 26, 2015.

53. Ibid.

54. Ibid.

55. Taylor, "How Male Trolls, Harassment, Sexism, and Racism Can Dominate Women's Web Experience."

56. Soraya Chemaly, interview with author, December 4, 2014.

57. Taylor, quoted in Rebecca Solnit, "How Male Trolls, Harassment, Sexism, and Racism Can Dominate Women's Web Experience."

58. Saul Levmore and Martha C. Nussbaum, introduction to *The Offensive Internet: Privacy, Speech, and Reputation* (Cambridge, MA: Harvard University Press, 2010), 6.

59. Citron, *Hate Crimes in Cyberspace*, 200.

60. Arthur Chu, "Trolls and Martyrdom: Je Ne Suis Pas Charlie," *Daily Beast*, January 9, 2104, http://www.thedailybeast.com/articles/2015/01/09/trolls-and-martyrdom-je-ne-suis-pas-charlie.html, accessed January 11, 2015.

61. Tim O'Reilly, "Code of Conduct: Lessons Learned So Far," Tim O'Reilly's blog Radar, April 11, 2007, http://radar.oreilly.com/2007/04/code-of-conduct-lessons-learne.html, accessed January 3, 2015.

62. Taylor, quoted in Rebecca Solnit, "How Male Trolls, Harassment, Sexism, and Racism Can Dominate Women's Web Experience."

63. Ibid.

64. Ally Fogg, quoted in Lewis, "This Is What Online Harassment Looks Like."

65. Soraya Chemaly, interview with author, December 4, 2014.

66. Citron, *Hate Crimes in Cyberspace*, 26.

67. Citron, "Civil Rights in Our Information Age," 46.

68. Penny, "A Woman's Opinion Is the Mini-Skirt of the Internet."

CHAPTER 9

1. "18 U.S. Code § 875 (c)—Interstate Communications," Cornell University Law School, Legal Information Institute, https://www.law.cornell.edu/uscode/text/18/875, accessed March 5, 2015.

2. Citron, "Civil Rights in Our Information Age," 43.

3. Wu, "I'm Brianna Wu, and I'm Risking My Life Standing Up to Gamergate."

4. Press Association, "Treat Trolling as Real-Life Abuse, MP Stella Creasy Urges Police," *Guardian*, October 29, 2013, http://www.theguardian.com/global/2013/oct/29/trolling-abuse-mp-stella-creasy-police-online, accessed October 12, 2014.

5. Stella Creasy, quoted in Alexandra Topping, "Online Trolling of Women Is Linked to Domestic Violence, Say Campaigners," *Guardian*, September 2, 2013, http://www.theguardian.com/society/2013/sep/03/online-trolling-women-domestic-violence, accessed August 15, 2014.

6. Anna Merlan, "Rep. Katherine Clark: The FBI Needs to Make Gamergate 'A Priority,'" Jezebel, March 10, 2015, http://jezebel.com/rep-katherine-clark-the-fbi-needs-to-make-gamergate-a-1690599361, accessed March 15, 2015; 18 U.S. Code § 2261A—Stalking, https://www.law.cornell.edu/uscode/text/18/2261A, accessed March 15, 2015.

7. Merlan, "Rep. Katherine Clark."

8. The definition of "fighting words" has been tightened over successive Supreme Court decisions. In a 1971 Supreme Court decision, fighting words were further restricted to only "those personally abusive epithets which, when addressed to the ordinary citizen, are, as a matter of common knowledge, inherently likely to provoke violent reaction." See *Cohen v. California*, 403 U.S. 15 (1971). Some legal commentators believe that the legal concept of "fighting words" is becoming less and less relevant as an increasingly diverse population makes it harder to make a clear determination as to which words should be reasonably considered to be provocative enough, "as a matter of common knowledge," to qualify as fighting words.

9. Citron, quoted in Chemaly, "'Hate Crimes in Cyberspace' Author."

10. Excerpt from Anthony Elonis's Facebook page, quoted in Martin Gould, "Criminal at Center of Landmark Supreme Court after Being Jailed for Telling Ex-Wife on Facebook That He Wanted Her 'Soaked in Blood and Dying' Is STILL Abusing People on Social Media," *Daily Mail*, December 5, 2014, http://www.dailymail.co.uk/news/article-2861283/Criminal-center-landmark-Supreme-Court-jailed-telling-ex-wife-Facebook-wanted-dead-abusing-people-social-media.html, accessed March 7, 2015.

11. Nina Totenberg, "Is a Threat Posted on Facebook Really a Threat?" *National Public Radio*, December 1, 2014, http://www.npr.org/2014/12/01/366534452/is-a-threat-posted-on-facebook-really-a-threat, accessed March 7, 2015.

12. Garrett Epps, "Does a True Threat Require a Guilty Mind?," *Atlantic*, June 2, 2015, http://www.theatlantic.com/politics/archive/2015/06/does-a-true-threat-require-a-guilty-mind/394643, accessed June 2, 2015.

13. Anthony Elonis, quoted in Adam B, "Supreme Court makes the Internet a Little Less Safe for Women," *Daily Kos*, June 1, 2015, http://www.dailykos.com/story/2015/06/01/1389529/-Supreme-Court-makes-the-Internet-a-little-less-safe-for-women?detail=email, accessed June 2, 2015.

14. *Elonis v. United States*, Supreme Court of the United States Blog, http://www.scotusblog.com/case-files/cases/elonis-v-united-states, accessed March 7, 2015.

15. Justice Samuel Alito, quoted in Adam B, "Supreme Court Makes the Internet a Little Less Safe for Women."

16. Adam B, "Supreme Court Makes the Internet a Little Less Safe for Women."

17. Amanda Marcotte, quoted in Adam B, "Supreme Court Makes the Internet a Little Less Safe for Women."

18. Sandra J. Badin, quoted in Soraya Chemaly, "Supreme Court Makes It Harder to Convict for Online Threats," Women's Media Center, June 2, 2015, http://www.womensmediacenter.com/feature/entry/supreme-court-makes-it-harder-to-convict-for-online-threats, accessed June 2, 2015.

19. Jessica Mason Pieklo, "More Domestic Violence Charges for Man in Supreme Court Facebook Threats Case," RH Reality Check blog, May 8, 2015, http://rhrealitycheck.org/article/2015/05/08/domestic-violence-charges-man-scotus-facebook-threats-case, accessed June 2, 2015.

20. Stella Creasy, quoted in Topping, "Online Trolling of Women Is Linked to Domestic Violence, Say Campaigners."

21. Brianna Wu, quoted in Aja Romano, "Gamergate Member Threatens Brianna Wu with Apparent Parody Video," *Daily Dot*, February 3, 2015, http://www.dailydot.com/geek/gamergate-brianna-wu-car-crash-video, accessed February 15, 2015.

22. Brianna Wu, quoted in Merlan, "The Cops Don't Care about Violent Online Threats."

23. Merlan, "The Cops Don't Care about Violent Online Threats."

24. Ibid.

25. Merlan, "Rep. Katherine Clark."

26. Ibid.

27. Ibid.

28. Quinn, "Dispatches from the Quinnspiracy."

29. Merlan, "The Cops Don't Care about Violent Online Threats."

30. Ibid.

31. Naomi Harlin Goodno, "Cyberstalking, A New Crime: Evaluating the Effectiveness of Current State and Federal Laws," *Missouri Law Review* 72, no. 1 (Winter 2007): 125–197.

32. Sarah Jameson, "Cyberharassment: Striking a Balance between Free Speech and Privacy," *CommLaw Conspectus: Journal of Communications Law and Policy*, 17, no. 1, (2009): 265.

33. Ibid.

34. Daniel J. Solove, "Speech, Privacy, and Reputation on the Internet," eds. Saul Levmore and Martha C. Nussbaum, *The Offensive Internet: Speech, Privacy, and Reputation* (Cambridge, MA: Harvard University Press, 2010), 23.

35. Ibid., 25.

36. Saul Levmore, "The Internet's Anonymity Problem," eds. Saul Levmore and Martha C. Nussbaum, *The Offensive Internet: Speech, Privacy, and Reputation* (Cambridge, MA: Harvard University Press, 2010), 64–65.

37. Citron, *Hate Crimes in Cyberspace*, 124.

38. Ibid., 137.

39. Ibid., 218.

40. Naomi Harlin Goodno, "Cyberstalking, A New Crime: Evaluating the Effectiveness of Current State and Federal Laws," *Missouri Law Review* 72, no. 125, (Winter 2007): 152.

41. Citron, *Hate Crimes in Cyberspace*, 218.

42. Goodno, "Cyberstalking, A New Crime": 160–1.

43. Solove, "Speech, Privacy, and Reputation on the Internet," 22.

44. Ibid., 23.

45. Citron, quoted in Chemaly, "'Hate Crimes in Cyberspace' Author."

46. Danielle Keats Citron, "Law's Expressive Valuing in Combating Cyber Gender Harassment," *Michigan Law Review*, 108 (2009): 373.

47. Citron, "Civil Rights in Our Information Age," 39.

48. 18 U.S. Code § 245(b)(C)(2006)—Federally Protected Activities, https://www.law.cornell.edu/uscode/text/18/245, accessed March 5, 2015.

49. Citron, "Civil Rights in Our Information Age," 41.

50. Ibid., 41–42.

51. See *Talley v. California*, 362 U.S. 60, 64 (1960) ("Anonymous pamphlets, leaflets, brochures and even books have played an important role in the progress of mankind."), cited in Jameson, "Cyberharassment," 239.

52. Martha C. Nussbaum, "Objectification and Internet Misogyny," eds. Saul Levmore and Martha C. Nussbaum, *The Offensive Internet: Speech, Privacy, and Reputation* (Cambridge, MA: Harvard University Press, 2010), 85.

53. Arthur D. Santana, "Virtuous or Vitriolic: The Effect of Anonymity on Civility in Online Newspaper Reader Comment Boards," *Journalism Practice*, 8, no. 1 (2014):18–33.

54. Ibid., 28.

55. Levmore, "The Internet's Anonymity Problem," 55.

56. Soraya Chemaly, interview with author, December 4, 2014.

57. Ingrid Lunden, "Facebook Will Give Up the Ghost on Real Identity in Future Apps," Tech Crunch, January 30, 2014, http://techcrunch.com/2014/01/30/facebook-will-give-up-the-ghost-on-real-id-in-future-apps, accessed September 26, 2014.

58. Levmore, "The Internet's Anonymity Problem," 60.

59. Ibid., 59.

60. Ibid., 57.

61. Citron, *Hate Crimes in Cyberspace*, 58.

62. Citron, "Civil Rights in Our Information Age," 223.

63. Chemaly, "Online Activism" panel presented at the Women in Secularism III conference, Alexandria, VA, May 16, 2014.

64. Mogilevsky, Ibid.

65. Suzanne LaBarre, "Why We're Shutting Off Our Comments," *Popular Science*, September 24, 2013, http://www.popsci.com/science/article/2013–09/why-were-shutting-our-comments, accessed March 1, 2015.

66. Lindy West, interview with author, May 26, 2014.

67. Lindy West, "A Feminist's Guide to Surviving the Internet," a talk delivered at the Women in Secularism III conference, Washington, DC, May 17, 2014.

68. Adrian Chen, "The Laborers Who Keep Dick Pics and Beheadings Out of Your Facebook Feed," October 23, 2014, *Wired* magazine, http://www.wired.com/2014/10/content-moderation, accessed February 2, 2015; Sam Frizell, "Google and Facebook Have Already Solved Twitter's Trolling Problem for It," *Time* magazine, February 5, 2014, http://time.com/3697077/twitter-trolls, accessed February 5, 2015.

69. Lindy West, interview with author, May 26, 2014.

70. Samantha Allen, "Will the Internet Ever Be Safe for Women?" *Daily Beast*, August 28, 2014, http://www.thedailybeast.com/articles/2014/08/28/will-the-internet-ever-be-safe-for-women.html, accessed November 27, 2014.

71. Frizell, "Google and Facebook Have Already Solved Twitter's Trolling Problem for It."

72. Arthur Chu, quoted in John Biggs, "'The *Jeopardy!* Guy.'"

73. Charles Arthur and Jemima Kiss, "Twitter Abuse: What Can Be Done to Stop Trolling?" *Guardian*, July 29, 2013, http://www.theguardian.com/technology/2013/jul/29/twitter-abuse-dealing-with-trolls-options, accessed October 15, 2014.

74. Adriana Lee, "Reporting Online Abuse on Twitter Just Got Easier," Read Write, December 2, 2014, http://readwrite.com/2014/12/02/twitter-abuse-blocking-reporting-tool-updates-zelda-williams, accessed March 1, 2015.

75. Amanda Hess, "Twitter Won't Stop Harassment on Its Platform, So Its Users Are Stepping In," *Slate*, August 6, 2014, http://www.slate.com/blogs/future_tense/2014/08/06/twitter_harassment_user_created_apps_block_together_flaminga_and_the_block.html, accessed February 12, 2015.

76. Kunova, "Netizens Come Together against Online Harassment of Women."

77. Caitlin Dewey, "Rape Threats, Then No Response: What It Was Like to Be a Woman on Twitter in 2014," *Washington Post*, December 17, 2014, http://www.washingtonpost.com/news/the-intersect/wp/2014/12/17/rape-threats-then-no-response-what-it-was-like-to-be-a-woman-on-twitter-in-2014, accessed February 11, 2015.

78. Dick Costolo, quoted in Mark Shrayber, "Twitter CEO: 'We Suck at Dealing with Abuse and It's All My Fault,'" Jezebel, February 4, 2015, http://jezebel

.com/twitter-ceo-we-suck-at-dealing-with-abuse-and-its-all-1683894216, accessed February 5, 2015.

79. Mina Farzad, "Twitter Increases Number of Staff on Their Moderation Team," Women, Action and the Media website, February 27 2015, http://www.womenactionmedia.org/2015/02/27/twitter-increases-number-of-staff-on-their-moderation-team, accessed March 1, 2015.

80. Hess, "Twitter Won't Stop Harassment on Its Platform."

81. Danilo Campos, "The Least Twitter Could Do," Danilo Campos's blog, July 30, 2014, http://danilocampos.com/2014/07/the-least-twitter-could-do.

82. Lindy West, quoted in Emily Greenhouse, "Twitter's Free-Speech Problem," *New Yorker*, August 1, 2013, http://www.newyorker.com/tech/elements/twitters-free-speech-problem, accessed January 18, 2015.

83. Martin Robbins, "I Am Now Officially a Transphobic Twitter Troll," *Vice*, August 8, 2014, http://www.vice.com/en_uk/read/whats-the-block-blot-martin-robbins-757, accessed March 1, 2015.

84. Soraya Chemaly, interview with author, December 4, 2014.

85. Danielle Citron, "The Facebook Justice System: The Social Network Needs to Change How It Deals with Reports of Abuse," *Slate*, August 6, 2014, http://www.slate.com/articles/technology/future_tense/2014/08/facebook_revenge_porn_lawsuit_social_network_should_change_abuse_reporting.html, accessed November 12, 2014.

86. Deni Kirkova, "Companies Pull Adverts from Facebook as Networking Site Refuses to Remove 'Anti-Women' Content: #FBRape Campaign Gets 50,000 Tweets of Support in Just One Week," *Daily Mail*, May 28, 2013, http://www.dailymail.co.uk/femail/article-2332028/FBRape-campaign-Companies-pull-adverts-Facebook-refuses-remove-anti-women-content.html, accessed March 1, 2015.

87. "Open Letter to Facebook," Women, Action & the Media website May 21, 2013, http://www.womenactionmedia.org/facebookaction/open-letter-to-facebook, accessed March 1, 2015.

88. Buni and Chemaly, "The Unsafety Net."

89. Ibid.

90. Soraya Chemaly, interview with author, December 4, 2014.

91. Citron, "The Facebook Justice System."

92. Ibid.

93. Allen, "Will the Internet Ever Be Safe for Women?"

94. Yoree Koh, "Twitter's Diversity Report: Women Make Up 30% of Workforce," *Wall Street Journal*, July 23, 2014, http://blogs.wsj.com/digits/2014/07/23/twitters-diversity-report-women-make-up-30-of-workforce, accessed March 28, 2015.

95. Lyndsey Gilpin, "The State of Women in Technology: 15 Data Points You Should Know," *Tech Republic*, July 8, 2014, http://www.techrepublic.com/article/

the-state-of-women-in-technology-15-data-points-you-should-know, accessed March 2, 2015.

96. Maxine Williams, "Building a More Diverse Facebook," June 25, 2014, Facebook, http://newsroom.fb.com/news/2014/06/building-a-more-diverse-facebook, accessed March 28, 2015.

97. Hayley Tsukayama, "No, Really. How Do We Get Girls to Code?" *Washington Post*, June 19, 2014, http://www.washingtonpost.com/blogs/the-switch/wp/2014/06/19/no-really-how-do-we-get-girls-to-code, accessed March 2, 2015.

98. "Making Google a Workplace for Everyone," Google, http://www.google.com/diversity/at-google.html#tab=tech, accessed March 28, 2015.

99. Taylor, quoted in Solnit, "How Male Trolls, Harassment, Sexism, and Racism Can Dominate Women's Web Experience."

100. Ibid.

101. Ibid.

102. Leah Burrows, "Women Remain Outsiders in Video Game Industry," *Boston Globe*, January 27, 2013, http://www.bostonglobe.com/business/2013/01/27/women-remain-outsiders-video-game-industry/275JKqy3rFylT7TxgPmO3K/story.html, accessed March 1, 2015.

103. Wu, "Rape and Death Threats Are Terrorizing Female Gamers."

104. Ibid.

105. Soraya Chemaly, interview with author, December 4, 2014.

106. Ashe Dryden, "You Asked: How Do I Deal with Online Harassment? How Do I Help the Targets of Online Harassment?" Ashe Dryen's blog, July 8, 2014, http://www.ashedryden.com/blog/you-asked-how-do-i-deal-with-online-harassment-how-do-i-help-the-targets-of-online-harassment, accessed January 2, 2015.

107. Amy Davis Roth, "Online Activism" panel presented at the Women in Secularism III conference, Alexandria, VA, May 16, 2014.

108. Soraya Chemaly, "Online Activism" panel presented at the Women in Secularism III conference, Alexandria, VA, May 16, 2014.

109. Atherton-Zeman, "How Some Men Harass Women Online and What Other Men Can Do to Stop It."

110. Lindy West, "A Feminist's Guide to Surviving the Internet," a talk delivered at the Women in Secularism III conference, Washington, DC, May 17, 2014.

111. Courtney Caldwell, "Machine Gun Misogynists: How Open Carry Texas Tried to Silence Me," Skepchick blog, May 27, 2014, http://skepchick.org/2014/05/machine-gun-misogynists-how-open-carry-texas-tried-to-silence-me, accessed January 2, 2015.

112. Ibid.

113. Press Association, "Treat Trolling as Real-Life Abuse, MP Stella Creasy Urges Police."

114. Lewis, "You Should Have Your Tongue Ripped Out."

115. Ashley Judd, "Forget Your Team: Your Online Violence toward Girls and Women Is What Can Kiss My Ass," *Mic*, March 19, 2015, http://mic.com/articles/113226/forget-your-team-your-online-violence-toward-girls-and-women-is-what-can-kiss-my-ass, accessed March 26, 2015.

116. Nussbaum, "Objectification and Internet Misogyny," 86.

117. Chemaly, "The Digital Safety Gap and the Online Harassment of Women."

118. Lindy West, "A Feminist's Guide to Surviving the Internet," a talk delivered at the Women in Secularism III conference, Washington, DC, May 17, 2014.

119. Quinn, "Dispatches from the Quinnspiracy."

120. Ibid.

121. Cath Elliot, quoted in Lewis, "You Should Have Your Tongue Ripped Out."

122. Wu, "Rape and Death Threats Are Terrorizing Female Gamers."

123. Ophelia Benson, interview with author, May 26, 2014.

124. Wu, "Rape and Death Threats Are Terrorizing Female Gamers."

125. Anita Sarkeesian, quoted in Amy Goodman interviewing Anita Sarkeesian, "'Women Are Being Driven Offline': Feminist Anita Sarkeesian Terrorized for Critique of Video Games," *Democracy Now*, October 20, 2014, https://www.youtube.com/watch?v=WRinZyeugfY&feature=youtu.be, accessed October 21, 2014.

126. Press Association, "Treat Trolling as Real-Life Abuse, MP Stella Creasy Urges Police."

127. McNally, "A Disheartening Account of the Harassment Going on in Gaming Right Now."

128. Kathy Sierra, quoted in "Blog Death Threats Spark Debate," *BBC News*, March 27, 2007, http://news.bbc.co.uk/2/hi/technology/6499095.stm, accessed March 16, 2015.

129. Chu, quoted in Biggs, "The *Jeopardy!* Guy."

130. Ibid.

131. Citron, "The Facebook Justice System."

132. Citron, *Hate Crimes in Cyberspace*, 95.

133. Nussbaum, "Objectification and Internet Misogyny," 85.

134. Solove, "Speech, Privacy, and Reputation on the Internet," 27.

135. Marcotte, "Harassment of Women Is Nothing New—The Internet Just Makes It Easier."

Index

Agustsdottir, Thorlaug, 177
Ahern, Shauna James, 30, 68, 123
Alito, Justice Samuel J., 198
Allen, Jay, 186
Allen, Samantha, 89, 109, 207
Anonymity, 131, 184, 186, 204–6
Anonymous, 5, 54, 65, 93–94
Anti-Semitism, 35, 152
Appropriation tort, 203–4
Asselin, Janelle, 29, 112–13
Astell, Mary, 133
Atherton-Zeman, Ben, 144, 147, 213
Aurenheimer, Andrew (weev), 182
AutoAdmit, 56, 60, 66, 104, 113, 205

Badin, Sandra J., 199
Baker, Katie J. M., 62
Baldwin, Adam, 83
Bates, Laura, 211
Beard, Mary, 29, 36, 44, 49, 137, 141, 142
Behn, Aphra, 161
Benson, Ophelia, 45, 93, 216
Black-hat hacking, 88
Blackman, Malorie, 36
Blockbot (blocking application), 210

BlockTogether (blocking application), 210
Bomb threats, 23, 49, 50, 102, 122, 196, 208
Brittain, Craig, 188
Brock, David, 169
Brownmiller, Susan, 151
/b/ section of 4chan, 4, 69, 93
Buck, Ken, 164

Caldwell, Courtney, 30, 44, 214
Campos, Danilo, 209
CDA. *See* Communications Decency Act
Chemaly, Soraya, 51, 94, 125, 152, 157, 190, 213, 214; on anonymity, 205; on comment moderation, 206; on diversity in technology companies, 212; Facebook rape campaign and, 210–11; on free speech, 110, 192–93; on hate crimes against women, 153
Chu, Arthur, 10, 89, 91, 94, 95, 157, 182, 183, 185, 186, 191, 217, 208
Citron, Danielle Keats, 9, 34, 94, 102, 156, 211, 217; on domestic

violence, 150, 157, 162, 166; on free speech, 187–88, 193, 196; on hate speech, 197; legal recommendations of, 203, 204, 206; on sexual harassment in the workplace, 152, 164, 165–66, 167, 173–74
Civil Rights Act of 1968 (18 U.S.C. § 245), 204
Civil rights law, 204
Clark, Representative Katherine, 196, 197, 200
Clementi, Tyler, 14
Comment moderation, 187, 206–7
Communications Decency Act (CDA), 202–3
Connors, Jace. *See* Rankowski, Jan
Costolo, Dick, 209
Creasy, Stella, 33, 49, 50, 53, 196, 199, 214, 217
Crews, Clyde Wayne, 187
Criado-Perez, Caroline, 32, 33, 47–51, 74, 104, 125, 208, 210
Culp-Ressler, Tara, 156
Cyberbullying, 13, 67
Cyberharassment, 13, 202
Cyberstalking, 13

Davis Roth, Amy, 33, 58, 75, 93, 101, 115, 119, 120, 121, 127, 128, 179, 213
DDoS. *See* Distributed Denial of Service attack
Denial of Service attack (DoS), 58, 59, 72
Dent, Grace, 33, 49
Depression Quest (video game), 83, 84, 181
Dewey, Caitlin, 56
Diels, Kelly, 58, 108
Digital Millennium Copyright Act, 188
Distributed Denial of Service attack (DDoS), 58, 59, 65, 105, 108
DoS. *See* Denial of Service attack

Doxxing, 24, 36, 57–59, 63, 65, 76, 86, 87, 88, 109, 122, 124, 139, 147, 178, 186, 201
Dragon Age: Inquisition (video game), 89
Dryden, Ashe, 105, 113, 213
Dzerins, Natalie, 43, 143

8chan, 87, 88, 92, 136, 185, 186, 202
18 U.S.C § 245. *See* Civil Rights Act of 1968
18 U.S.C. § 875. *See* Interstate Communications Act
18 U.S.C. § 2261A. *See* Federal Cyberstalking Statute
Elam, Paul, 95, 167, 172
Elevatorgate (event), 78
Elevatorgate (person), 69, 70, 80
Elliot, Cath, 56, 144, 180, 215
Elonis v. United States, 197–99
Encyclopedia Dramatica, 58, 65
Epps, Garrett, 197
Evans, Ched, 169
Everyday Sexism Project, 211

Facebook, 8, 101, 107, 108, 126, 201, 213, 214; real-name policy of, 205; recommendations to improve, 207, 209, 210–11, 212; responses to reports of abuse, 52, 177; use of in *Elonis v. United States* case, 197; use of in gendertrolling attacks, 12, 24, 35, 44, 51, 52, 58, 66, 68, 69, 72, 76, 78, 79, 120, 131, 177
Facebook Rape Campaign. *See* #FBRape
Fae, Jane, 146
False flag, 178, 181
Farrow, Caroline, 30, 43, 104
#FBRape (Facebook Rape Campaign), 211
Federal Bureau of Investigation (FBI), 9, 74, 153, 197, 201; increased training about cyberharassment for, 196, 199, 201; women seeking

help from, 40, 67, 74, 79, 88, 119, 120, 128, 177, 178
Federal Cyberstalking Statute (18 U.S.C. § 2261A), 196, 203
Feminist Frequency (blog), 54
Fighting words, 189, 197, 256 n.8
Filipovic, Jill, 59–60, 101, 103–4, 113, 125
First Amendment, 191, 193, 196, 197, 198, 204
Fish, Phil, 147
Flaminga, 210
Fogg, Ally, 192
Foster, Dawn, 29, 43, 58, 112, 142, 143
4chan, 88, 178, 186, 201; anonymity on, 186; harassers/cybermobs coordinating on, 23, 55, 65, 68, 69, 84, 88, 92, 93; men's rights activists/Gamergaters on, 79, 185, 208; rickrolling on, 5; trolls on, 4
Freeman, Hadley, 33, 49
Free speech, 17, 110, 139, 183, 190, 191–93, 202, 207, 214; credible threats and, 196, 197, 200; *Elonis v. United States* and, 197; techno-libertarians' views on, 184, 185, 187–88, 189
Friedman, Jaclyn, 211
Futrelle, David, 95, 96, 136

#GameOverGate, 88
Gamergate, 83–90, 108–9, 181, 185, 188, 189, 208, 216, 217; Gamergaters' tactics and motivations in, 83–90, 95, 178, 181, 182, 183; law enforcement ineffectiveness, 200; women targeted in, 27, 73, 83–90, 114, 124, 136, 147, 177, 178, 188, 189, 200
Gandy, Imani, 35
Gjoni, Eron, 83, 84, 147
Golden, Jamie Nesbitt, 145, 146
Goodno, Naomi Harlin, 203
Google, 6, 24, 72, 103, 188, 207, 212

Grant, Linda, 108
Green, David Allen, 144

Halligan, Ryan, 14
Haniver, Jenny, 32
Hardaker, Claire, 9, 10
Harry, Sydette, 146
Hate crimes, 101, 153, 197, 199
Hate speech, 56, 177, 192, 193, 197, 199, 210, 211
Hendren, Trista, 76, 177
Hensley, Melody, 33, 43, 70, 76, 91, 93, 140, 176
Hepler, Jennifer, 89
Herrman, John, 183
Hess, Amanda, 32, 54, 122, 148, 209
Hill, Anita, 155, 156, 160, 162, 169, 172
Howe, Adrian, 165

Idle No More, 36
Instagram, 66, 69, 212
International Game Developers Association, 74
Internet-induced suicides, 13, 14, 202
Interstate Communications Act (18 U.S.C. §875), 196

Jameson, Sarah, 202
Jennings, Robert, 165, 170
Jones, Feminista, 22–28, 31, 145
Judd, Ashley, 29, 44, 52, 214

Kane, Shanley, 67, 75, 81, 106, 114, 124, 139
Kendall, Mikki, 35, 102, 115
Kendzior, Sarah, 106
Kilstein, Jamie, 147
Kimmel, Michael, 173
Kotaku, 84, 85, 86, 88
Kover, Chris, 36, 53, 56, 135, 187
Kunova, Marcela, 57, 108, 140

League of Legends (video game), 217
Lee, Erica, 36

Lepine, Marc, 62, 73
Levmore, Saul, 203, 205, 206
Lewis, Helen, 210, 214
Lewis, Jone Johnson, 138
Lewis's law, 210
Locke, Chris, 183, 184

Mack, Darren, 172
MacKinnon, Catharine, 152, 154, 155, 165
Manosphere, 69, 92
Marcotte, Amanda, 131, 132, 140, 198, 218
Mardoll, Ana, 70
Mason, Priscilla, 138
Massively Multiplayer Online Role-Playing Games (MMORPGs), 8, 135
Maxwell, Zerlina, 34, 35
May, Emily, 106
Mayer, Catherine, 49, 102, 122
McCreight, Jennifer, 108
McEwan, Melissa, 58, 59
McNally, Victoria, 217
Mensch, Louise, 54
Men's rights, 93, 94, 95, 96, 172; men's rights activists (MRAs), 34, 61, 69, 90, 95, 97, 136, 167, 172, 185
Men's rights movement, 79, 92, 95
Merlan, Anna, 86, 118, 119, 200, 201
Miller, Laura, 10
Miller, Nancy, 125
MMORPGs. *See* Massively Multiplayer Online Role-Playing Games
Mogilevsky, Miri, 45, 52, 75, 126, 145, 206
Montreal Massacre, 62, 73
Moore, Suzanne, 49
Moran, Caitlin, 49, 208
Morrison, Lt. Gen. David, 173
Moulitsas, Mark, 179
MRAs. *See* Men's rights: men's rights activists
Myren, Allie, 151, 170

Naber, Jill, 14
National Organization for Men against Sexism, 144, 213
Nelson, Robin, 35
Nerdlove, Dr. *See* O'Malley, Harris
Norton, Jim, 38, 39, 40
#NotAllMen, 171
Notice-and-takedown remedies, 188, 202, 203
Nussbaum, Martha, 205, 214, 218

O'Hagan, Eleanor, 32, 33, 91, 110, 139, 142
O'Malley, Harris (Dr. Nerdlove), 37, 112
O'Neill, Brendan, 180, 184
Open Carry Texas, 30, 44, 214
O'Reilly, Tim, 192

Palmer, Janay, 31, 160
Pankhurst, Christabel, 161
Parsons, Rehtaeh, 13, 162
Penny, Laurie, 28, 36, 44, 49, 51, 105, 134, 193
Pew Research Center Internet Project, 10, 11
Phillips, Whitney, 10
Pickup artists, 61, 90, 92, 93, 96
Pistorius, Oscar, 170
Polansky, Lana, 116
Poole, Christopher, 88
Post-traumatic stress disorder (PTSD), 15, 27, 43, 81, 115, 176
Pozner, Jennifer, 42, 60
Privacy, 197, 202–3; settings for, 213
PTSD. *See* Post-traumatic stress disorder
PUAHate.com, 61, 62, 79, 92

Quinn, Zoe, 95, 110, 136, 177–78, 200, 215; fleeing home, 86, 114; law enforcement ineffectiveness, 177–78, 200–201; role in Gamergate, 83–90, 114, 147, 178, 181

Racism, 23, 34–36, 96
Ramzan, Iram, 123, 143
Rankowski, Jan (Jace Connors), 188
Rape blackmail videos, 13, 14
Reddit, 66, 88, 135, 188, 213; anonymity on, 186; harassers/cybermobs on, 68, 84, 88, 92; men's rights activists/Gamergaters on, 61, 69, 79, 95, 185, 208; trolls on, 4
Revenge pornography, 13, 14, 188
Rice, Ray, 31, 161
Richards, Adria, 92, 108
Rickrolling. See Trolling, generic
Roberts, Shoshana, 161
Rodger, Elliot, 61, 62, 73, 94, 95, 96, 119, 171
Roosh V. See Valizadeh, Daryush
Ryerson, Liz, 110, 181

Sarkeesian, Anita, 35, 71–74, 95, 109–110, 178–79, 180, 183, 216, 217; criticism of portrayal of women in videogames, 32, 71–74, 147; harassment of and threats against, 54, 71–74, 95, 114, 126, 178–79, 200; role in Gamergate, 73, 83, 89, 90, 114, 189
Saudi Arabia, street harassment in, 167–68
Scalzi, John, 144
Schafer, Tim, 147
Scoble, Robert, 102, 144
Seelhoff, Cheryl Lindsey, 32, 54, 64–66, 91, 93
Shafiq, Shamina, 13
Sierra, Kathy, 31, 105, 136, 144, 176, 179, 181–82, 184, 217; doxxing of, 57; endorsement of comment moderation, 187; on law enforcement ineffectiveness, 122; threats made against, 31, 105, 115, 176; withdrawal from Internet, 109, 115
#SilentNoMore, 125
Simpson, Nicole Brown, 171

Simpson, O. J., 171
Skepchick (blog), 30, 100, 101, 115, 119, 213
Slymepit, 78, 79, 92, 93
Smith, S. E., 75, 114
Smurthwaite, Kate, 42, 58, 76, 103, 112
Sodini, George, 62
Solnit, Rebecca, 91
Solomon, Barbara Miller, 138
Solove, Daniel J., 202, 203, 204, 218
Sottek, T. C., 84, 85, 182
Southern Poverty Law Center, 92, 153
Spender, Dale, 132, 133, 134, 138, 142, 161
Steenkamp, Reeva, 170
Steubenville, 161, 169–70
Stewart, Patrick, 169
Stoeffel, Kat, 61
Stone, Lucy, 138
Storify, 12, 66, 69, 70
Swatting. See Trolling, generic

Taylor, Astra, 91, 145, 179, 186, 187, 189, 190, 192, 212
Techno-libertarians, 184, 185, 186, 187, 188, 189, 190, 191, 192
Tekobbe, Cindy, 139
#TheatoftheDay, 125
This American Life, 126, 209
Thomas, Clarence, 155, 159, 160, 162, 169, 171
Thorson, Matt, 74
Todd, Amanda, 14
Tosh, Daniel, 38, 39
Totilo, Stephen, 88
TowerFall (video game), 74
Traceable anonymity, 206
Trolling, generic, 10–11, 12, 23, 66, 81, 94, 157, 177, 220; advice, 6; bait and switch, 5; concern, 5–6; flaming, 7; griefing, 8; impersonation, 8; IRL trolling, 9, 59–60; practical jokes, 6–7; raiding, 8; rickrolling, 5; RIP,

8; shock trolling, 8; sock puppets, 6, 8; swatting, 9, 139
Tumblr, 12, 66, 86, 126, 207
Twitter, 10, 30, 51, 59, 88, 101, 102, 106, 107, 108, 110, 112, 122, 139, 145, 200, 207, 212, 214; blocking applications on, 69, 76, 91, 208, 209, 210, 213; bomb threats made on, 49, 50, 102; campaigns using, 22, 125, 128, 171; recommendations for improvement of, 207–10, 212–13; report abuse button on, 50, 75, 209, 210; responses to reports of abuse, 50; use of in gendertrolling attacks, 12, 24, 25, 27, 30, 33, 34, 35, 36, 39, 40, 44, 48, 49, 50, 53, 54, 57, 66, 67, 68, 69, 72, 75, 76, 78, 87, 89, 118, 123, 124, 131, 147, 181

Upskirting, 13, 14
Urwin, Rosamund, 104

Valenti, Jessica, 40
Valizadeh, Daryush (Roosh V), 92, 93, 96
Violence against Women Act (VAWA), 204
Voice for Men, A (blog), 92, 93, 167
Voyeurism, 163

Wagner, Kyle, 85, 181, 183
Watson, Rebecca, 29, 33, 34, 75, 77–81, 90, 91, 93, 100, 115, 126; Elevatorgate (event) and, 78; Elevatorgate (person) and, 69, 70; on law enforcement ineffectiveness, 79–80, 119–120; rape and death threats made against, 52, 70, 78–80
Weev. *See* Aurenheimer, Andrew

We Hunted the Mammoth (blog), 95, 136
West, Lindy, 35, 38–41, 42, 61, 69, 90, 92, 93, 94, 96, 100, 123, 141, 213, 214; criticism of rape jokes and comedy, 32, 38; endorsement of comment moderation, 206–7; featured on *This American Life* podcast, 126–27, 209; rape and death threats against, 32, 39; video of rape threats made by, 126
WHOA. *See* Working to Halt Online Abuse
Wikipedia, 12, 65, 66, 68, 71, 72, 80
Williams, Zelda, 208
Wollstonecraft, Mary, 134, 138, 161
Women, Action, and the Media, 209, 211
Women in Media and News, 42, 60
Woolley, Chelsea, 127
Working to Halt Online Abuse (WHOA), 11, 66
Wu, Brianna, 108–9, 124, 136, 178, 181, 183, 188, 212, 216; fleeing home, 86, 88, 114, 136; on law enforcement ineffectiveness, 196, 199–200; rape and death threats made against, 87, 88, 124; role in Gamergate, 86–87, 89, 90, 147, 108–9, 114, 178, 189

#YesAllWomen, 171
Yiannopoulos, Milo, 182
#YouOKSis, 22, 24
YouTube, 5, 6, 35, 67, 101, 187, 201, 209, 213; use of in gendertrolling attacks, 12, 39, 53, 54, 66, 68, 71, 72, 75, 78, 84, 101, 201

Zimmerman, Frank, 54

About the Author

KARLA MANTILLA is a longtime collective member of *off our backs* (a feminist newsjournal that was in publication from 1970 through 2008) and the managing editor at *Feminist Studies*, an interdisciplinary women's studies journal. She has taught sociology, research methods, and statistics at George Mason University, Gettysburg College, McDaniel College, and the University of Maryland, College Park.

Lightning Source UK Ltd.
Milton Keynes UK
UKOW06n0801030915

257982UK00009B/61/P